The Encyclopedia of Small Business Forms and Agreements

A Complete Kit of Ready-to-Use Business Checklists, Worksheets, Forms, Contracts, and Human Resource Documents With Companion CD-ROM

THE ENCYCLOPEDIA OF SMALL BUSINESS FORMS AND AGREEMENTS: A COMPLETE KIT OF READY-TO-USE BUSINESS CHECKLISTS, WORKSHEETS, FORMS, CONTRACTS, AND HUMAN RESOURCE DOCUMENTS WITH COMPANION CD-ROM

Copyright © 2011 Atlantic Publishing Group, Inc.
1405 SW 6th Avenue • Ocala, Florida 34471 • Phone 800-814-1132 • Fax 352-622-1875
Website: www.atlantic-pub.com • E-mail: sales@atlantic-pub.com
SAN Number: 268-1250

Library of Congress Cataloging-in-Publication Data

Maeda, Martha, 1953-
   The encyclopedia of small business forms and agreements : a complete kit of ready-to-use business checklists, worksheets, forms, contracts, and human resource documents with companion CD-ROM / by Martha Maeda.
      p. cm.
   Includes bibliographical references and index.
   ISBN-13: 978-1-60138-248-1 (alk. paper)
   ISBN-10: 1-60138-248-0 (alk. paper)
   1. Small business--United States--Forms. 2. Small business--Law and legislation--United States--Forms. I. Title.
   HF5371.M284 2010
   651'.29--dc22
                                 2010027217

Printed in the United States

PROJECT MANAGER: Melissa Peterson
PEER REVIEWER: Marilee Griffin
PROOFING: C&P Marse • bluemoon6749@bellsouth.net
EDITORIAL INTERNS: Brad Goldbach and Shayna Bouker
INTERIOR DESIGN: Jackie Miller • millerjackiej@gmail.com
FRONT & BACK COVER DESIGN: Jackie Miller • millerjackiej@gmail.com

Printed on Recycled Paper

We recently lost our beloved pet "Bear," who was not only our best and dearest friend but also the "Vice President of Sunshine" here at Atlantic Publishing. He did not receive a salary but worked tirelessly 24 hours a day to please his parents. Bear was a rescue dog that turned around and showered myself, my wife, Sherri, his grandparents Jean, Bob, and Nancy, and every person and animal he met (maybe not rabbits) with friendship and love. He made a lot of people smile every day.

We wanted you to know that a portion of the profits of this book will be donated to The Humane Society of the United States. *–Douglas & Sherri Brown*

The human-animal bond is as old as human history. We cherish our animal companions for their unconditional affection and acceptance. We feel a thrill when we glimpse wild creatures in their natural habitat or in our own backyard.

Unfortunately, the human-animal bond has at times been weakened. Humans have exploited some animal species to the point of extinction.

The Humane Society of the United States makes a difference in the lives of animals here at home and worldwide. The HSUS is dedicated to creating a world where our relationship with animals is guided by compassion. We seek a truly humane society in which animals are respected for their intrinsic value, and where the human-animal bond is strong.

Want to help animals? We have plenty of suggestions. Adopt a pet from a local shelter, join The Humane Society and be a part of our work to help companion animals and wildlife. You will be funding our educational, legislative, investigative and outreach projects in the U.S. and across the globe.

Or perhaps you'd like to make a memorial donation in honor of a pet, friend or relative? You can through our Kindred Spirits program. And if you'd like to contribute in a more structured way, our Planned Giving Office has suggestions about estate planning, annuities, and even gifts of stock that avoid capital gains taxes.

Maybe you have land that you would like to preserve as a lasting habitat for wildlife. Our Wildlife Land Trust can help you. Perhaps the land you want to share is a backyard— that's enough. Our Urban Wildlife Sanctuary Program will show you how to create a habitat for your wild neighbors.

So you see, it's easy to help animals. And The HSUS is here to help.

THE HUMANE SOCIETY
OF THE UNITED STATES.

2100 L Street NW • Washington, DC 20037 • 202-452-1100
www.hsus.org

TABLE OF

Contents

Chapter 7: Purchasing and Managing Supplies and Inventory.............................. 197

Chapter 8: Human Resources: Hiring and Managing Employees 209

Introduction

This book contains checklists, worksheets, forms, contracts, human-resource documents, and sample letters to help you manage every aspect of your small business. You will find everything you need to plan a business startup, organize your finances, buy or lease real estate, set up a bookkeeping system, interact with your customers and clients, keep track of inventory and supplies, create and maintain a project schedule, hire and manage employees, and deal with setbacks and complications. The documents in this book represent the experience of thousands of business owners, accountants, attorneys, and consultants who have learned how to succeed in their fields.

Putting Everything in Writing

Before you go to the grocery store, you do not necessarily have to write down a shopping list; you can compose a mental list of the items you need, or you can just push your cart along the aisles and pick up things as they catch your eye. But what happens when you get home and find you forgot a crucial ingredient for tonight's dinner, or you get to the cash register and do not have enough money to pay for everything in your cart? A business agreement does not have to be put in writing to be legal; it can be a verbal agreement or a relationship that is just understood. But what do you do when your business partner fails to show up for an important job or does not hand over your share of a payment? What happens when a tenant does not pay his rent, a supplier fails to deliver goods on schedule, or a manufacturer sends you the wrong items? Writing everything down helps you organize your thoughts, anticipate your expenses, and ensure that everyone involved in a business transaction clearly understands their roles and responsibilities. Written contracts and agreements spell out exactly what actions will be taken if one party fails to fulfill its obligations.

Save time and get organized

Using lists, written procedures, and standardized documents saves time and helps you organize your business processes effectively. For example, numbered purchase orders, invoices, and receipts are used in accounting systems to track all of a business's transactions and make it easy to look up information quickly. Following a checklist of cash register procedures ensures that sales are properly recorded and important security measures are never overlooked. Hundreds of people can read and follow written instructions without having to be personally taught how to do a task.

Every business has needs and requirements similar to those of other businesses. You do not need to "reinvent the wheel" every time you start a new business or implement a new process. Benefit from the experience of all those who have gone before you by adapting the plans, contracts, and documents they have already developed and used successfully in their businesses. You have so much to accomplish that you do not have time to think your way carefully through every contingency of your new business. Instead, build on someone else's success strategies by using standardized checklists, documents, and legal contracts. Then devote your valuable time to finding new customers and developing your product.

Make it legal

A contract or legal agreement clarifies exactly what is expected of each of the parties to a business transaction, and what the consequences will be if any party fails to fulfill those expectations. Each party involved in the agreement knows it can be taken to court if certain conditions are not met. Legal contracts protect you from harm when something goes wrong. Each clause in a contract is designed to cover a specific eventuality. For example, a real estate mortgage contract often includes a clause requiring insurance to be taken out on the property in case it is damaged in a fire or flood. This protects both the borrower and the lender from losing money if the property is destroyed. The words in a contract determine who will have to pay if a project overruns its budget, or if a manufacturer delivers substandard goods.

Manage and control

Written contracts and agreements have an authority of their own. Everyone who signs an agreement acknowledges that he or she accepts its terms. Anyone who breaks the terms of a contract knows what the consequences will be. Contracts are an effective method for establishing and maintaining standards. For example, if you sign an agreement to buy materials of a certain standard from a manufacturer and the manufacturer fails to meet that standard, you have legal grounds to return the materials and refuse payment. Employees who sign a code of conduct or an Internet-use agreement know they can be disciplined or terminated for disregarding it. When such agreements are regularly enforced, all employees know what is expected of them. An employee fired for violating such a contract cannot claim unfair termination.

How to Use This Book

The documents in this book are ready-to-use; all you have to do is fill in the blanks or change a few words to suit your particular business needs. All of the documents can be printed from the companion CD-ROM, which also contains numerous additional legal forms, sample documents, and letters, including IRS and other government forms to supplement each section of the book. The title of each document explains its purpose, and many are accompanied by brief explanations. Read each document carefully before using it to make sure it is appropriate for your business needs, and make any necessary changes. Some of the documents in this book are legally binding contracts and agreements, while others, such as invoices and receipts, are simply official records of transactions. Consult a lawyer, accountant, or real estate agent before signing any document that commits you to important legal obligations. Although many simple contracts and transactions do not require a lawyer's services, you will save time and money by getting legal advice if your situation is complicated.

CD-ROM also contains bonus forms for property managers and landlords, building contractors, project management, hospitality, nonprofit management, and marketing and public relations.

CHAPTER

Starting a Business

Every entrepreneur knows it is a long journey from the first inspiration for a new business to its realization as a profitable enterprise. A business cannot succeed without a business plan — a blueprint detailing exactly how it will operate, how much it will cost to get started, and what steps must be taken to establish it. Checklists and guides help you do the necessary research, make realistic estimates and calculations, and include all the necessary elements for success.

The forms, checklists, worksheets, and sample documents in this section will guide you through the steps of starting a new business or expanding an existing one.

Evaluating Your Business Idea

The first step in turning your business idea into a reality is deciding what form your new business will take. Are you building on an existing business you are already experienced in, or are you venturing into an entirely new field? Should you start from scratch, buy into a franchise, or purchase an established business? This personality quiz will help you evaluate your skills and aptitudes.

Business Evaluation Personality Quiz

1. I am happiest when I am completely in charge of a project and using my own ideas.

   ☐ Yes   ☐ Sometimes   ☐ No

2. I prefer to have a group of people brainstorm alternatives and then come to a group consensus to set priorities and make decisions.

   ☐ Yes   ☐ Sometimes   ☐ No

3. I like to have someone else with more experience set my targets and goals, so I can meet or exceed them.

   ☐ Yes   ☐ Sometimes   ☐ No

4. I am excited about starting from scratch.

   ☐ Yes   ☐ Sometimes   ☐ No

5. I enjoy building teams as long as I am the leader.

   ☐ Yes   ☐ Sometimes   ☐ No

6. I feel uptight if someone asks me a question, and I do not immediately know the answer.

   ☐ Yes   ☐ Sometimes   ☐ No

7. I enjoy pleasing the people I work for.

   ☐ Yes   ☐ Sometimes   ☐ No

8. I want to help my employees feel successful, and I know how to encourage others.

   ☐ Yes   ☐ Sometimes   ☐ No

9. My primary goal is to make a lot of money fast and have lots of leisure time.

   ☐ Yes   ☐ Sometimes   ☐ No

10. I like the idea of coming to work later in the morning and seeing my employees already working.

    ☐ Yes   ☐ Sometimes   ☐ No

11. I know I do not know how to do everything, but I am willing to ask for advice and even pay for it.

    ☐ Yes   ☐ Sometimes   ☐ No

12. I would rather learn on the job by trial and error than pay for help.
    ☐ Yes   ☐ Sometimes   ☐ No

13. I would rather sit in my office making phone calls and setting appointments than working outside, getting sweaty.
    ☐ Yes   ☐ Sometimes   ☐ No

14. I do not care if I have to follow someone else's rules if I benefit from their expertise and make more money faster.
    ☐ Yes   ☐ Sometimes   ☐ No

15. I work and play outdoors. It is my favorite place to be.
    ☐ Yes   ☐ Sometimes   ☐ No

16. I hate being cooped up in an office.
    ☐ Yes   ☐ Sometimes   ☐ No

17. I have excellent mechanical skills.
    ☐ Yes   ☐ Sometimes   ☐ No

18. I know I am good at what I do, but I know my limits.
    ☐ Yes   ☐ Sometimes   ☐ No

19. I am orderly by nature. I live by the motto: "A place for everything, and everything in its place."
    ☐ Yes   ☐ Sometimes   ☐ No

20. Even if my work area seems messy, it is organized to suit my needs.
    ☐ Yes   ☐ Sometimes   ☐ No

21. I like the challenge of getting along with difficult people.
    ☐ Yes   ☐ Sometimes   ☐ No

22. One of my goals is to inspire others to succeed. I want to be a role model in my community.
    ☐ Yes   ☐ Sometimes   ☐ No

23. I would like a job where I can get my hands dirty.
    ☐ Yes   ☐ Sometimes   ☐ No

24. I prefer the wilderness to a manicured golf course.
    ☐ Yes   ☐ Sometimes   ☐ No

25. I keep my checkbook balanced and promptly reconcile bank statements.
    ☐ Yes   ☐ Sometimes   ☐ No

26. I pay my taxes on time.
    ☐ Yes   ☐ Sometimes   ☐ No

27. I know the local regulations for the business I want to open.
    ☐ Yes   ☐ Sometimes   ☐ No

28. I feel comfortable negotiating prices with customers and vendors.
    ☐ Yes   ☐ Sometimes   ☐ No

29. I like to associate with people from different backgrounds.
    ☐ Yes   ☐ Sometimes   ☐ No

30. I will tell an employee the result I want, and let him/her figure out how to achieve it.
    ☐ Yes   ☐ Sometimes   ☐ No

31. I am rarely satisfied, and I always strive for improvement.
    ☐ Yes   ☐ Sometimes   ☐ No

32. I have always enjoyed working with numbers.
    ☐ Yes   ☐ Sometimes   ☐ No

33. I am willing to change any business practice or product at a moment's notice if I hear of something that might work better.
    ☐ Yes   ☐ Sometimes   ☐ No

34. I hate having someone else tell me what to do or how to do it.
    ☐ Yes   ☐ Sometimes   ☐ No

35. I am done with formal education forever.
    ☐ Yes   ☐ Sometimes   ☐ No

36. I will ask customers for feedback regularly. If I do not hear complaints, I will not change anything in the business.
    ☐ Yes   ☐ Sometimes   ☐ No

37. I like to shop for bargains.
    ☐ Yes   ☐ Sometimes   ☐ No

38. I do not take chances; I plan for all possibilities.
    ☐ Yes   ☐ Sometimes   ☐ No

39. I can be fine without a regular paycheck for a while.
    ☐ Yes   ☐ Sometimes   ☐ No

40. I am eager to open this business. It is like a parachute jump — a leap into the unknown.
    ☐ Yes   ☐ Sometimes   ☐ No

41. I have enough of my own money and resources to start this business immediately.
    ☐ Yes   ☐ Sometimes   ☐ No

42. I know where to get more money if I need it.
   ☐ Yes   ☐ Sometimes   ☐ No

43. I am living from paycheck to paycheck now. I am tired of it.
   ☐ Yes   ☐ Sometimes   ☐ No

44. I want customers ready and waiting the day I open my doors.
   ☐ Yes   ☐ Sometimes   ☐ No

45. I have many ideas about marketing my business, and I know how to get it done.
   ☐ Yes   ☐ Sometimes   ☐ No

46. I already have a company name picked out.
   ☐ Yes   ☐ Sometimes   ☐ No

47. I already know what kind of customers I want to serve.
   ☐ Yes   ☐ Sometimes   ☐ No

48. I dream about this business at night.
   ☐ Yes   ☐ Sometimes   ☐ No

49. I have a picture in my head of me running my own business.
   ☐ Yes   ☐ Sometimes   ☐ No

50. My family and friends are supportive of my business ideas.
   ☐ Yes   ☐ Sometimes   ☐ No

Scoring:

Business ownership may be appropriate for you if you answered "yes" on Questions 1, 4, 5, 8, 12, 33, 34, 39, 41, 42, 48, 49, and 50. This response shows you have an independent spirit and are willing to take full responsibility for the job you are undertaking. A "yes" response on Question 2 suggests you might want to form a partnership or at least consider having employees, family, or other advisers help you make business decisions.

A person well-suited to franchise ownership might answer "yes" to Questions 3, 14, and 50. Someone who answers "yes" to 41, 42, and 44 may find purchasing an existing business more appropriate than starting from scratch. Delegating skills are highlighted by "yes" answers to Questions 18 and 30.

A good attitude that will be helpful in business is demonstrated by "yes" answers to Questions 11, 21, 22, 38, and 40. Skills and affinities useful to business operation are shown in "yes" answers to 15, 16, 17, 19, 20, 23, 25, 26, 27, 28, 29, 31, 32, 37, 45, 46, and 47.

Finally, those who answer "yes" to Questions 9, 10, 13, 24, 35, 36, and 43 may find the reality of business ownership difficult. This does not mean you cannot run a successful business, just as a "no" to certain questions in the skills and affinities group does not mean you cannot succeed. But, it does mean you may need to select partners, advisers, or get some specific training yourself to make the path of your business growth possible and realistic. It is always helpful to consider delegating work in an area where your skills are not supreme. Also, remember that showing your employees you are dedicated to doing the job will inspire them to make their best effort, too.

Questions to Ask About a Franchise

Franchises are individually owned businesses operated under the name and rules of a large chain, called the franchisor. The franchisor has perfected a successful business method and has created a business plan for franchisees to implement. Everything is standardized; the franchisor sells the franchisee the right to operate a business using the company's name, logo, reputation, and selling techniques. The franchisor might sell a franchisee "marketing rights" to certain areas or zones of the country. Typically, you pay a set price for the franchise and a percentage of gross sales on each sale you make. You also may need to pay into a national marketing fund, and the franchisor may require you to purchase marketing materials from specific vendors to maintain brand consistency and image. **If you are interested in purchasing a franchise, ask the franchisor the following questions**:

1. How long has the company been in business? _____

   _____

2. How many franchisees does the company currently have? _____

   _____

3. How many franchisees are in your area? _____

   _____

4. How is a franchisee's business territory defined? _____

   _____

5. Is the area you would be interested in available? If not, what areas are available? _____

   _____

6. What are the costs, including the initial cost to purchase the franchise, the royalties, and the marketing fees? _____

7. How do the royalty fees work, and how long do you pay them? _____

   _____

8. Are the royalty fees a percentage of sales or a set fee? _____

   _____

9. What is the marketing fee? _____

10. How will the franchise company assist you with marketing? _____

    _____

11. What assistance will the franchisor give you if you purchase? Is the assistance given just during the startup phase or on a consistent basis? _____

    _____

12. How much control do you have as a franchisee on what you sell or how you run your business? _____

13. Can you speak to an existing owner? _____

    _____

THE ENCYCLOPEDIA OF SMALL BUSINESS FORMS AND AGREEMENTS

The Federal Trade Commission requires companies selling franchised businesses to provide a franchisor disclosure to any prospective franchisee ten business days before any papers are signed or fees are paid. Official guidelines for a Uniform Franchise Offering Circular (UFOC) can be found on the website of the North American Securities Administrators Association (NASAA) (**www.nasaa. org/content/Files/UniformFranchiseOfferingCircular.doc**). Request a copy of the franchisor's disclosure document and review it carefully. It should include this information:

Franchisor's Disclosure Document Checklist

☐ Franchisor name

☐ Business experience of key officials

☐ Litigation record

☐ Bankruptcy record

☐ Initial franchise fee

☐ Other fees

☐ Initial investment, including franchise fee, equipment, and any other costs

☐ Any requirements about where to purchase products and services

☐ Franchisee's obligations

☐ Franchisor's obligations

☐ Territories, including exclusivity and growth options

☐ Trademarks

☐ Patents, copyrights, and property information

☐ Obligation to participate in operating the business

☐ Restrictions on what the franchisee may sell

☐ Contract renewal, termination and transfers, and dispute resolution

☐ Earnings claims — estimates of what the franchisee may earn

☐ List of all franchise outlets, with contact names and numbers

☐ Franchisor's audited financial statements

☐ Receipt — signed proof that the prospective franchisee received a UFOC

☐ Use of public figures — payment to celebrities or high-profile persons and/or their investment in the system

Creating Your Business Plan

A business plan transforms your idea into reality. A good business plan is essential for success. It lays out, on paper, why you are in business, who your customers and competitors are, what your strengths and weaknesses are, how you plan to finance and run your business, and what you have to do to get started. Creating a business plan helps you develop your ideas and foresee all eventualities. You are forced to consider every aspect of your new business, including how much you will spend to establish and operate it, assets and skills you can contribute to the business, sales and profit expectations, strategies for expanding and growing the business, and how you will exit the business. A business plan is also your sales pitch to prospective investors and partners, lenders, and suppliers who might extend you credit. A well-constructed business plan shows you understand your business thoroughly and are planning for the future. Finally, a business plan serves as a yardstick to measure your progress and help you adjust goals and expectations as the business progresses.

The forms and checklists in this section will help you organize information and formulate your business plan. The worksheets for an overall business plan are followed by individual worksheets that cover details of the plan's various sections.

Elements of a Business Plan

I. Cover sheet

II. Statement of purpose

III. Table of contents

   i. The business

      1. Description of business

      2. Marketing

      3. Competition

      4. Operating procedures

      5. Personnel

      6. Business insurance

   ii. Financial data

      1. Loan applications

      2. Capital equipment and supply list

      3. Balance sheet

      4. Break-even analysis

      5. *Pro forma* income projections (profit and loss statements)

         a. Three-year summary

         b. Detail by month, first year

        c. Detail by quarters, second, and third years

        d. Assumptions upon which projections were based

    6. *Pro forma* cash flow

        a. Follow guidelines for Number 5

  iii. Supporting documents

    1. Tax returns of principals for past three years

    2. Personal financial statement (all banks have these forms)

    3. In the case of a franchised business, a copy of franchise contract and all supporting documents provided by the franchisor

    4. Copy of proposed lease or purchase agreement for building space

    5. Copy of licenses and other legal documents.

    6. Copy of résumés of all principals

    7. Copies of letters of intent from suppliers, etc.

IV. The body of the business plan can be divided into four distinct sections:

   i. The description of the business

  ii. The marketing plan

 iii. The management plan

  iv. The financial management plan

Addenda to the business plan should include the executive summary, supporting documents, and financial projections.

Description of the business

The business description section is divided into three primary parts. Section 1 describes your business; Section 2, the product or service you will be offering; and Section 3, the location of your business and why this location is desirable (if you have a franchise, some franchisors assist in site selection).

Section 1: Description of business

When describing your business, you should explain:

- Business form: proprietorship, partnership, or corporation. What licenses or permits you will need.

- Business type

- What your product or service is.

- Business character. Is it a new independent business, a takeover, an expansion, a franchise?

- Why your business will be profitable. What are the growth opportunities? Will franchising impact growth opportunities?

- When your business will be open. What days? Hours?

- What you have learned about your kind of business from outside sources (trade suppliers, bankers, other franchise owners, franchisor, publications).

A cover sheet precedes the description. It includes the name, address, and telephone number of the business and the names of all principals. In the description of your business, emphasize any special features, and explain how and why these features will appeal to customers. Clearly identify the business's goals and objectives, and clarify why you are or why you want to be in business.

Section 2: Product/services

Describe the benefits of your goods and services from your customers' perspective. Successful business owners know or at least have an idea of what their customers want or expect. This foresight can be helpful in building customer satisfaction and loyalty, and it is a good strategy for beating the competition or retaining your competitiveness.

Describe:

- What you are selling.

- How your product or service will benefit the customer.

- Which products / services are in demand.

- What is different about the product or service your business is offering.

Section 3: Location

The location of your business can play a decisive role in its success or failure. Remember the old maxim, "Location, location, location." Your location should be built around your customers; it should be accessible; and it should provide a sense of security. Consider these questions when addressing this section of your business plan:

- What are your location needs?

- What kind of space will you need?

- Why is the area desirable? The building desirable?

- Is it easily accessible? Is public transportation available? Is street lighting adequate?

- Are market shifts or demographic shifts occurring?

Marketing plan

Marketing is vital to successful business ventures. How well you market your business, along with a few other considerations, will ultimately determine your degree of success or failure. The key element of a successful marketing plan is knowing your customers — their likes, dislikes, and expectations. By identifying these factors, you can develop a marketing strategy that will arouse and fulfill their needs.

Identify your customers by their age, sex, income / educational level, and residence. At first, target only those customers who are most likely to purchase your product or service. As your customer base expands, you may need to modify the marketing plan to include other customers. (Potential franchise owners will have to use the marketing strategy the franchisor has developed.) Your marketing plan should be part of your business plan and should contain answers to these questions:

- Who are your customers? Define your target market(s).

- Are your markets growing? Steady? Declining?

- Is your market share growing? Steady? Declining?

- If a franchise, how is your market segmented?

- Are your markets large enough to expand?

- How will you attract, hold, increase your market share? If a franchise, will the franchisor provide assistance in this area? How will you promote your sales?

- What pricing strategy have you devised?

Advertising and public relations

Having a good product or service and not advertising and promoting it is like not having a business at all. Advertising and promotions are the lifeline of a business. Your marketing plan should include a public relations strategy and an advertising budget. Your public relations strategy should identify the characteristics, age, and physical location of your target customers and the best ways to get their attention and attract them to your business. It should also include plans for expanding your business into new target markets once you have successfully established your initial customer base.

Competition

Competition is a way of life in business. It is important to know your competitors and the relative advantages and disadvantages of your business. Answer the following questions:

- Who are your five nearest direct competitors?

- Who are your five nearest indirect competitors?

- How is their business? Steady? Increasing? Decreasing?

- What have you learned from their operations? From their advertising?

- What are their strengths and weaknesses?

- How do their products or services differ from yours?

Pricing and sales

Your pricing strategy can improve your overall competitiveness. Get a feel for the pricing strategy of your competitors and determine whether your prices are in line with theirs and whether they are in line with industry averages. Some pricing considerations are:

- Product / service cost and pricing

- Competitive position

- Pricing below competition

- Pricing above competition

- Price lining

- Multiple pricing

- Service components

- Material costs
- Labor costs
- Overhead costs

Have a well-planned strategy, establish your policies, and constantly monitor prices and operating costs to ensure profits. Even in a franchise where the franchisor provides operational procedures and materials, it is a good policy to keep abreast of the changes in the marketplace because these changes can affect your competitiveness and profit margins.

Operating procedures: Management and personnel

The management plan

Your personnel management plan, along with your marketing and financial management plans, sets the foundation for and facilitates success. Employees and staff will play an important role in the total operation of your business. Evaluate the skills you do and do not possess, because you will have to hire personnel to supply the skills you lack.

Your management plan should answer questions such as:

- How does your background / experience help you in this business?
- What are your weaknesses, and how can you compensate for them?
- Who will be on the management team?
- What are their strengths / weaknesses?
- What are their duties?
- Are these duties clearly defined?
- If a franchise, what type of assistance can you expect from the franchisor?
- Will this assistance be ongoing?
- What are your current personnel needs?
- What are your plans for hiring and training personnel?
- What salaries, vacations, and holidays will you offer? If a franchise, are these issues covered in the management package the franchisor will provide?
- What benefits, if any, can you afford at this point?
- If the business is to be a franchise, the operating procedures, manuals, and materials devised by the franchisor should be included in this section of the business plan.

Financial management plan

A sound financial management plan ensures that your business will be able to meet its financial obligations. This plan should contain a realistic budget, including the amount of money needed to open your business (startup costs) and the amount needed to keep it open (operating costs). Your startup budget will include one-time-only costs, such as major equipment, utility deposits, and down payments.

Startup budget

- Personnel (costs prior to opening)
- Legal / professional fees
- Occupancy
- Licenses / permits
- Equipment
- Insurance
- Supplies

- Advertising / promotions
- Salaries / wages
- Accounting
- Income
- Utilities
- Payroll expenses

Operating budget

Your operating budget should include money to cover the first three to six months of operation, allowing for these expenses:

- Personnel
- Insurance
- Rent
- Depreciation
- Loan payments
- Advertising / promotions
- Legal / accounting
- Miscellaneous expenses

- Supplies
- Payroll expenses
- Salaries / wages
- Utilities
- Dues / subscriptions / membership fees
- Taxes
- Repairs / maintenance

The financial section of your business plan should include any loan applications you have filed, capital equipment and supply list, balance sheet, break-even analysis, *pro forma* income projections (profit and loss statement), and *pro forma* cash flow. The income statement and cash-flow projections should include a three-year summary, detail by month for the first year, and detail by quarter for the second and third years. Include an explanation of all projections. Unless you are thoroughly familiar with financial statements, get help in preparing your cash flow and income statements and your balance sheet.

This section also describes the accounting system and the inventory-control system you will use. If your business is a franchise, the franchisor may stipulate these systems in the franchise contract. A financial adviser can assist you in developing this section of your business plan.

Business Plan and Strategic Plan Worksheet

Use this tool to plan your business and prioritize everything you need to do and where you want to focus your efforts.

What does it take to start your business?

Startup to-do list:

1. _____

2. _____

3. _____

4. _____

5. _____

What is it going to take to run your business?

This list is for *you*. What do *you* need to be able to run your own business full time or part-time? What do *you* need to be doing to focus on your clients and be able to support yourself?

1. _____

2. _____

3. _____

4. _____

5. _____

Business plan planner

Introduction

- Introduce the plan. Explain who wrote it, when, and for what purpose.

Mission statements

- What are the central purposes and activities of the business?

- What are its major objectives, key strategies, and primary goals?

Product / service offerings

- Provide short, concise descriptions of the products / services you are offering.

- What makes them special?

Profiles of target markets

- Define the size, segments, trends, and competitors that impact your business.

- Establish a customer profile for your primary and secondary markets.

Marketing strategies, sales plans, and projections

- How will the business market its products / services and sell to customers?

- What sales will be achieved in its main markets?

- How will you deal with competitors?

Operational plans

- Establish your plans for service activities.
- What services are you going to provide?
- How are you going to organize your services?
- What resources are you going to apply toward your operations?

Management and administration

- Identify your proposed management team.
- Identify your proposed structure.

Financial projections

- What key financial projections impact your business plan?
- What are your profit and loss projections for the next five-year period?
- What are the key rationalizations for your financial projections?
- Establish a balance sheet for your business.

Funding requirements and proposals

- How much money do you need to get started?
- How much money are you going to need to manage for six to 12 months?

Conclusion

- Why will the business succeed?
- Why should it be supported?

Strategic plan planner

Assess the current situation for your business:

- Internal strengths
- Internal weaknesses
- External threats
- External opportunities

Explain your vision of business in one- to five-years' time:

- What do you want the business to achieve?
- Where do you see it going in the next year / two years / five years?

Establish your mission statement for your business:

- What will the business be doing?
- What activities will it perform?
- What makes the business special/competitive?

Set out key long-term objectives that are your primary underlying reasons for being involved in the business:

1. _____

2. _____

3. _____

Identify key strategies for your business and major functional areas:

1. _____

2. _____

3. _____

Assess possible future scenarios:

- Internal strengths
- Internal weaknesses
- External threats
- External opportunities

Specify major goals achievable over the next one to five years:

1. _____

2. _____

3. _____

Define strategic action programs:

Target _____

_____

Priority _____

_____

Who? _____

_____

What? _____

_____

Where? _____

_____

When? _____

_____

How? _____

_____

Business Plan Checklist

Your business plan should contain the following sections:

- ☐ Executive summary

- ☐ Mission statements

- ☐ Company objectives

- ☐ Personal evaluation of the business owner

- ☐ Description of services and products

- ☐ Company overview (a review of location, personnel, and resources)

- ☐ Market analysis (a review of the business niche and competitors)

- ☐ Advertising and marketing summaries

- ☐ Financial projections (startup costs and profit/loss statements for at least the first two years of business)

Questions to ask yourself:

1. When your business closes down, how are you going to divide the assets? Do you want to pass your business on to someone? Do you want to sell your business? _____

   _____

   _____

   _____

2. How are you going to let go of your office? Do you want to dispose of it entirely, or do you want to hold on to it and secure rent from it? _____

   _____

   _____

   _____

3. What are you going to do about your clients when you decide to close down your business? Are you prepared to help them find another company that will be able to meet their needs?

   _____

   _____

   _____

4. What are you going to do if one of your clients decides to sue you? Are you adequately protected? _____

   _____

   _____

Sample Business Plan

This sample business plan for a lawn-care company includes all the elements in the checklist on the preceding page. Your plan might be written differently to reflect the nature of your business, but it should contain specific information and inspire the confidence of potential investors or partners.

This example plan makes certain assumptions about the business's structure, financials, and equipment needs. Your plan must reflect your needs, marketing conditions, funding, and the advice you receive from your attorney and accountant.

Executive summary

Lance's Lawn Care and Nursery is a residential and commercial landscaping service offering basic-to-advanced lawn services, gardening, and landscape design to homeowners, property managers, and developers. Lance's Lawn Care and Nursery will target upper-income homeowners and upscale commercial areas, which need and can afford quality services of this nature. Real estate prices in this area have remained strong, despite the turnout in other sections of the country, and demand remains high, thus offering growth opportunities.

Lance's Lawn Care and Nursery will begin as a limited liability company (LLC) owned entirely by Lance Lingering. Lance has worked as a lawn care and gardening specialist for the past eight years as supervisor for Bob's Yards and Patios, and, more recently, as a master nursery supervisor at Elaine's Plants and Patios. Lance is a certified lawn maintenance quality-control specialist.

Lance's will open for business at the beginning of the region's lawn care season, which typically runs for seven months — April through October. During that time, Lance will hire one part-time helper to work up to 20 hours per week. Lance estimates his own workweek at 60 to 80 hours. If business warrants, Lance will hire a second part-time worker.

Lance forecasts initial business at 20 to 30 residential customers requiring weekly yard maintenance, plus spring and fall services such as cleanup, mulching, and trimming. The average lawn maintenance fee will be $50, with some fees being higher or lower depending on yard size and services required. Spring and fall services will be in the $100 to $300 range. Anticipated monthly revenues during the first season from residential customers are expected to be $6,000, plus an additional $2,000 to $3,000 per month in April, May, and October from yard cleanup and preparation. We do not anticipate significant commercial contracts during the first season of business; however, we will market aggressively for commercial work for the following season, using the first year as a period of development and networking. Our first-year revenues are forecast at $49,500.

The above numbers are fictional, but serve as a good example. The summary explains the thinking that justifies the company and its future.

Market analysis

Lance's service area has experienced strong, sustained growth in population and property values over the past decade, even during recent setbacks in the real estate industry nationally. The growth of upper-income homes has been pronounced in communities with large lots. These homeowners a) have the financial resources to pay for first-class landscaping, and b) little desire to do this type of work themselves. County planners expect more than 300 such homes to be sold and occupied in the coming 12 months, adding to the more than 1,000 such homes now occupied. Lance will target all of these residences, so our estimate of 30 customers is modest. We expect to exceed that number quickly.

In addition, several retirement communities are under construction, and Lance will market to the developers and management companies that oversee landscaping and maintenance. Lance has joined several professional groups that network decision makers in this segment.

Again, the idea here is to explain the market you intend to pursue.

Company description

Formally explain the business structure you have selected. This example is a limited liability corporation, or LLC. In your specific case, you may elect something else. In this portion of your business plan, explain that structure, stating your officers, managers, and so on.

Organization and management

Be specific about how your company will be operated. Lance will be owner and general manager. If he plans to hire his wife or sister to do some daily bookkeeping, mention it here. If Lance's office will be at home, list it here. Where will equipment be stored? Will Lance need a storage facility? Be specific. Personnel and sales goals can also be mentioned here and will be expanded upon later in this plan.

Marketing and sales management

Lance's Lawn Care and Nursery, LLC, will rely primarily on door-to-door marketing during its first quarter. We will distribute fliers at each home in our target area once a week for four weeks, approximately 4,000 fliers during the first month of operation. Each home will receive the flier at least twice. Two of our target communities permit solicitors to knock on doors, and Lance will personally knock on these doors on Saturday mornings for two hours each week to help him establish personal contact with potential customers and to offer on-the-spot consultations and estimates to build the initial customer base. Lance's initial marketing will focus on spring cleanup special offers.

Lance will also pass out business cards to developers, property managers, and other potential commercial customers, establishing potential relationships in the commercial arena.

This is where the plan meets the real world. Think this through and understand that this is the key part of your plan to make your business successful. All of your research and planning will focus on sales and marketing. Explain an entire year's worth of market planning — canvassing, networking, phone directories, professional organizations, and any other advertising you plan to use.

Do not expect miracles from your marketing. Fliers generate a 1 percent to 2 percent response rate, meaning out of every 100 fliers you distribute, you will get one or two calls. You should close more than half of these responses. The response rate goes up with frequency. Each time a potential customer sees your flier, the higher the likelihood that person will respond. Everything you do will add up to a total marketing strategy that will bring customers to your business.

Services and products

Expand on what you will do for your customers. If, for the purposes of this example, you live in an area with a short lawn season and a long, snowy winter, you may want to provide snow removal in the cold months. Determine how much income you can project for your services given the number of customers you can realistically anticipate in your first six months or year.

Research all of your services. Be aware of your competition, their prices, and the market. Do you plan to operate a nursery to sell plants and related products to the public, in addition to landscaping or yard maintenance? If so, you will need a separate business plan for that, including a commercial site, permits, and products.

Financials

Here is where you make your financial projections for your first three years. These are estimates based on solid information and market conditions, but, as with all business activities, nothing is guaranteed. Nevertheless, this is a financial blueprint.

First, make a column of all of the services you plan to offer and forecast sales for them.

Service	Year 1	Year 2	Year 3
Service ex. 1	$7,500	$10,000	$12,500
Service ex. 2	$42,000	$50,000	$55,000
Products			
Product 1	$5,000	$6,500	$7,000
Product 2	—	—	—

Next, list your costs. These would include cost of goods (not equipment, which is a capital expense), rent, phone, marketing, insurance, fuel, equipment maintenance, and other costs of doing business.

Costs			
Storage rental	$8,000	$8,000	$8,000
Phone	$600	$625	$700
Insurance	$2,000	$2,100	$2,200
Ad / marketing	$5,000	$6,000	$8,000
Fuel	$1,800	$2,000	$2,000

Make a good faith effort at predicting your costs. Your actual expenses may be higher or lower than your initial projections, so track your expenses monthly to allow for adjustments. For instance, you may increase or decrease your marketing expenses according to projected costs versus actual expenses.

Labor

List your labor expenses. How much are you going to pay yourself and your employee(s)? If you have employees, you must pay unemployment insurance, workers' compensation insurance, and possibly other fees, depending on your state's laws.

Startup costs

List here what you anticipate the cost of opening your business will be: Include the cost of locating, leasing, and furnishing a site; office supplies, licenses and fees; furniture and equipment; advertising and promotional costs; staring salaries for employees; and so on.

Funding requests

If you are going to borrow the money needed to start the business, you must provide a detailed financial statement in addition to the information you already have in your business plan. This is the same information you would provide for any substantial loan from a bank or other financial institution. You must provide assurance that you can and will pay back the loan and offer a form of security. This might be your home or other assets such as savings, stocks, or real estate. Your business and its assets will be part of the security package.

If you are purchasing a franchise, you likely will not be able to use the franchise as collateral because franchisors typically retain sole rights to award franchises, and therefore, may not honor any claims against the franchise. This means if you put your business up as collateral and default on the loan, the lender cannot take over your franchise, so it is useless as collateral.

If you are considering purchasing a franchise, the law requires that the franchisor provide you with a detailed report explaining every aspect of the business. This is a requirement of the Federal Trade Commission (FTC) that advises all prospective franchisees to carefully read these reports. A meticulous review will protect yourself and your investment. Employ a lawyer or accountant who is aware of FTC regulations to double-check these documents for potential problems.

You may have noticed the words *lawyer* and *accountant* again. As stressed earlier, these two professionals can save you from trouble and losing money. One more option many startup companies have used, especially in the past, is using credit cards. If you have good personal credit and a high enough limit, you may be able to borrow the money from yourself. Be wary of high interest rates, and be sure you will be able to pay the monthly fees. Talk to your accountant and your banker about loan details. If you lend money to your company, you may be entitled to interest on the loan, as well as repayment.

Format for Business Proposal

Startup Proposal	Other Business Proposals
Executive summary	Executive summary
General company description	Introduction and background
Product / service plan	Goals and objectives
Demographic analysis	Methods and tasks
Competitive analysis	Timelines
Marketing and promotion plan	
Management plan	
Operating plan	
Financial plan and financial spreadsheets	
Conclusion and request for funding	Conclusion
Supporting financial statements and other appendixes	Appendixes

Elevator Pitch

Describe, in *only* 150 words and 60 seconds, everything most prospective investors would want to know before asking to see your business plan:

1. Your company _____

_____

_____

2. Your product _____

_____

_____

3. Your market_____

_____

_____

_____

4. Your market/product differentiation; that is: "Why us?" _____

_____

_____

_____

5. Your revenue model _____

_____

_____

_____

6. Your personal qualifications _____

_____

_____

7. How much money you need _____

_____

_____

8. What you would do with the money if you get it _____

_____

_____

_____

Startup Costs

Before you can begin making money with your new business, you will need to rent or purchase an office or building, purchase equipment and supplies, set up your business, print business cards and stationery, turn on electricity and water, pay for Internet and phone lines, and hire employees. These initial expenses are your "startup costs." The following worksheets will guide you through the process of calculating how much startup money you will need.

Estimated Startup Costs Worksheet

Estimated Startup Costs	
Description	*Estimated cost*
Property expenses	
Deposit	
First three months' rent	
Merchandise expenses	
Initial inventory	
Three months' inventory	
Business insurance (one year)	
Legal expenses	
Franchising fee	
Trademark licensing	
Business license	
Fictitious name (DBA) paperwork	
Corporation / partnership agreement	
Communication expenses	
Telephone installation	
Website address registration	
Website hosting, **yearly**	
Internet access, **yearly**	
Equipment and supplies	
Vacuum cleaner	
Cleaning supplies	
Office supplies	
Delivery vehicle	

Shelving and displays	
Computer and software	
Cash register	
Point-of-sale system	
POS subscription, **yearly**	
Personal expenses	
Lost wages (if leaving a job) for one year	
Health insurance, yearly	
Personnel expenses for one year	
Wages	
Advertisements for employees	
Training	
Taxes	
Health insurance	
Marketing expenses	
Outdoor signs	
Advertisements	
Interior design expenses	
Carpeting	
Interior signs	
Paint	
Furniture	
Decorations	
Other expenses	
TOTAL (add above)	

Startup Expenses Worksheet

Company

Sources of capital	Value	Description
Owners' investment		
Your name and percent ownership	$	
Other investor	$	
Other investor	$	
Other investor	$	
Total investment	$	
Bank loans		
Bank 1	$	
Bank 2	$	
Bank 3	$	
Bank 4	$	
Total bank loans	$	
Other loans		
Source 1	$	
Source 2	$	
Total other loans	$	
Startup expenses	*Value*	*Description*
Buildings/real estate		
Purchase	$	
Construction	$	
Remodeling	$	
Other	$	
Total buildings/real estate	$	
Leasehold improvements		
Item 1	$	
Item 2	$	
Item 3	$	
Item 4	$	
Total leasehold improvements	$	
Capital equipment list		
Furniture	$	

THE ENCYCLOPEDIA OF SMALL BUSINESS FORMS AND AGREEMENTS

Equipment	$	
Fixtures	$	
Machinery	$	
Other	$	
Total capital equipment	$	
Office and admin expenses		
Rental	$	
Utility deposits	$	
Legal and accounting fees	$	
Prepaid insurance	$	
Pre-opening salaries	$	
Other	$	
Total location and admin expenses	$	
Opening inventories		
Category 1	$	
Category 2	$	
Category 3	$	
Category 4	$	
Category 5	$	
Total inventory	$	
Advertising and promotional expenses		
Advertising	$	
Signage	$	
Printing	$	
Travel/entertainment	$	
Other	$	
Total advertising and promotional expenses	$	
Other expenses		
Other expense 1	$	
Other expense 2	$	
Total other expenses	$	
Reserve for contingencies	$	

Working capital (from 12-month cash flow)	$	
Summary statement	*Value*	*Description*
Sources of capital		
Investments	$	
Bank loans	$	
Other loans	$	
Total source of funds	$	
Startup expenses		
Buildings / real estate	$	
Leasehold improvements	$	
Capital equipment	$	
Location / administration expenses	$	
Inventory	$	
Advertising / promotional expenses	$	
Other expenses	$	
Contingency fund	$	
Working capital	$	
Total startup expenses	$	
Security and collateral for loan proposal		
Collateral for loans	**Value**	**Description**
Real estate	$	
Other collateral	$	
Other collateral	$	
Other collateral	$	
Owners		
Your name here		
Other owner		
Other owner		
Loan guarantors (other than owners)		
Loan guarantor 1		
Loan guarantor 2		
Loan guarantor 3		

Estimated Startup Cost Shortfall

Estimated Startup Cost Shortfall	
Description	*Amount*
Estimated startup costs	a.
Personal financial contribution	b.
Shortfall (subtract b from a)	

Sample Startup Expenses Worksheet

Item	Estimated Cost	Actual Cost
Laptop or standard PC	$2,000-$3,000	$2,599
Printer	$200-$300	$225
Scanner / fax / copier	$125-$200	$175
Digital camera	$100-$300	$200
Cell phone	$200-$500	$350
Attorney fees	$500-$1,000	$750
Accountant fees	$500-$1,000	$500
Insurance	$50-$1,000	$950
Software	$200-$2,250	$1,800
Business cards	$25	$19.99
Phone line installation	$75-$125	$100
Office furniture	$200-$300	$250
Office supplies	$50-$150	$75
Startup advertising	$200-$400	$300
Total	**$4,425-$10,550**	**$8,294**

Creating an Operating Budget Worksheet

Once your business is up and running, you will need to calculate how much it will cost you to operate the business every month. These worksheets and checklists will help you determine how much money you must bring in every month to make a profit.

Before beginning work on a detailed annual or monthly budget, answer the following questions:

1. How much money do you have?_____

_____

_____

2. How much money will you need to effectively run your business? _____

_____

_____

3. How much money will you need to purchase equipment? _____

_____

_____

4. If you will be hiring employees or independent contractors, how much capital will you need so you can pay them? _____

_____

_____

5. What is the total of all your startup costs?_____

_____

_____

6. What are your expected profits on a monthly basis? _____

_____

7. What are your day-to-day costs? _____

_____

_____

8. How much money must you make to keep your business running smoothly? _____

_____

_____

Answer each question honestly and directly. Your answers will help determine whether you can afford to hire employees or realistically pay for the office property you are considering.

Budgeting Worksheet

Use this list to create your monthly budget. Items and services you must have should go into your startup budget and take precedence in your regular monthly budget. Other expenses, should-haves, or would-like-to-haves, take secondary and tertiary positions.

Must-haves

List items and services you *must* have for your business:

_____

_____

_____

_____

_____

_____

Should-haves

List items and services you *should have* for your business:

_____

_____

_____

_____

_____

_____

Would-like-to-haves

List items and services you *would like to have* for your business:

_____

_____

_____

_____

_____

Based on your determinations, use the following worksheets to draw up the budget and expenses for your company.

Startup Expenses Estimate Worksheet

Item	Estimated Cost	Actual Cost
Total		

THE ENCYCLOPEDIA OF SMALL BUSINESS FORMS AND AGREEMENTS

Operating Expenses Worksheet

Item	Estimated Cost	Actual Cost
Total		

Sample Operating Expenses Worksheet

Item	Estimated Cost	Actual Cost
Office rent*	$2,500-$4,000	$2,750
Utilities	$100-$350	$195
Internet	$40-$100	$70
Phone / fax	$50-$150	$75
Cell phone	$40-$150	$100
Travel	$70-$200	$150
Attorney fees	$50-$1,000	$250
Accountant fees	$500-$1,000	$500
Advertising	$50-$200	$120
Office supplies	$30-$100	$75
Staff (assistant)	$200-$1,600	$400
Total	**$3,630-$8,850**	**$4,685**

Checklist for Cutting Costs

This checklist covers several effective ways to reduce costs for your small business.

___ **Do you buy used?** If you have to furnish your office, buy used furniture rather than brand new furniture. You may save hundreds of dollars, especially considering that office furniture loses approximately 25 percent of its value the minute you take it out of the store.

___ **Do you buy local?** If you need to purchase products (e.g., printer ink, office supplies, computer software, and the like), go to stores in your area rather than ordering online or from a catalog. That way you will save on shipping costs.

___ **Do you buy in bulk?** Join Costco, BJ's, or whatever warehouse store is in your area, and purchase in bulk.

___ **Do you comparison shop?** Do not purchase the first product or service you research. Check prices and get quotes from at least three vendors. Choose the one that offers the services you need at the best price. Every few months, review how much you are paying for services and shop around for better deals.

___ **Do you negotiate?** If you are buying a product or service, talk with the seller, and try to negotiate a lower price. You might be surprised at how willing some people are to negotiate in order to get your business.

___ **Do you attend trade shows?** In many instances, vendors at trade shows offer attendees big discounts on products.

___ **Do you buy generic?** You do not need brand-name paper, pens, or other office supplies. Save money by buying generic, store-brand products. In many instances, those products are made by the same manufacturers as the brand-name ones.

___ **Do you shop around for insurance on a yearly basis?** It is common for people to pick an insurance company and allow the policy to renew automatically every year. You may be able to save money by getting quotes from other insurers when it is time to renew.

___ **Invest in a postage scale.** Purchasing a postage scale and ensuring that it is programmed with the correct postage rates can result in significant savings on your mailing costs.

___ **Buy your business checks anywhere but the bank.** You can find a much better deal on business checks elsewhere. Look online for deals, or find a coupon in a local coupon book.

___ **Request discounts.** If you consistently work with a vendor, ask whether he will give you a discount if you pay your invoices with a check or if you make your payment before the due date.

___ **Always pay your bills on time** to ensure you do not incur late penalties.

___ **Reconsider the organizations you are part of.** Many self-employed people belong to industry associations. A writer, for example, may belong to the National Writers Union, the Chamber of Commerce, and several other writing-industry associations. What associations do you belong to that require you to pay dues? Do you actively take part in those organizations, and do you benefit from them in some way? Or do you just write a check to cover the fees every year? If you answered yes to the latter, consider dropping out of those organizations.

Checklists for Evaluating a Business Location

This section includes several checklists to help you evaluate whether a particular location suits your business plans.

Location Analysis

You often hear the business phrase: "Location is everything." Large retailers and restaurant chains conduct extensive research before deciding on a location for a new store because they already know the type of area where they are most likely to succeed. When you shop around for a property for your new business, consider factors beyond the monthly rent and the building's physical appearance. This worksheet will help you determine whether a particular area, shopping center, or building is a location where your business can succeed.

Location Analysis						
Read the descriptions and circle the number that best describes the location.						
Local trends						
The local population is declining.	1	2	3	4	5	The location is having a population boom.
There are not many people in the area in the income bracket of my target market.	1	2	3	4	5	The average income for the area is the same as that of my target market.
There are not many people in the area in the age range of my target market.	1	2	3	4	5	The majority of the population is at or below the age of my target market.
Traffic						
The store is out of the way. Customers would have to make a special trip to get there.	1	2	3	4	5	Current traffic patterns take many people past the store.
Future construction will have traffic bypassing the store.	1	2	3	4	5	Future construction will bring more traffic past the store.
Competition						
Several stores nearby offer the same or similar merchandise.	1	2	3	4	5	This is the only store of its type in the area.
Visibility						
The store is not visible from the road.	1	2	3	4	5	The store is visible for several blocks.

There is no signage.	1	2	3	4	5	Signage is large, highly visible, and does not need upgraded.
Accessibility						
The store is difficult to get to. You have to know where you are going.	1	2	3	4	5	The entrance of the store is clearly marked and easy to find.
The parking is inadequate and will need to be improved immediately.	1	2	3	4	5	There is plenty of parking — more than enough for employees and customers.
The store is not handicap-accessible. It has stairs, steps, or narrow walkways that would make it impossible for a customer in a wheelchair.	1	2	3	4	5	The store is fully accessible. Enabling equipment has been installed to make the parking lot, entrance, selling floor, and restrooms easily navigable for customers with a range of disabilities.
Convenience						
The store is a long distance from my home. Commuting will be difficult.	1	2	3	4	5	The store is close to home. I can go back and forth several times a day.
Services such as accounting, shipping, and printing are not available in the area.	1	2	3	4	5	The store is close to all services I will use regularly.
Image						
The location's image is substantially different than the image of the intended clientele.	1	2	3	4	5	The location's image is identical to that of the intended clientele.
I would be embarrassed to own a business in this area.	1	2	3	4	5	I would be proud to own a business in this area.
The outside of the store would not attract customers. It needs immediate improvement.	1	2	3	4	5	The outside of the store is attractive and matches the image of the business.

Potential Location Checklist

Use this checklist to determine whether a prospective business site meets your requirements.

Potential Location Checklist	
Location	
The site…	✓
is the right size for my business.	
is passed by an adequate amount of traffic.	
fits the image I want for my store.	
would attract my target market.	
is near other successful businesses.	
is near other businesses that cater to my target market.	
has adequate parking.	
is visible from the road.	
is handicap-accessible.	

Proposed Location Rating

Proposed Location Rating	
Use this score sheet to rate the proposed location. Grade each: "A" = excellent, "B" = good, "C" = fair and "D" = poor.	
Factor	*Grade*
1. Good location for your target market	
2. The products you need are readily available	
3. Evaluate local competition situation	
4. Proximity to area attractions	
5. Employee qualifications	
6. Local wages for employees	
7. Parking facilities	
8. Adequate utilities are available	
9. Traffic flow	
10. Taxation burden	
11. Quality police and fire protection	
12. Housing availability for employees	
13. Details about schools and community activities	
14. Is the building suitable for your business?	
15. Type and cost of building / business	
16. Are there possibilities for future expansion?	
17. Estimate of site suitability in 10 years	

Legal Business Structures

This section includes checklists and information to help you determine which legal structure to use and documents to help you organize your new business.

Legal forms of business

When organizing a new business, one of the most important decisions is choosing its structure. Factors influencing this decision include:

- Legal restrictions

- Liabilities assumed

- Type of business operation

- Earnings distribution

- Capital needs

- Number of employees

- Tax advantages or disadvantages

- Length of business operation

You can find detailed information about the different legal structures for a business online in the Department of Housing and Urban Development's *Small Business Resource Guide* in *Chapter 11: Starting a Small Business* (**www.hud.gov/offices/osdbu/resource/guide/chap11.cfm**).

The advantages and disadvantages of sole proprietorship, partnership, corporation, and the hybrid limited liability company (LLC) are as follows:

Sole proprietorship

This is the easiest and least costly way of starting a business. You will probably need to pay for business name registration, a fictitious name certificate, and other necessary licenses. Attorney fees for starting the business will be less than those of the other business structures because less preparation of documents is required, and the owner has absolute authority over all business decisions.

Partnership

The two most common types of partnerships are general and limited partnerships. A general partnership can be formed simply by an oral agreement between two or more persons, but a legal partnership agreement drawn up by an attorney is highly recommended. Legal fees for drawing up a partnership agreement are higher than those for a sole proprietorship, but may be lower than incorporating. A partnership agreement could be helpful in solving any disputes. But partners are responsible for the other partners' business actions, as well as their own.

In a partnership, all profits and losses are shared among the partners. A profit is the positive gain after expenses are subtracted, while a loss occurs when a company's expenses exceed revenues. In a partnership, not all partners necessarily have equal ownership of the business. Typically, the extent of financial contributions toward the business determines the percentage of each partner's ownership.

A Partnership Agreement should include the following:

- Type of business
- Amount of equity invested by each partner
- Division of profit or loss
- Partners' compensation
- Distribution of assets upon dissolution
- Duration of partnership
- Provisions for changes or dissolving the partnership
- Dispute settlement clause
- Restrictions of authority and expenditures
- Settlement in case of death or incapacitation

Corporation

A corporation can be established as public or private. A public corporation is owned by its shareholders (also known as stockholders) and is public because anyone can buy shares of company stock through public stock exchanges. Control depends on stock ownership. Persons with the largest stock ownership — not the total number of shareholders — control the corporation. With control of stock shares or 51 percent of stock, a person or group is able to make policy decisions.

A private corporation is owned and managed by a few individuals who are normally involved in the company's day-to-day decision-making and operations. If you own a relatively small business, but still wish to run it as a corporation, a private corporation legal structure would allow you to stay closely involved in the operation and management.

Whether private or public, a corporation is a legal entity capable of entering into binding contracts and being held directly liable in any legal issues. Its finances are not directly tied to anyone's personal finances, and taxes are addressed completely separately from its owners.

A business may incorporate without an attorney, but legal advice is highly recommended. The corporate structure is usually the most complex and is more costly to organize than the other two business forms.

Control is exercised through regular board of director meetings and annual stockholders' meetings. Records must be kept to document decisions made by the board of directors. Small, closely held corporations can operate more informally, but record keeping cannot be eliminated entirely. Officers of a corporation can be liable to stockholders for improper actions. Liability is generally limited to stock ownership, except where fraud is involved.

You may want to incorporate as a "C" or "S" Corporation. Under IRS regulations, "S" Corporation means "small business corporation." An "S" Corporation is taxed similarly to a partnership or sole proprietorship, rather than being taxed like a corporation. Under the "S" Corporation legal structure, the shareholders' income taxes are directly impacted by the business's profit or loss.

Profits or losses are passed through to the shareholders, who report them on their own income tax returns. According to the IRS, shareholders must pay taxes on the profits the business realized for that year in proportion to the stock they own.

In order to qualify as an "S" Corporation under IRS regulations, the following requirements must be met:

- It cannot have more than 100 shareholders.

- Shareholders must be U.S. citizens or residents.

- All shareholders must approve operating under the "S" Corporation legal structure.

- It must be able to meet the requirements for an "S" Corporation the entire year.

- Additionally, Form 2553, "Election by a Small Business Corporation," must be filed with the IRS within the first two months and 15 days of the corporation's fiscal year.

Limited liability company (LLC)

An LLC is not a corporation, but it offers many of the same advantages. Many small-business owners and entrepreneurs prefer LLCs because they combine the limited liability protection of a corporation with the "pass through" taxation of a sole proprietorship or partnership.

LLCs have additional advantages over corporations:

- LLCs allow greater flexibility in management and business organization.

- LLCs do not have the ownership restrictions of "S" Corporations, making them ideal business structures for foreign investors.

- LLCs accomplish these aims without the IRS restrictions for an "S" Corporation.

LLCs are available in all 50 states and Washington, D.C. If you have other questions regarding LLCs, speak with a qualified legal and/or financial adviser.

Regulations and procedures affecting the formation of LLCs differ from state to state. Find them on the Internet in the "corporations" section of your secretary of state office's website.

Business Entity Chart

Legal entity	Costs involved	Number of owners	Paperwork	Tax implications	Liability issues
Sole proprietorship	Local fees assessed for registering business; generally between $25 and $100	One	Local licenses and registrations; assumed name registration	Owner is responsible for all personal and business taxes	Owner is personally liable for all financial and legal transactions
Partnership	Local fees assessed for registering business; generally between $25 and $100	Two or more	Partnership agreement	Business income passes through to partners and is taxed at the individual level only	Partners are personally liable for all financial and legal transactions, including those of the other partners
LLC	Filing fees for articles of incorporation; generally between $100 and $800, depending on the state	One or more	Articles of organization; operating agreement	Business income passes through to owners and is taxed at the individual level only	Owners are protected from liability; company carries all liability regarding financial and legal transactions
Corporation	Varies with each state; can range from $100 to $500	One or more; must designate directors and officers	Articles of incorporation to be filed with state; quarterly and annual report requirements; annual meeting reports	Corporation is taxed as a legal entity; income earned from business is taxed at individual level	Owners are protected from liability; company carries all liability regarding financial and legal transactions

Ownership Structure of Business Entities

	Ownership	Liability	Tax	Formalities
Sole proprietorship	One owner	Unlimited	Pass through to owner	None required
General partnership	Any number and type of general partners (at least two)	Unlimited	Pass through to general partners	None required, but partnership agreement recommended
Limited partnership	Any number and type of owners — at least one general partner, at least one limited partner	Unlimited for general partner(s); limited for limited partners	Pass through to both types of partner	File with state; agreement and annual meeting not required, but recommended
Limited liability company	Any number and type of owners — called members	Generally no personal liability for members	Pass through to members (unless they elect otherwise)	File with state; agreement and annual meeting not required, but recommended
"S" Corporation	Up to 100 shareholders — all to be U.S. citizens	Generally no personal liability for shareholders	Pass through to shareholders	File with state; bylaws and annual meetings required
"C" Corporation	Any number of shareholders	Generally no personal liability for shareholders	Corporation taxed; shareholders taxed on dividends	File with state; bylaws and annual meetings required

Checklist for Choosing and Registering a Business Name

☐ 1. Make a list of four or five possible names you like. One suggestion is to use your last name in the business name. Unless you have a common name such as Jones or Smith, it is often easier to remember a real name as opposed to a fictitious one.

_____

_____

_____

_____

_____

☐ 2. Perform searches to make certain your name is not already in use. Search at the local, state, and possibly federal level if you have chosen to do business as a corporation. Places you can check for business names that already exist:

- Phone directories

- County clerks, who have a Local Deed Registry

- Libraries, who will do name searches sometimes for a small fee

- Newspaper classified advertisements

- Trade journals (magazines for your industry)

☐ 3. After you have determined your name is not being used at the local level, register it with the county. Although there may be a small fee for this, registering at the county level is a smart move to ensure no one else can legally register or use your company's name.

☐ 4. Most business owners go on to register their name at the state level. You may be able to do the search portion yourself online (by entering "secretary of state" and your state name into any search engine to find the correct site and the search process) or for a small fee at the secretary of state's office. You will need documented proof your name is not in use before you can file for state registration. After you pay a small registration fee and fill out the official paperwork, your business name will be yours to use.

☐ 5. The Department of Commerce in your state can help answer and / or direct your questions to the proper registration agency.

Articles of Organization for an LLC

Two main documents are normally filed when establishing an LLC. One is an Operating Agreement, which addresses issues such as the management and structure of the business, the distribution of profit and loss, the method of how members will vote, and how changes in the organizational structure will be handled. Not every state requires the Operating Agreement.

Every state, however, does require Articles of Organization, and the necessary form is generally available for download from your state's website. The purpose of the Articles of Organization is to legally establish your business by registering with your state. It must contain, at a minimum, the following information:

- The limited liability company's name and the address of the principal place of business

- The purpose of the LLC

- The name and address of the LLC's registered agent (the person who is authorized to physically accept delivery of legal documents for the company)

- The name of the manager or managing members of the company

- An effective date for the company and signature

Articles of Organization for an LLC filed in the state of Florida will look like the sample on the following page.

Articles of Organization for an LLC filed in the state of Florida will look like this:

ARTICLE I — Name

The name and purpose of the Limited liability company is:

Name: International Trading Company, LLC

Purpose: To conduct...

ARTICLE II — Address

The mailing address and street address of the principal office of the limited liability company is:

Street Address:	1234 International Trade Drive
	Beautiful City, FL 33003
Mailing Address:	P.O. Box 1235
	Beautiful City, FL 33003

ARTICLE III — Registered Agent, Registered Office, and Registered Agent's Signature

The name and the Florida street address of the registered agent are:

> John Doe
>
> 5678 New Company Lane
>
> Beautiful City, FL 33003

Having been named as registered agent and to accept service of process for the above stated limited liability company at the place designated in this certificate, I hereby accept the appointment as registered agent and agree to act in this capacity. I further agree to comply with the provisions of all statutes relating to the proper and complete performance of my duties, and I am familiar with and accept the obligations of my position as a registered agent as provided for in Chapter 608, Florida Statutes.

Registered Agent's Signature

ARTICLE IV — Manager(s) or Managing Member(s)

Title	Name & Address
"MGR" = Manager	"MGRM" = Managing Member
MGR	Jane Doe
	234 Manager St.
	Beautiful City, FL 33003
MGRM	Jim Unknown
	789 Managing Member Drive
	Beautiful City, FL 33003

ARTICLE V — Effective Date

The effective date of this Florida limited liability company shall be January 1, 2010.

Required Signature: Signature of a member or an authorized representative of a member

Guidelines for Articles of Incorporation

A corporation is the most common form of business organization and is chartered by a state under its laws. Forming a corporation can be a lengthy and costly process. In addition to startup costs, you will have additional ongoing maintenance costs, as well as legal and financial reporting requirements not found in partnerships or sole proprietorships.

To legally establish your corporation, you must register with the state the business is created in by filing Articles of Incorporation. Filing fees, information to be included, and actual format vary from state to state. Some of the information most commonly required includes:

- Name of the corporation

- Address of the registered office

- Purpose of the corporation

- Duration of the corporation

- Number of shares the corporation will issue

- Duties of the board of directors

- Status of the shareholders, such as quantity of shares and responsibilities

- Stipulation for the dissolution of the corporation

- Names of the incorporator(s) of the organization

- Statement attesting to the accuracy of the information contained therein

- Signature line and date

Alabama's format for filing the Articles of Incorporation can be accessed through the Secretary of State's website. The site contains instructions for filling out and submitting the document along with corresponding filing fees.

Sample Filing for Articles of Incorporation

State Of Alabama Domestic For-Profit Corporation Articles Of Incorporation Guidelines

Instructions:

Step 1: Contact the office of the secretary of state at (334) 242-5324 to reserve a corporate name.

Step 2: To incorporate, file the original, two copies of the articles of incorporation, and the certificate of name reservation in the county where the corporation's registered office is located. The secretary of state's filing fee is $40. Please contact the judge of probate to verify filing fees.

Pursuant to the provisions of the Alabama business corporation act, the undersigned hereby adopts the following articles of incorporation.

Article I   The name of the corporation:

Article II   The duration of the corporation is "perpetual" unless otherwise stated.

Article III   The corporation has been organized for the following purpose(s):

Article IV   The number of shares, which the corporation shall have the authority to issue, is

_____

Article V   The street address (NO P.O. BOX) of the registered office:

_____

_____

                  and the name of the registered agent at that office:

_____

Article VI   The name(s) and address(es) of the Director(s):

_____

_____

Article VII   The name(s) and address(es) of the Incorporator(s):

Type or Print Name of Incorporator _____

Signature of Incorporator _____

Any provision that is not inconsistent with the law for the regulation of the internal affairs of the corporation or for the restriction of the transfer of shares may be added.

IN WITNESS THEREOF, the undersigned incorporator executed these Articles of Incorporation on this the _____ day of _____, 20_____.

Printed Name and Business Address of Person Preparing this Document:

_____

Statement of Intention to Conduct Business Under an Assumed or Fictitious Name

The undersigned party does hereby state his/her intention to carry on the business of
_____, at the business location of _____, in the
City of _____, in the state of _____, under the assumed or
fictitious name of: _____.

The owner's name, home address, and percentage of ownership of the above-named business are
as follows:

Name: _____

Address: _____

Percentage of Ownership: 100 percent

Signed on _____, 20___

_____

Business owner signature

_____

Business owner printed name

Financial Statement Requirements for Business Entities

Financial Statement Requirements and Disclosure at a Glance by Business Structure

Business type	Regulatory requirement	Management requirement	Investor and lender requirement
Sole proprietors	None	Generally rely on common accounting software and reports. Financial statements are not relied on and audited statements are rare.	Lenders normally limit loan sizes and rely on owner's income tax returns and other personal information when making loan decisions. Loans are backed by the sole proprietor's personal property, in addition to business assets.
Partnerships	None	May rely on common accounting software. May have an accounting firm compile financial statements if a particular need arises.	Similar to the sole proprietor, except two or more partners provide personal resources to guarantee loans.
Private "C" Corp	Generally none. Some states require annual disclosure of total assets and liabilities, but not a full set of financial statements.	Typically the largest of the private business structures. Senior management uses financial statements to manage daily operations, to provide the board of directors with ability to oversee the entire company, to keep investors informed, as a requirement of bylaws, and to obtain loans. Stock option programs may make audited statements a requirement in the process of valuing the company and establishing a stock price.	Lenders frequently require GAAP-conforming audited financial statements and include covenants about the total amount a company can borrow from all sources against assets. Investors normally require unaudited quarterly statements and audited annual statements to track financial performance.

Private "S" Corp	Generally none. Some states require annual disclosure of total assets and liabilities, but not a full set of financial statements.	The need for financial statements is made at management discretion. Accounting software may or may not give adequate oversight of the business, and with up to 100 investors the corporate bylaws may mandate annually audited statements.	Similar to Private "C" Corps. Lenders frequently require annual audited statements depending on loan sizes and associated risk. Investors that do not actively manage the business may require statements to verify management is competent.
Private LLC	Generally, none. Some states require annual disclosure of total assets and liabilities, but not a full set of financial statements.	Generally, the same as Private "S" Corps, but there can be more investors influencing the need.	Generally, the same as Private "S" Corps, but there can be more investors influencing the need.
Public "C" Corp	All financial statements publicly disclosed as defined by the SEC. Includes annual audited and quarterly unaudited reports along with other requirements.	Management regularly relies on financial statements to guide decision making. Extensive public analysis requires that management thoroughly understand information behind the numbers and be able to explain significant changes. Board of directors determines the outside firm to conduct the annual audit.	Lender requirements are similar as those for Private "C" Corps. Investors can obtain copies from the SEC EDGAR database and have an opportunity to ask questions of management at the annual shareholders meeting.

Worksheet for a Successful Partnership

Before entering into a partnership, all partners must understand each other's expectations and agree on important matters such as compensation, decision making, and reinvestment in the business. Write down your responses to these questions, and have your partner do the same. Trade worksheets and discuss your answers.

1. My philosophical vision for the company: _____

2. My business strategy: _____

3. I came to this strategy through the following education, practice, and life lessons: _____

4. My work ethic: _____

5. What "commitment to the business" means to me: _____

6. My talents are:_____

7. My partner's talents are: _____

8. My skills are:_____

9. My partner's skills are: _____

10. My role as I see it in the company:_____

11. My partner's role in the company: _____

12. Our method of compensation for partners is as follows: _____

13. Our compensation plan for key employees and other employees is as follows: _____

    _____

14. Our record keeping will be done through _____ (method) or by

    _____ (person): _____

15. We plan to create capital by:_____

16. We will finance debt through these methods:_____

17. We will deal with OSHA regulations and safety by: _____

18. When big decisions need to be made, we will:_____

19. If we disagree on a decision that has a major impact on the company, we will:_____

    _____

20. Things we enjoy outside of working hours include: _____

    _____

How to Obtain an Employer Identification Number

All employers, partnerships, and corporations must have an employer identification number (EIN), also known as a federal tax identification number. You must obtain your EIN from the IRS before you conduct any business transactions or hire any employees. The IRS uses the EIN to identify the tax accounts of employers, certain sole proprietorships, corporations, and partnerships. The EIN is used on all tax forms and other licenses. You can obtain an EIN by submitting an application on the IRS website (**www.irs.gov/businesses/small/article/0,,id=102767,00.html**). Your application will be validated, and you will receive your EIN immediately. You can also get an EIN assigned to you by telephone, at 1-800-829-4933, or by filling out Form SS-4, obtainable from the IRS at **www.irs.gov/businesses/small/article/0,,id=99198,00.html.** A copy of this form is included on the companion CD-ROM. If you are in a hurry to get your number, you can get an EIN assigned to you by telephone, at 800-829-4933. There is no charge.

Also, request the following publications:

- Publication 15, Circular E, "Employer's Tax Guide," download at **www.irs.gov**.

- Several copies of Form W-4, "Employer Withholding Allowance Certificate." Each new employee must fill out one of these forms. Download at **www.irs.gov**.

- Publication 334, "Tax Guide for Small Businesses," download at **www.irs.gov**.

- Request free copies of "All about OSHA" and "OSHA Small Business Handbook." Depending on the number of employees you have, you will be subject to certain regulations from this agency. You can access publications from the OSHA website (**www.osha.gov**) or by writing to: OSHA, U.S. Department of Labor, Washington, D.C. 20210.

- Request a free copy of "Handy Reference Guide to the Fair Labor Standards Act." Contact: Department of Labor, Washington, D.C. 20210 (**www.dol.gov**) or download it at **www.dol.gov/whd/regs/compliance/wh1282.pdf**.

IRS Forms and Publications

View and download IRS forms and publications at **www.irs.gov** or call 1-800-829-3676 to order forms and publications through the mail at no cost. Many of these publications are available in the reference section of public libraries. The IRS recommends these publications for small businesses:

- Pub 15 Circular E Employers Tax Guide

- Pub 334 Tax Guide for Small Businesses (available on companion CD-ROM)

- Pub 463 Travel, Entertainment, Gift, and Car Expenses

- Pub 505 Tax Withholding and Estimated Tax (available on companion CD-ROM)

- Pub 531 Reporting Tip Income

- Pub 535 Business Expenses

- Pub 583 Starting a Business and Keeping Records

- Pub 587 Business Use of Your Home

- Pub 946 How to Depreciate Property (available on companion CD-ROM)

- Pub 966 Electronic Choices to Pay All your Federal Taxes

- Pub 1779 Independent Contractor or Employee

- Pub 1872 Tips on Tips: A Guide to Tip Income Reporting

- Pub. 1932 How to Make Correct Federal Tax Deposits

- Pub 3402 Tax Issues for Limited Liability Companies

- Pub 3995 Recognizing Illegal Tax Avoidance Schemes

- Pub 4132 Pay Taxes Online! "Easy As 1-2-3"

The IRS also recommends these resources, available on **www.irs.gov** when you type the suggested keyword in the search box:

- Starting, Operating, or Closing a Business — (Keyword: Starting, Operating, or Closing)

- Business Taxes — (Keyword: Business Taxes)

- Checklist for Starting a Business — (Keyword: Checklist)

- Employer ID Number — (Keyword: EIN)

- Self-Employed — (Keyword: Self-employed)

- Business Expenses — (Keyword: Business Expenses)

- Employment Taxes — (Keyword: Employment Taxes for Businesses)

- Tax Information for Specific Industries / Professions — (Keyword: Industries/Professions)

- Electronic Federal Tax Payment System (EFTPS) — (Keyword: EFTPS) or 800-555-4477

- e-File for Small Business — (Keyword: e-File for Business)

- Common Errors — (Keyword: Tax Gap)

- State Resources for Small Businesses — (Keyword: State Links)

- Business-related News — (Keyword: Business-related News)

Call these numbers for assistance with tax questions:

- e-Help — 866-255-0654

- National Taxpayer Advocate Help Line — 877-777-4778

- Information Return Reporting — 866-455-7438

- Report Tax Schemes — 866-775-7474

The Small Business Resource Guide on the U.S. Department of Housing and Urban Development website is designed to assist small-business owners and those who are just starting up new business ventures. This guide can be found at **www.hud.gov/offices/osdbu/resource/guide.cfm**.

Creating an Exit Plan

At some point in the future, you will want to leave your business. You will be ready to retire, sell the business and move on, go out of business, or leave the business to your heirs. When you are ready to sell, you will understand the importance of building a profitable, saleable business. When you start your business, you should already be thinking about your exit.

Your exit plan will not require as much detail as your business plan, but develop it now because it will influence some of your decisions as your business progresses. The way you plan to exit your business will affect how you decide to finance it, what accounting system you adopt, how you handle taxes, whether you buy or lease property and equipment, and the extent to which you develop and train your employees. As your business situation inevitably changes from year to year, review your exit plan and make necessary revisions.

Some owners pass their businesses on to family members or heirs. There are tax implications in such situations, including inheritance tax, trusts, and tax-free gifts. Consult with your attorney, banker, estate planner, and accountant to make sure the transition is handled well. The U.S. Chamber of Commerce (**www.uschamber.com**) offers advice on leaving a business to your heirs, and the Business Owner's Toolkit (**www.toolkit.com**) also has helpful articles.

You might not have family members who are interested in carrying on the business without you. Another option is to pass or sell the business to your partners or employees. They will need to have adequate financing, and you will require the assistance of your attorney or accountant to carry out the transfer correctly. Ways to handle this transaction include transferring your business to a worker co-op or transferring directly to employees. Information on these types of transfers is available from the National Center for Employee Ownership (**www.nceo.org**) and Foundation for Enterprise Development (**www.fed.org**). The process might become personally challenging because you feel uncomfortable negotiating financial issues with friends. Also, the employees buying your business might have different plans and ideas from yours for operating the business in the future.

Exit Plan Worksheet

1. Your best-case scenario: Do you know when you want to retire? Decide whether you want to sell the business or leave it for your family to manage. _____

   _____

   _____

2. Current value: If you were to sell your business today, what is it worth?_____

   _____

   _____

3. Enhancing business value: What changes would make your business more appealing for a buyer? Consider these carefully and realize there might be some changes that you do not necessarily want to make but that will enhance the value of the business when it is time to sell. _____

   _____

   _____

4. Worst-case scenario: If you had to get out of the business today, what could be done? _____

   _____

   _____

5. Preparing for the sale: Be aware of the tax implications of the sale._____

   _____

   _____

6. Leaving: Are you in a partnership or corporation with others, and if so, how does this affect how you leave your business? _____

   _____

   _____

7. Financial health for your family: Prepare a will. Is your family trained and prepared to run the business without you?_____

   _____

   _____

Consult an attorney and an accountant for advice about how to create a realistic exit plan. Guidance for creating an exit plan can be found on the Family Business Experts website (**www.family-business-experts.com/exit-planning.html**).

CHAPTER 2

Buying or Selling a Business

These checklists and sample documents will guide you through the process of searching for and purchasing an existing business or selling your own business.

Checklist for Putting Together a Search Plan

Search Plan for _____

☐ Type of Industry

    a. _____

    b. _____

☐ Type of Business

    a. _____

    b. _____

☐ Size of Business (in relation to investment capability)

    _____

    _____

☐ Are you willing to relocate if necessary?

    _____

    _____

☐ What are your geographical preferences?

    a. _____

    b. _____

    c. _____

☐ What is your risk level?

    _____

    _____

☐ Do you want to actively manage, or will you be an absentee owner?

    _____

    _____

☐ What are the time constraints for purchase completion?

    _____

    _____

Selling Memorandum

A selling memorandum is a public proposal to sell a business, setting forth the conditions under which the company will be sold and giving information about the business.

Elements of a Selling Memorandum

Table of contents

I. Conditions of acceptance

II. The proposed transaction

III. Executive summary/company profile

IV. The company

V. Financials

VI. Growth strategies

VII. Conclusion

I. Conditions of acceptance

This memorandum contains certain statements, estimates, and projections provided by Company B with respect to its anticipated future performance. Such statements, estimates, and projections reflect assumptions by Company B concerning anticipated results, which assumptions may or may not prove to be correct. No representations are made as to the accuracy of such statements, estimates, or projections.

Further, this section also uses strong language regarding the importance of keeping all confidential material confidential and, if there is a selling agent involved, that all communications relating to these materials should be directed to that agent. Management at Company B should not be contacted under any circumstances.

II. The proposed transaction

Recipients of this memorandum should determine their degree of interest in acquiring Company B. If, upon review of this information, it is decided that there is no further interest, it is requested that the memorandum be returned to _____. Such parties are reminded that they will continue to be bound by the Confidentiality Agreement.

Interested parties are asked to advise _____ of their interest, including a preliminary range of value and a suggested time frame for closing a transaction.

From those expressing interest, a small number will be invited to meet the management and tour the facility. Proposals will be invited from those making the tour, following which a buyer will be selected. Final negotiations will be concluded followed by a letter of intent, purchase and sell agreement, and a closing.

While price will be an important consideration, interested parties are advised that other conditions will also be important in selecting the successful bidder. Such conditions may include payment terms, timing, availability of necessary financing, etc.

III. Executive summary/company profile

Company B

Any Street

Any Town, USA 11111

Ownership and Organization:

Business:

Financial Highlights:

Historical Performance and Projections:

IV. The company

History:

Markets:

Products:

Competition:

Management:

Real Estate:

V. Financials

VI: Growth strategies

Summary Investment Considerations:

Reason for Selling:

VII: Conclusion

Three-Year Financial Worksheet

Fill in the figures for each year your business is in operation. Lenders and investors use a three-year projection to evaluate the business's performance and potential for growth.

Item	Year 1	Year 2	Year 3
Assets			
Cash			
Accounts receivable			
Notes receivable			
Inventory			
Prepaid expenses			
Total current assets			
Land and buildings			
Machinery and equipment			
Less depreciation			
Goodwill			
Total assets			
Liabilities			
Notes payable			
Accounts payable			
Taxes payable			
Accruals			
Total current liabilities			
Capital			

Long-term debt			
Stock			
Paid-in-surplus			
Total capital			
Total liabilities and capital			
Income			
Gross sales			
Less returns / allowances			
Net sales			
Cost of goods sold			
Materials			
Labor			
Gross profit			
Expenses			
General and administrative expense			
Selling expenses			
Total expenses			
Operating profit			
Interest			
Taxes			
Net profit after tax			

Agreement for Purchase and Sale of a Business

Date: _____

Purchaser: _____

Address: _____

City: _____ State: _____ ZIP code: _____

Seller: _____

Permanent address: _____

City: _____ State: _____ ZIP: _____

This agreement is entered into on _____ (date) between _____

_____ (Seller), doing business as _____

_____, with its primary place of business at _____

_____ _____

_____, AND _____

_____ (Purchaser) residing at _____

_____.

The Seller is the owner of a business known as _____, with its

principal office situated at:

Address: _____

City: _____ State: _____ ZIP: _____

involving the retail sales of _____ and other

miscellaneous items, and in operating this business, has developed a reputation and following and has

accumulated certain assets more fully described hereafter.

The Purchaser has expressed an interest in the acquisition of the business of the Seller; and the Seller

desires to sell to Purchaser, and Purchaser desires to purchase from Seller, the _____

_____ under the terms and conditions set forth

in this Agreement.

In consideration of the mutual promises and conditions contained in this Agreement, and intending to be

legally bound by it, the parties agree as follows:

1. Sale of business. The Seller agrees to sell to the Purchaser, and the Purchaser agrees to purchase and

acquire from the Seller, all of the right, title, and interest of the Seller in and to the retail sales business,

_____, including without limitation, all inventory and stock-in-trade, as listed in Exhibit "A" attached to this document; certain equipment, as listed in Exhibit "B" attached to this document; office equipment, furniture, computers, software, signage, shelving, cabinets, supplies, and all other items of tangible property located in the Seller's place of business and utilized in conjunction with the operation of the partnership of the Seller, as listed in Exhibit "C" attached to this document; and the good will of the Seller, together with the customer records and customer files and the manufacturer records and manufacturer files that the Seller has maintained in conjunction with the operation of the sole proprietorship.

2. Purchase price. The total purchase price to be paid by Purchaser to Seller shall be_____

($_____) U.S. dollars.

3. Payment of purchase price. Upon the execution of this Agreement, the Purchaser shall pay to the Seller the sum of _____ ($_____) Dollars, against the purchase price ("Purchase Price"), with the balance of the Purchase Price ($_____) to be paid by the Purchaser to the Seller at the Closing as follows:

a)_____ dollars ($_____) to be paid by certified funds, cashier's check, wire transfer, or other acceptable means of payment; and

b) A Note, attached as Exhibit "D" to this document, to the Seller from the Purchaser for _____ dollars ($_____), which shall be secured by a security interest in the inventory on-hand at the store at_____ _____, as documented in a Security Agreement, attached as Exhibit "E" to this document, and a Financing Statement, attached as Exhibit "F" to this document.

The term of the Note shall be ten (10) years with a two- (2) year balloon payment from the date of Closing. If the Purchaser pays the remaining principal balance in full within twelve (12) months after the date of Closing, the Seller shall discount the remaining principal balance then owed by five percent (5%). The first payment due on the Note shall be sixty (60) days after the date of Closing.

4. Allocations. The Seller and the Purchaser hereby agree that the Purchase Price shall be allocated as provided in this Agreement, and that the following allocations are fair and reasonable and the product of the terms of this sale negotiated between the Seller and the Purchaser:

Inventory	$_____,000.00
Fixtures, Signage & Computers	$_____,000.00
Goodwill, Trademark	$_____,000.00
Noncompete Covenant	$_____,000.00
Total	$_____,000.00

5. Goodwill. At the Closing, the Seller shall transfer all of the Seller's good will to the Purchaser with respect to the Seller's operation of the business, including the trade name _____ and the domain name www._____.com. Furthermore, at Closing the Seller shall assign to the Purchaser, all of the right, title, and interest of the Seller in and to the telephone number utilized by the Seller with respect to the Seller's business.

6. Seller assistance & training. The Seller agrees to assist and train the Purchaser with respect to the operation of the business known as _____ following the date of Closing for a period of three-hundred sixty (360) days and shall endeavor to make the acquisition by the Purchaser as smooth as possible. The Seller shall familiarize the Purchaser with all aspects of the business of the Seller's customers so as to develop the best possible rapport between the Purchaser and the customers of the Seller.

7. Warranties. The Seller warrants and represents to the Purchaser, both now and after the Closing, that the Seller is the sole owner of the business and its assets, free and clear of any and all liens and encumbrances and free and clear of the claims of any person. The Seller makes no other warranties except any that might be set forth in this agreement, and all other warranties, express or implied, are hereby disclaimed.

The Seller hereby expressly disclaims any and all other express or implied warranties. Any affirmations of fact or promises made by the Seller shall not be deemed as any express guarantee that the tangible property will conform to any such affirmation or promise. Any description of the tangible property is for the sole purpose of identifying the tangible property, and shall not be construed as an express warranty that the tangible property shall conform to the description. No affirmation or promise, or description, shall be considered as part of the agreement between the parties hereto. The Seller further expressly disclaims any implied warranty of merchantability and any warranty of fitness of the tangible property for any particular purpose, and the parties agree that there are no warranties that extend beyond the provisions of this paragraph. The tangible property is sold "as is" and "where is."

8. Accounts receivable. The Seller shall retain all accounts receivable from the operation of the business, except for items on layaway at the time of Closing, for which the Purchaser shall be entitled to receive any remaining payment(s) due on that merchandise from the date of Closing and thereafter. The Seller shall be entitled to collect all accounts receivable at any and all times following the Closing. The Purchaser shall fully cooperate with the Seller with respect to the Seller's efforts to collect all accounts receivables due the Seller.

9. Transfer documents. The Seller shall transfer title to the partnership and the assets thereof to the Purchaser, by means of a Bill of Sale and an Assignment, copies of which are attached as Exhibits "G" and "H" to this document.

10. Liabilities. The Seller shall pay all trade debts and any other liabilities incurred by the operation of the business at, or prior to, the Closing. Any trade debts or similar liabilities materializing after the Closing that are lawfully the responsibility of the Seller shall be presented to the Seller for immediate payment.

11. Lease of building contingency. If prior to Closing, the Purchaser, after reasonable good-faith efforts, has not been able to negotiate a new five- (5) year lease with an optional five- (5) year extension between the Purchaser and Landlord of the business premises for _____ dollars ($_____) per month for the first five- (5) year term plus the reasonable cost of utilities attributable to_____ _____, then this Agreement shall be null and void, and the Purchaser's deposit money of $1,000 shall be refunded by _____, 20__.

12. Financing Contingency. If prior to Closing, the Purchaser, after reasonable good-faith efforts, has not been able to secure a personal loan for at least _____ dollars ($____,000) so as to enable the Purchaser to make the first payment at Closing in accordance with provision a) of Paragraph 3 of this Agreement, then this Agreement shall be null and void, and the Purchaser's deposit money of $1,000 shall be refunded by _____, 20____.

13. Further assurances and mutual cooperation. Each of the parties to this Agreement assures the other that they will mutually cooperate in all respects at any and all times hereafter, and that they will further execute and deliver to each other all documents requested, within reason, to substantiate and document the proper, expedient, and convenient sale of the business of the Seller and the transition as set forth in this Agreement.

14. Conduct of business. The Seller shall continue to conduct the business as normal in every respect through the date of the sale.

15. Bulk sales compliance. The Seller shall comply with all bulk sales requirements with regard to the sale of the business of the Seller to the Purchaser as provided for in this Agreement.

16. The closing and closing date. The Closing shall occur on _____, 20___ ("Closing Date"), at the offices of_____ located at: _____ _____.

17. Noncompete covenant. In consideration of the business being undertaken by the Purchaser under the terms of this Agreement, the Seller hereby agrees that they will not, directly or indirectly, for their own account or for the account of others, engage in a similar business, for a period of five (5) years following the Closing, in _____ County or in any county adjacent thereto.

18. Notices. Any notice, communication, request or reply (severally and collectively called "Notice") required or allowed by this Agreement to be made by either party to the other must be in writing and may be served by registered or certified mail, return receipt requested, or by delivering the notice in person to such party to the addresses set forth in opening paragraphs of this Agreement, or to any other address indicated in writing by either party. Notice sent by mail as described above shall be effective only when received by the party to be notified.

19. Headings. Headings contained in this Agreement are for reference purposes only and shall not affect in any way the meaning or interpretation of this Agreement.

20. Counterpart execution. This Agreement may be executed in two or more counterparts, each of which shall be considered an original, but all of which together shall constitute one and the same instrument.

21. Parties in interest. All the terms and provisions of this Agreement shall be binding on and enforceable by Purchaser and Seller, their heirs, executors, administrators, successors, and assigns.

22. Integrated agreement. This Agreement constitutes the entire agreement between the parties concerned, and there are no agreements, understandings, restrictions, warranties, or representations between the parties other than those set forth within this document.

23. Amendment and waiver. This Agreement may be amended or modified at any time and in all respects by an instrument in writing executed by Purchaser and Seller.

24. Expenses. Each of the parties shall be responsible for any and all expenses incurred by them in connection with this Agreement and in the consummation of the transactions contemplated hereby and in preparation thereof.

25. Choice of law. This Agreement, the construction of its terms, and the interpretation of the rights and duties of the parties shall be governed by the laws of the state of _____.

26. Survival of obligations. All covenants and obligations of the Purchaser and Seller as set forth in this Agreement shall survive Closing and any termination of this Agreement.

PURCHASER: _____

WITNESS: _____

SELLER: _____

WITNESS: _____

STATE OF _____, COUNTY OF _____

The foregoing instrument was acknowledged before me, this ___ day of _____, 20 ___.

Notary Public _____

(SEAL) State of _____

My Commission Expires: _____

Checklist for New Owner of a Business

Transitioning employees

___ Inform about the sale prior to complete switchover.

___ Inform about ongoing involvement of seller (if applicable).

___ Discuss employee concerns.

___ Distribute, in writing, any changes in employment terms.

___ Distribute, in writing, any changes in store policies and procedures.

Transitioning business associates

___ Make a list of suppliers, service providers, and subcontractors.

___ With an attorney, review any contracts.

___ Draft and send a letter regarding the change.

___ Personally call associates as needed.

___ Draft new contracts as needed.

Transitioning customers

___ Decide on a strategy for publicizing change to customers

___ Implement strategy.

Transitioning general public

___ Send a press release to business editor of local newspaper.

___ Purchase an ad in local paper. Include a coupon if possible.

___ Place a "new ownership" sign outside of store.

CHAPTER

3

Setting Up and Running a Corporation

S etting up your business as a corporation will protect you from being personally liable for losses caused by the business. A corporation must be set up according to the business-law requirements of the state where the business is located. Obtain the forms for incorporation from your secretary of state's office; most states have downloadable forms on their websites and typically, charge a small fee. You also can buy or download commercial incorporation kits, and numerous companies charge a fee to prepare and file the articles of incorporation for you. If your business is not complicated, there is no reason why you cannot prepare and file the forms yourself. Many states try to keep the process as simple as possible for small businesses. Consult a lawyer if your business organization is complicated.

Articles of Incorporation

Articles of incorporation may vary from state to state, but a basic format contains:

1. The corporation's name, including a corporate suffix such as Corporation, Corp., Incorporated, Inc., Company, or Co. A professional association must contain the word "chartered" or "professional association" or "P.A."

   _____

2. The corporation's principal place of business and mailing address. The principal address must be a physical address. The mailing address, if different, can be a P.O. box.

   _____

   _____

   _____

3. The number of shares of stock the corporation is authorized to issue. _____

4. The specific purpose for which the corporation is being formed. _____

   _____

   _____

5. The names, addresses and titles of the Directors / Officers (optional). The names of officers / directors may be required to apply for a license, open a bank account, or purchase real estate.

   _____

   _____

   _____

6. Additional provisions for managing the corporation's affairs in accordance with state laws.

   _____

   _____

7. The name, street address (in the state of incorporation), and signature of the person authorized to represent the company as its Registered Agent. The Registered Agent must sign in the space provided and type or print his / her name accepting the designation.

   _____

   _____

   Signed: _____

8. The name, address, and signature of the Incorporator.

   _____

   _____

   Signed: _____

Roles of Shareholder, Director, Officer, and Employee

One or two individuals can fulfill all of the legal roles in a small corporation. A larger corporation might have hundreds of shareholders and a dozen or more directors.

- **Shareholders**: Shareholders own stock (called shares or ownership interests) in the corporation and have the exclusive right to:

  - Elect and remove directors

  - Amend the articles of incorporation and bylaws

  - Approve the sale of all or substantially all of the corporate assets

  - Approve mergers and reorganizations

  - Dissolve the corporation

State laws typically require shareholders to hold an annual meeting. In many states, shareholders can do this through a "written consent" or "consent resolution" — a document signed by all of the shareholders — instead of a physical meeting.

- **Directors**: The board of directors sets policy for the corporation and makes major financial decisions. Among other things, the directors:

  - Authorize the issuance of stock

  - Elect the corporate officers

  - Decide the salaries of officers and key employees

  - Decide whether to mortgage, sell, or lease real estate

  - Approve loans to or from the corporation

  - Create committees and allocate authority to them

  - Adopt business policies and plans

  - Approve mergers, joint ventures, and reorganizations

  - Approve the adoption of pension, profit sharing, and other employee-benefit plans and stock-option plans

Many states require directors to hold regular meetings; most states allow these meetings to be held in a telephone conference call. Directors can take actions by signing a consent resolution or written consent.

In a small company, most shareholders are also directors and officers, but they must still observe the formalities required by law by acting in different capacities at different times.

- **Officers**: State laws usually require a corporation to have at least a president, a secretary, and a treasurer (sometimes called a chief financial officer, or CFO). In most states, the same person can hold all of the required offices. Officers are responsible for the corporation's day-to-day operation and management. The president is usually the chief operating officer (COO) of the corporation, and the secretary is responsible for maintaining corporate records. The treasurer, or chief financial officer (CFO), is responsible for the corporate finances, although everyday accounting duties are often delegated to a bookkeeper.

- **Employees**: The owners of small corporations are usually also employees of the corporation, and they receive most of their financial reward from the business in the form of a salary and other compensation they receive as corporate employees.

Shareholder, Director, Officer, and Employee Worksheet

Use this worksheet to list shareholders, directors, officers, and employees for your corporation.

1. Shareholders:

_____

_____

_____

_____

2. Board of directors:

_____

_____

_____

_____

3. Officers:

President: _____

Secretary: _____

Treasurer: _____

_____

_____

4. Employees:

_____

_____

_____

_____

_____

Corporate Minutes

As a corporation owner, you are required to hold shareholders' and directors' meetings, maintain corporate records, and document major corporate decisions in the form of minutes of shareholder and director meetings. If you neglect these formalities and creditors or the IRS later question your decisions, or if the business becomes involved in a lawsuit, a court could decide to disregard your corporate status and hold you and the other shareholders personally responsible for the corporation's debts. Corporate minutes also serve as a historical record of how and why certain decisions were made.

Decisions that require formal director or shareholder participation and should be recorded in written minutes or consent resolutions include:

- Proceedings of annual meetings of directors and shareholders
- Issuance of stock to new or existing shareholders
- Purchase of real property
- Approval of a long-term lease
- Authorization of a substantial loan or line of credit
- Adoption of a stock option or retirement plan
- Making important federal or state tax decisions

If your small business makes these decisions in small, informal meetings, you should still write up meeting minutes or unanimous written consents (signed by all the directors in lieu of a meeting) indicating that the actions were approved.

In addition to keeping records of important business decisions, your corporation must record financial transactions in a double-entry bookkeeping system and keep other necessary financial records so it can file an annual corporate tax return.

Form for Corporate Minutes

Minutes of the _____ of the _____
           [Annual Meeting / Special Meeting]   *[Shareholders / Directors]*

of _____ on _____
           [Name of Corporation]   *[Date]*

The _____ meeting of the _____ of _____
    [Annual / Special]   *[Directors / Shareholders]*   *[Name of Corporation]*

was held on the date and at the time and place specified in the written notice of the meeting or the waiver

of notice signed by the _____and attached to the minutes of this meeting.
           [Shareholders / Directors]

The following _____ were present:
           [Shareholders / Directors]

The meeting was called to order and it was moved, seconded and carried that _____
           [Name]

act as Chairman and _____ act as Secretary.
    [Name]

Minutes of the preceding meeting of the _____ held on
           [Shareholders / Directors]

_____ were read.
    [Date]

Upon motion duly made, seconded, and carried, the following resolutions were adopted:

_____

_____

_____

_____

_____

           [Detailed description of the decisions made at the meeting]

There being no further business, the meeting adjourned on _____ at _____
           [Date]   *[Time]*

_____

Secretary

Approved:

_____

CHAPTER 4

Contract Basics

A written contract is a legal document signed by two or more parties to indicate that they and / or the organizations they represent agree to abide by the terms of the stated agreement. It can be a simple purchase order or a complex agreement laying out the obligations of a contractor undertaking a building construction project. A good contract is designed to ensure that all the parties involved receive the benefits they expect from the business transaction and that no party is harmed by the transaction. For example, the seller of a product wants to sell it at a price that guarantees a profit and to receive payment on time; the buyer wants the product to be delivered on time, in good condition, and in the quantity requested. Each party signing the contract is confident it can fulfill its promise. If something goes wrong, however, such as delivery of the wrong product or a late payment, a good contract spells out how the injured party will be compensated by the other party.

A contract's words and phrases become very important when a legal dispute arises. A single clause, inaccuracy, or omission could result in substantial losses for your business. For this reason, review contracts carefully before signing them, and include all the elements necessary to protect your company. Sample legal contracts for various businesses are included in some of the other chapters of this book. This chapter is a general explanation of the important components of a contract. The checklists will help you review contracts and confirm that the language they contain is in the best interests of your business

Getting the Signature Right

The way a contract is signed is also crucial in determining who is responsible for fulfilling its terms. Businesses are organized as corporations and LLCs in order to protect the owners from becoming personally liable for actions the business performs. If you are signing as a representative of a corporation, partnership, or LLC, make that clear by listing the company name above your signature and your title or position in the company underneath it.

When someone signs a contract as a representative of a partnership, company, or organization, verify that he or she is legally authorized to represent the organization before signing the document yourself. A person signing a major contract on behalf of a corporation should have a written grant of authority to do so.

Signature Boxes

Signature Box for a Sole Proprietorship without Fictitious Name

Date: _____

By: _____ (Printed Name of Owner)

Owner's Address:

_____

_____

Signature Box for Sole Proprietorship with Fictitious Name

Date: _____

By: _____ (Printed Name of Owner)

Doing business as: _____

Owner's Address:

_____

_____

or

Date: _____

_____ (Fictitious Name)

A Sole Proprietorship

By: _____ (Printed Name of Owner)

Owner's Address:

_____

_____

Signature Box for General Partnership without a Fictitious Name

_____(Partnership Name), a _____ (State) partnership

_____ (Name or Names of Owner or Owners)

_____ (Address or Addresses of Owner or Owners)

Date: _____

By: _____ (Printed Name of Signer)

_____ (Title of Signer)

Signature Box for General Partnership with a Fictitious Name

_____(Partnership Name), a _____ (State) partnership,

doing business as _____

_____ (Name or Names of Owner or Owners)

_____ (Address or Addresses of Owner or Owners)

Date: _____

By: _____ (Printed Name of Signer)

_____ (Title of Signer)

Signature Box for Corporation without a Fictitious Name

_____ (Corporation Name), a _____ (State) corporation

_____ (Corporation Address)

Date: _____

By: _____ (Printed Name of Signer)

_____ (Title of Signer)

(Repeat for additional signers)

Signature Box for Corporation with a Fictitious Name

_____ (Corporation Name), a _____ (State) corporation

doing business as _____

_____ (Name of Owner or Owners)

_____ (Address or Owner or Owners)

Date: _____

By: _____ (Printed Name of Signer)

_____ (Title of Signer)

(Repeat for additional signers)

Signature Box for Limited Liability Company (LLC) without a Fictitious Name

_____ (LLC Name), a _____ (State) limited liability corporation

_____ (Address)

Date: _____

By: _____ (Printed Name of Signer)

_____ (Title of Signer)

(Repeat for additional signers)

Signature Box for Limited Liability Company with a Fictitious Name

_____ (LLC Name), a _____ (State) limited liability corporation

doing business as _____ (Fictitious Name)

_____ (Address)

Date: _____

By: _____ (Printed Name of Signer)

_____ (Title of Signer)

(Repeat for additional signers)

Reviewing a Contract

Never sign a legally binding agreement without reading through it carefully and thoroughly understanding the obligations it imposes on you. Some contracts are full of lengthy paragraphs of legal terminology that may seem bewildering at first, but once you become familiar with the vocabulary, you will find many of those paragraphs are standard clauses protecting specific legal rights.

The following checklist will help you quickly review a contract and determine whether it is satisfactory to you. During the review, you may discover some terms are unacceptable or unnecessarily burdensome and need to be negotiated with the other party. A business deal is nothing more than an agreement in which all parties believe they will gain something.

Use the same checklist to examine the contract forms in this book and accompanying CD-ROM, and any ready-made contracts purchased or downloaded from the Internet, to confirm they are appropriate for your business.

Checklist for Reviewing a Contract

1. Identify your five top priorities for this contract. For example, you might want to purchase an item at a set price, have deliveries or payments made within a specific time interval, receive quick service when repairs are needed, protect yourself from lawsuits, or ensure that a tenant pays rent on time and reimburses you for any damage done to your property. Does this contract address all five of your priorities? What weaknesses have you found? What terms can you add to remedy these weaknesses?

    a. _____

    b. _____

    c. _____

    d. _____

    e. _____

2. Does the contract contain any of the following terms? Anytime you see this language, take a closer look, and consider rewriting the clause.

    ____ Time is of the essence. This term means all dates and deadlines in the contract are absolute, and any failure to meet them could be construed as a breach of contract. If this term does not apply equally to all parties, or if you are not confident you can keep to this standard over the life of the contract, consider changing or dropping it.

    ____ Best efforts. Best efforts is a very high legal standard and means your company agrees to employ every means and spare no expense to accomplish whatever the contract is requiring it to do. This term can be replaced with "reasonable effort," which means the effort a reasonable person would make to accomplish the task; "diligent effort," which is more than a reasonable effort but still within limits; or "good faith effort," which means at least trying to meet the contract's obligations.

___ Sole determination. If the other party is permitted to make a "sole determination" about some aspect of the contract, it can make that decision for any reason at all or even without a reason. Without the words "sole determination" in the contract, the party must have a reasonable basis for making a decision.

___ Automatic renewal. An automatic renewal provision means that when it expires, the contract will automatically renew for another term unless your company notifies the other party by a certain date that it wants to terminate the contract. The deadline is usually well before the expiry date, and it is easy to overlook.

___ Satisfactory. The contract may contain phrases such as "mutually satisfactory," "satisfactory to all parties," or "in form and substance satisfactory to (the other party's name)." In a dispute, it is difficult to determine exactly what "satisfactory" means because it can be very subjective. Actions that are satisfactory according to your company's standards might be deemed unsatisfactory by the other party. If the term "satisfactory" is used in the contract without some way of clearly defining what "satisfactory" means, replace it with a more concrete term such as "in form and substance customary for transactions of this type" or "reasonably satisfactory."

3. Is the contract written to benefit you or the other party?

    a. Who must perform the majority of the duties under the contract? A contract typically benefits the party with fewer duties. _____

    b. Who benefits the most from the payment arrangements? For example, if payments are made after services are rendered, the contract benefits the party buying the services. Payment in advance benefits the seller._____

    c. Who has the most responsibilities under the standard clauses in the contract? The contract benefits the party with fewer responsibilities. _____

4. Use the checklists on the following pages to make sure all aspects of the business transaction are covered by the contract.

5. Add missing elements and fine-tune your contract. If the checklist has uncovered weaknesses in your contract, draft additional clauses to make it stronger. Some provisions may seem unnecessarily cumbersome for the type of business you are engaged in. Narrow their scope by inserting words such as "material," which means the provision applies only when the business is significantly affected by an event or circumstance; or "reasonable," which means no effort is required beyond what would be considered reasonable by a majority of people.

6. Sign the contract and have all parties initial each page in colored ink. This will prevent any party from substituting pages with altered text later on.

Checklist for Reviewing a Contract for Consulting or Services

☐ Are the legal names and addresses of the parties correct?_____

☐ What is the date of the contract? _____

☐ What date does the contract take effect? _____

☐ What date does the work begin (if different)? _____

☐ How long is the contract for?_____

☐ Is there a detailed description of your duties, including specifications for the expected final products or deliverables? _____

☐ What standards will be used to evaluate the final products?_____

☐ Does the contract include deadlines or project milestones? _____

☐ Does the contract spell out the client's duties, such as providing necessary information, acquiring legal permits, and meeting deadlines for approval of plans or estimates? _____

☐ How will you communicate with the client? _____

☐ What materials or labor will you be responsible for supplying?_____

☐ What materials or labor will the client supply? _____

☐ What are the payment arrangements? _____

☐ Will you receive a deposit or retainer if you are not being paid until the job is finished? _____

☐ When will payment be due?_____

☐ How will payment(s) be made? _____

☐ Will there be late fees or other charges if payment arrangements are not met? _____

☐ Is there a confidentiality clause? _____

☐ Is the client required to return confidential or proprietary material?_____

☐ Is there a noncompete clause or a clause prohibiting the client from hiring your employees away from you? _____

☐ Are you permitted to hire a subcontractor to do some of the work?_____

☐ What is the procedure for resolving disputes? _____

☐ Who is responsible for legal costs in case of litigation? _____

☐ Does the contract contain all applicable standard clauses? _____

   ☐ Force majeure

   ☐ Indemnity or hold harmless

   ☐ Cumulative rights

   ☐ Entire agreement

   ☐ Limit of liability

   ☐ Survival

   ☐ Termination

   ☐ Termination on insolvency

   ☐ Waiver

   ☐ Written modification

☐ Does the contract state that your relationship with the client is one of independent contractor? _____

☐ What are the provisions for terminating the agreement?_____

☐ Are you permitted to use the client's name in publicity or promotion? _____

☐ Are the signature blocks correct?_____

☐ Is the contract signed and initialed on each page by all parties with colored ink? _____

Checklist for Reviewing a Contract for Buying or Selling Goods

☐ Are the legal names and addresses of the parties correct?_____

☐ What is the date of the contract? _____

☐ How long is the contract for, and is there an expiration date?_____

☐ Detailed description of the goods — quantity, size, stock number, etc. _____

☐ How will orders be made, and what procedure will the seller follow in accepting orders? Standing order, individual purchase orders, etc. _____

☐ Provisions for rejection of goods — time limit, reasons for rejection? Can goods be rejected after final payment has been made?_____

☐ What is the process for changing an order? Can orders be cancelled? _____

☐ How will goods be priced?_____

☐ If buyer and seller purchase orders have different terms, which one will take precedence? _____

☐ Shipping arrangements and pricing — insurance, storage costs, choice of carrier?_____

☐ Packaging and labeling requirements?_____

☐ Will the buyer be supplying any packaging materials or equipment to seller?_____

☐ Delivery date or time frame? _____

☐ Procedure for returning goods? _____

☐ Does the seller offer any warranty, such as free from defects, repair service, or replacement of defective goods? What procedure will be followed?_____

☐ What are the payment arrangements? _____

☐ When will payment be due?_____

☐ How will payment(s) be made? _____

☐ Will there be late fees or other charges if payment arrangements are not met? _____

☐ Is there a confidentiality or patent protection clause? _____

☐ Is information, such as pricing schedules, confidential? How will this information be protected?

☐ What is the procedure for resolving disputes?_____

☐ Is the seller permitted to subcontract or assign some of the work?_____

☐ Who is responsible for legal costs in case of litigation? _____

☐ What laws will govern this contract? Under what jurisdiction will legal proceedings take place?

☐ Does the buyer require compliance with any specific laws?_____

☐ Does the contract contain all applicable standard clauses? _____

    ☐ Force majeure

    ☐ Indemnity or hold harmless

    ☐ Cumulative rights

    ☐ Entire agreement

    ☐ Limit of liability

    ☐ Survival

    ☐ Termination

    ☐ Termination on insolvency

    ☐ Waiver

    ☐ Written modification

☐ Is the seller permitted to enter into a joint venture or association with another seller? _____

☐ Is the seller permitted to sell to a competitor?_____

☐ What are the provisions for terminating the agreement?_____

☐ Are you permitted to use the other party's name or logo for publicity or promotion? _____

☐ Are the signature blocks correct?_____

☐ Is the contract signed and initialed on each page by all parties with colored ink? _____

Making Changes to a Contract

Modify, extend, or correct a contract by appending a document known as an "amendment," "supplement," or "modification." In order for the restatement to be valid, all parties who signed the original contract must sign the new version.

Amendment to a Contract

Amendment _____ to _____ dated _____
    (One, or consecutive number)   *(Name of Contract)*   *(Date of Contract)*

This Amendment deletes, replaces, and amends the following paragraphs as described below in

_____ dated _____ between
      (Name of Contract)   *(Date of Contract)*

_____ and _____
    (Legal Name of Party 1)   *(Legal name of Party 2).*

Paragraph_____, _____is replaced by:
    (Number of paragraph being replaced)   *(Title of paragraph being replaced)*

_____

(New paragraph)

Paragraph _____, _____ is amended to read:
    (Number of paragraph being amended) *(Title of paragraph being amended)*

_____

(New text or addition)

(Signature of Party 1, using correct signature format) _____

(Date) _____ *(Signature of*

Party 2, using correct signature format) _____

(Date) _____

Purchase orders and sales agreements, which frequently need to be altered, are often replaced with new purchase orders. To avoid confusion, each new purchase order or sales agreement should contain the clause:

These Purchase Order terms and conditions, effective March 5, 2010, supersede the Purchase Order terms and conditions dated September 9, 2000.

When the changes being made to a contract exceed 25 percent of the original text, it is less confusing to simply restate the entire contract. The new contract should be titled:

"Amended and restated (Name of Contract) dated (Date of Contract)."

UCC: A Ready-Made Sales Contract

Even if you did not sign a sales agreement with your supplier or customer and even if neither of you issued a purchase order, a sales contract still exists between you, governed by your state's Uniform Commercial Code (UCC). The Code, first published in 1952, is a comprehensive set of laws governing commercial transactions, including the borrowing of money, leases, contracts, and the sale of goods in and between U.S. states and territories. The Code is a long-term, joint project of the National Conference of Commissioners on Uniform State Laws (NCCUSL) and the American Law Institute (ALI). All 50 states have adopted it, each with its own terms and variations. If your business involves the purchase and sale of goods, familiarize yourself thoroughly with your state's UCC. Obtain a copy of the Code from your secretary of state (links and addresses are available at **www.statelocalgov.net/50states-secretary-state. cfm**). The Cornell University Law School has posted the entire UCC online, including its application in each state, at **www.law.cornell.edu/uniform/ucc.html**.

What Documents Need to be Notarized?

A notary public is licensed to act as a witness that the person signing a document is the individual named in the signature. Only a few types of documents need to be notarized to be legally enforceable. Deeds and any other documents, including wills and trusts, that transfer ownership of tangible physical assets from one person (corporation) to another must be notarized. When two parties cannot be present in the same physical location to sign a contract, each signature can be notarized, with the notary acting as a witness that the person signing is the party named in the contract and is signing voluntarily. A Power of Attorney (POA), a document that authorizes another party to act on your behalf, must be notarized in order for banks, corporations, and courts of law to accept it. Each state's laws determine which documents of public record, such as wedding certificates, must be notarized.

CHAPTER

5

Buying, Selling, and Leasing Real Estate

Review legal documents governing the ownership and occupancy of real estate property very carefully. When you sign an agreement to purchase or lease a commercial property, you are committing yourself to a long list of obligations that may seriously impact your business. In addition to making regular payments, you could be required to purchase insurance, pay for maintenance and renovations, and take on liability for the actions of your employees and customers. Some commercial leases dictate the hours your business must be open, restrict the types of activities allowed on the premises, tell you how and where you can place advertising and signs, and even prohibit you from selling merchandise that might compete with another tenant. Avoid unpleasant surprises. Before signing the agreement, confirm that its provisions coincide with your business plans and that your budget includes any financial obligations the contract outlines.

Although a real estate contract imposes many duties on you, it also requires the landlord, seller, or buyer to meet requirements that benefit you, such as guaranteeing that the property is well maintained and that the land has been properly surveyed. Real estate contracts typically require a landlord to notify a tenant before entering or inspecting the premises and promise the tenant "quiet enjoyment" of the property, meaning use of the property without interference.

The sample contracts in this section have been written to benefit both parties and represent the types of contracts in general use in the United States. Before using one, make sure it complies with any state and local regulations in your region.

Retail and Office Lease Agreement

Date: _____

Landlord: _____

Address: _____

City: _____ State: _____ ZIP code: _____

Tenant: _____

Permanent Address: _____

City: _____ State: _____ ZIP code: _____

ARTICLE I

1.01 Premises: By virtue of this document, Landlord leases to Tenant, and Tenant leases from Landlord, for the rent specified in this Lease and subject to the provisions of this Lease, the specific parcel of vacant land ("Premises") described in Appendix "A" attached to and made a part of this Lease agreement; and / or shown on a Site Plan, marked Appendix "B", and attached to and made a part of this Lease agreement. Landlord and Tenant agree that a Building will be constructed on the Premises according to the terms of the Development Agreement attached to this document as Appendix "C." This Building and related improvements shall be constructed in accordance with plans and specifications approved by Landlord and Tenant, as set forth in Appendix "C." If, upon completion of the Building and any related improvements outlined in the following agreement, the actual square footage of the building is more or less than planned, this Lease and its provisions shall be considered to be amended, pro rata, to reflect the actual square footage of the Building, and, if applicable, to reflect the contributions made by the Landlord to the Tenant's Improvements while carrying out the provisions in Appendix "C."

ARTICLE II

2.01 Term: The term of this Lease shall be for (____) years, beginning on the Commencement Date as defined in this document, and ending at 12:00 noon on a date (_____) years later ("Expiration Date"), unless the Landlord terminates the lease sooner according to the provisions in this document. After the Expiration Date, the Tenant shall be given (____) Option Periods to extend the lease (____) years per Option Period, according to terms and conditions mutually agreeable to Landlord and Tenant.

2.02 Possession: If on the Commencement Date any of the following "Rental Abatement Conditions" have occurred and are continuing, rent under this Lease Agreement will be abated. Rental Abatement Conditions are strictly limited to any event or item that either a) prohibits the Landlord from delivering to Tenant a legally defensible leasehold interest in the premises; or b) results from delays of any review and response required by Landlord that exceeds the deadlines set out in the Development Agreement (Appendix "C"). Neither the Landlord nor the Landlord's agents will be liable for any claim, damage resulting from such a delay, loss, liability, or expense associated with failure to complete construction by the deadline or tender possession. This Lease shall not be void or voidable, except at the express option of the Landlord.

2.03 Commencement date: The Commencement Date shall be whichever date occurs earlier: (a) the 45th day immediately following the later of the following two dates: (i) the date on which the architect supervising construction certifies in writing to the Landlord and to the Tenant that the Building and all of its facilities are complete and ready for use, except for any personal property to be installed or supplied by the Tenant, or (ii) the date on which the appropriate governmental authority issues a temporary certificate of occupancy for the entire Building; or (b) the date on which the Tenant commences business at the Building. After the Commencement Date has been determined, upon the request of either the Landlord or the Tenant, both Landlord and Tenant will sign and record a written declaration stating the specific commencement and termination dates of the initial term of this lease.

ARTICLE III

3.01 Annual base rent: In accordance with any adjustments to the Base Rent set forth in this Lease Agreement, the Tenant agrees to pay to Landlord a base annual rental ("Base Rent") for the first lease year of _____ U.S. DOLLARS, payable in monthly installments of _____ U.S. DOLLARS on the first day of each calendar month of the first lease year. The tenant will remit Base Rent to Landlord in U.S. Dollars, without imposition of any notice, demand, deduction, offset, or abatement, to the place or person designated by the Landlord, or to any other person or place that the Landlord may from time to time, designate in a written notice.

3.02 Annual rent escalation: The Base Rent agreed to in Article 3.01 shall be increased annually on the anniversary of the Commencement Date ("Escalation Date") and on each annual anniversary of the Commencement Date during the term of the Lease. The amount of this increase in the Base Rent shall be whichever is greater: (i) _____ percent (%) of the Base Rent charged for the year immediately preceding the Escalation Date, or (ii) an amount calculated as follows: The calendar month ending immediately prior to _____ months before each Escalation Date during the term of the Lease shall be used as the "Comparative Month." The increase in the Consumer Price Index (meaning the Consumer Price Index for all Urban Consumers, All Cities Average, all items (1967 = 100), not seasonally adjusted, published and issued by the Bureau of Labor Statistics of the United States Department of Labor (the "Bureau of Labor Statistics") for the _____ -month period immediately preceding the Comparative Month, shall be calculated as a percentage (Percentage Increase). The Base Rent charged for the year immediately preceding the Escalation Date shall then be multiplied by this Percentage Increase to determine the amount of the annual rent escalation. (If the Consumer Price Index ceases to use the 1967 average of One Hundred (100) as its basis of calculation, or if a change is made in the terms of particular items contained in the Consumer Price Index, the Consumer Price Index may be adjusted, at the Landlord's discretion, to the figure that would have been arrived at if the changes had not been made to the method of computing the Consumer Price Index that was in effect at the Commencement Date of the Lease term. If a Consumer Price Index, or substituted Consumer Price Index, is not available, a reliable governmental or other nonpartisan publication, evaluating the purchase power of money, may be used at the discretion of Landlord.)

The increase in the Base Rent shall be paid in _____ monthly installments in advance on the first day of each calendar month, beginning on the Escalation Date and continuing until the next Escalation Date. The Landlord must give the Tenant written notice of the increase in Base Rent as soon as reasonably possible after the increase has been determined. If the tenant does not receive this written notice until after the Escalation Date, any increased amounts that were due but not paid since the Escalation Date shall be payable within _____ days after the Tenant receives written notice.

3.03 Initial term rental: The Landlord and the Tenant agree that the property is leased for an amount equal to the number of years of the initial term multiplied by the Annual Base Rental, as adjusted, for the term of this Lease. This amount is payable at the time of the signing of this Lease, and the provisions contained in this Lease for the payment of rent in installments are only for the convenience of the Tenant. If the Tenant defaults in the payment of the rent as specified in this lease, or defaults on any of the terms of this Lease, the entire rent, as adjusted on the date of default, remaining unpaid for the full term of the Lease will immediately become due and payable without any notice or demand from the Landlord.

3.04 Security deposit/escrow deposit: The Tenant has deposited the sum of U.S. $ _____ with the Landlord as a "Security Deposit" and / or "Escrow Deposit." After the commencement date of the Lease, this amount will be treated as a Security Deposit and as an Escrow Deposit. If the Tenant fails to comply with any provisions of this Lease, the Landlord has the authority to apply all or any part of the Security Deposit to the default, without obligation and without consideration of any other deposit or account held by the Landlord on the Tenant's behalf. Once all or part of the Security Deposit has been used to pay off a default, the Tenant shall, at the Landlord's request, deposit additional cash with Landlord to restore the original amount of the Security Deposit. The Tenant's failure to do so will be considered a material breach of this Lease.

The Landlord is not required to keep the Security Deposit in a separate fund and may commingle it with other funds. The Tenant is not entitled to interest on the Security Deposit. The Security Deposit or any balance of it will be returned to Tenant within ___ days after the Expiration Date of the Lease, if the Tenant is not in default. The Tenant does not have the right to use the Security Deposit to offset or satisfy any payments due to Landlord under this Lease.

An Escrow Deposit, the amount paid by the Tenant to the Landlord referred to in this section, will be held by Landlord as security to ensure that the Tenant meets all the conditions of the Development Agreement, (Appendix "C") prior to the Commencement Date of this Lease. If the Tenant defaults under the Development Agreement, the Landlord may retain all or an agreed amount of the Escrow Deposit, as liquidated damages for the breach of this Lease. Upon the Commencement Date of the Lease, this Escrow Deposit shall automatically become a Security Deposit as described above.

ARTICLE IV: ADDITIONAL RENT

4.01 Net lease: The Landlord and Tenant agree that the payments made to Landlord under the terms of this Lease shall be made in full to the Landlord, and that the Premises Expenses, as defined below in this Lease, will be the obligation of Tenant rather than Landlord.

4.02 Sales tax on rents: The Tenant agrees to pay Sales Tax (and any other applicable tax) on all rentals payable under this Lease, including, without limitation, Base Rent, all increases to Base Rent, and Additional Rent, to the Landlord as part of the Additional Rent.

4.03 Tenant's premises expenses:

a. In each calendar year of the term, or portion of a calendar year, Tenant shall pay the following additional rent to the Landlord:

    ii. All Common Area Costs described in Section 4.04 of this Lease;

    iii. All real estate and other ad valorem taxes and assessments of every kind relating to the Premises; and

    iv. All premiums, charges, and / or assessments paid or owed by Landlord for insurance on the Premises and on personal property used in the maintenance of the Premises (collectively referred to as the "Premises Expenses").

        The Landlord will deliver a written estimate of Tenant's Premises Expenses prior to or on the Commencement Date and from time to time throughout the term of the Lease. In addition to Base Rent, Tenant shall pay the Landlord installments equal to _____ of this estimated amount in advance on the first day of each calendar month during the term of this Lease. The first of these installments is due on the Commencement Date.

b. Within _____ days after the end of each calendar year of the term, or portion of a calendar year, the Landlord will deliver a statement of the actual Premises Expenses, certified by the Landlord, to the Tenant. At the time Landlord delivers this statement to the Tenant, the Landlord will refund any amount paid by the Tenant in excess of the actual Premises Expenses for that period. If the Tenant's actual Premises Expenses are greater than the total amount paid by the Tenant, the Tenant shall pay the difference within _____ days after receipt of Landlord's statement.

If Premises Expenses increase at any time during the term of the Lease, the Landlord reserves the right to increase the Tenant's Premises Expenses by providing written notice of the amount of this increase to the Tenant. The Tenant, who retains the right to audit Premises Expenses, agrees to begin payment of this increase in the next due monthly installment. Tenant, at its own cost and expense, has the right to examine or audit Landlord's records pertaining to Premises Expenses once each year, within the ____ day period following the date on which the Landlord delivers the statement of the actual Premises Expenses to the Tenant.

The obligations of Landlord and Tenant under this Article IV shall remain in force until the expiration of the term of this Lease.

4.04 Common area: "Common Area" refers to all areas, facilities, and improvements provided by Landlord and / or the adjoining shopping center that may be constructed from time to time for the convenience and use of the Tenant of the Premises, and its subtenants, agents, concessionaires, employees, customers, invitees, and licensees. The Common Area includes, without limitation, all parking areas, sidewalks, service corridors, truckways, loading docks, delivery areas, ramps, landscaped areas, public bathrooms, access and interior roads, retaining walls, and lighting facilities. The Tenant agrees that the Landlord and a master maintenance association (as described below) shall at all times have the right to make a reasonable determination of the nature and extent of the Common Areas, whether within or adjacent to the Premises. The Landlord and the master maintenance association shall have the right to make any changes, rearrangements, additions, or reductions to these areas that are deemed to be desirable from time to time by their reasonable judgment, or that are required by law.

a. **Master maintenance association:** The Landlord and the Tenant agree that the property upon which the Premises is located is or will be subject to a master maintenance association (the "Association") that will administer Tenant's pro rata share of association expenses and provide consistent management of the Common Areas within the adjoining shopping center. To the extent that Landlord is required to be a member of an association formed for the purpose of administering common areas, the Tenant may be required to be a member of the same association. A portion of the Common Area Costs shall be charged to administration and overhead and shall be included within Premises Expenses as defined in 4.03 above.

4.05 Utilities: It is the sole responsibility of the Tenant to apply and be solely responsible for all charges for water, heat, electricity, sewer, telephone, and any other utility used on, or provided to, the Premises. These charges should be promptly paid by the Tenant, who holds the Landlord harmless from any charge or liability for same. The Landlord is not liable for any interruptions in utility services and shall not be in breach or default under this Lease as long as the Landlord acts diligently to restore any failure or defect that impedes the provision of utility services after receiving written notice of such a failure or defect.

4.06 Leasehold and personal property taxes: The Tenant is responsible for the timely payment of any and all taxes levied, or assessed and payable during the term of this Lease on all of the Tenant's equipment, furniture, fixtures, and personal property located in the Premises.

4.07 Real estate taxes: The Tenant will pay all real estate taxes levied, assessed, or imposed on the Premises during the term of this Lease as soon as they become due.

ARTICLE V

5.01 Use: The Tenant shall use the Premises only for the purposes and activities specified in the attached Appendix "D," including activities and programs related to the operation of the premises, which the Tenant carries out in other similar facilities operated by the Tenant. Approval must be obtained from the Landlord in writing before the Premises can be used for any other purpose. The Tenant shall not allow Premises to be used for any improper, immoral, unlawful, or objectionable purpose. The Tenant shall not cause, or allow any public or private nuisance in, on, or about the Premises, including but not limited to, objectionable or harmful noises and odors. Except for reasonable wear and tear, the Tenant shall not damage or allow damage to be done to the Premises. The Tenant will not permit anything that conflicts in any way with any private restrictive covenant, law, statute, ordinance; any rule or regulation of the Landlord; or any governmental or quasi-governmental authority that is now in force or may be enacted or promulgated in the future; to be done in the Premises. The Landlord must demonstrate to the Tenant that, under applicable zoning laws and present covenants of record, there is no impediment to the use of the Premises as specified in this Lease. During the term of this Lease and any extension of it, the Landlord will not agree to any private restrictive covenant or enact any rule or regulation that would impair the ability of Tenant to use the Premises as specified in this Lease.

ARTICLE VI

6.01 Alterations and additions: From the Commencement Date, the Tenant will make no alterations, installations, additions, or improvements in or to the Premises without the prior written consent of Landlord. From the date of execution of this Lease, any improvements, including the Building, and any alterations, installations, additions, or improvements in or to the Premises, except movable furniture and movable trade fixtures, will become a part of the Premises and belong to Landlord. They will be surrendered with the Premises at the expiration of this Lease, or when the Tenant's right to possession of the Premises is terminated. The Landlord may require Tenant to remove any alterations, installations, additions, or improvements made by Tenant at Tenant's sole cost and expense. Prior to the expiration or termination of this Lease, Tenant shall remove all Tenant's property and all of the property that the Landlord has designated for removal from the Premises. The Tenant must make any repairs necessitated by the removal of this property or reimburse the Landlord for the costs of such repairs.

6.02 Tenant repairs: In taking possession of the Premises, the Tenant accepts the Premises as being in good, sanitary order, condition, and repair. Except as provided in Section 6.03 of this Lease, the Tenant, at its own cost and expense, will maintain the Premises and any associated property, wherever it is located, including without limitation the interior portion of all doors, door checks, windows, window frames, plate glass, storefront, all plumbing facilities within the Premises, signs, fixtures, and electrical systems (located in the Premises or outside), sprinkler systems, walls, floors, and ceilings, in good order and repair (including the replacement of parts and equipment, if necessary).

The tenant shall maintain in good order and repair (including the replacement of parts and equipment, if necessary) the heating and air conditioning systems associated with the Premises. Before taking occupancy of the Premises, the Tenant shall enter into a maintenance contract in a form and with a subcontractor approved by Landlord, to properly maintain the heating and air conditioning systems, naming Landlord as an additional loss payee or co-beneficiary. A copy of this maintenance contract must be provided to Landlord as a condition of taking possession of the Premises together with evidence that the premiums of other fees necessary to activate the maintenance contract have been paid. Annually on each anniversary date of this Lease, evidence that this maintenance contract has been renewed or replaced shall be provided to the Landlord. The obligation to provide a maintenance contract does not limit the Tenant's duty to maintain the heating and air conditioning systems, but is in addition to that duty.

The Tenant is required to maintain the Premises in a clean, sanitary, and safe condition in accordance with state and federal laws and in accordance with all directions, rules, and regulations of health officers, fire marshals, building inspectors, or regulatory jurisdiction over the Premises. The Tenant shall comply with all laws, regulations, and ordinances affecting the premises, including without limitation, all laws, regulations, and ordinances applicable to (*enter type of business*) facilities. The Tenant will install and maintain fire extinguishers and other fire protection devices and comply with all the requirements of any insurance policies and the insurance underwriters insuring the Premises.

The Tenant shall carry out a program of regular maintenance and repair to the Premises, including painting or refinishing of all areas of the interior to keep it in an attractive condition and to prevent, as much as possible, deterioration through ordinary wear and tear. At the termination of this Lease, Tenant shall surrender the Premises in good condition, except for reasonable wear and tear or loss by fire or other casualty.

The Tenant shall maintain the foundation, exterior walls, and roof of the Premises, as well as the structural portions of the Premises (including the doors, door frames, door checks, windows, and window frames located in exterior building walls) in good repair. Any repairs, maintenance, or the like that affect the exterior appearance of the Premises must be approved by the Landlord.

If the Tenant fails to perform any of the duties under the terms of this Section 6.02 for a period of ____ business days after the Landlord has delivered a written demand, the Landlord or its authorized representatives may, but are not obligated to, perform these duties without liability to Tenant for any resulting loss or damage that may result to Tenant's stock or business. If the Landlord performs, or causes to be performed, any of Tenant's responsibilities under this Article, the Tenant's default under this Lease will not be waived, and the Tenant shall be liable for all of the Landlord's costs and expenses, plus interest on these costs at the rate specified in Section 9.04 from the date that the costs and expenses are incurred until Tenant reimburses Landlord. Failure of the Tenant to reimburse the Landlord for such costs upon demand shall be considered a breach of this lease, and the Landlord will have the right to use all of the remedies specified in Article IX of this Lease.

The Landlord agrees that Tenant may accept possession of the Premises subject to a punch list and latent defects, but this punch list or latent defects shall not alter the Tenant's obligation to pay rent as required in this Lease. The Landlord will repair or replace any items that are defective in materials or workmanship within one year after the Commencement Date. If applicable, Landlord will assign to Tenant all extended warranties provided by contractors, subcontractors, suppliers, and material men.

6.03 Landlord repairs: The Landlord shall have no duty to repair or maintain the Premises or any part of the Premises. Neither the Landlord nor the Tenant shall erect a fence or barrier that segregates or separates the Premises from the Common Area, as set out in Section 4.04, will be erected by either the Landlord or the Tenant.

ARTICLE VII

7.01 Tenant's insurance: The Tenant is responsible, at Tenant's sole expense, to obtain and keep in force during the term and any extension or renewal of this Lease:

a. Fire and extended coverage insurance, with vandalism and malicious mischief endorsements and a sprinkler leakage endorsement (where applicable), on the Premises, insuring the building for not less than 100% of its replacement cost;

b. Comprehensive general liability insurance, including contractual liability coverage (according to the terms in Section 7.03 below), insuring the Landlord (as an additional insured) and the Tenant against any liability arising out of the ownership, use, occupancy, or maintenance of the Premises and all associated areas. The insurance companies must be approved by Landlord, shall cover a minimum of $ ____ for any loss of or damage to property from any one accident and $_____ for death of or injury to any one person from any one accident.

c. If not previously covered by the insurance in (i) above, contents and personal property insurance sufficient to provide full coverage in the event of loss or damage. The limits of this insurance shall not limit the liability of the Tenant. This insurance may be carried by the Tenant under a blanket policy, provided that a Landlord's protective liability endorsement is attached to it. The Landlord, and any mortgagee of which the Tenant has been given written notice as mortgagee, shall be named as insured parties under the fire and extended coverage insurance on the building. In the event that the Tenant fails to procure and maintain such insurance, the Landlord, may, but is not obligated to, procure and maintain it at the expense of Tenant.

Before occupying the Premises, the Tenant shall deliver to the Landlord copies of the policies of liability insurance required in Article 7.01. or certificates documenting the existence and amounts of such insurance, with loss payable clauses satisfactory to Landlord. No insurance policy shall be cancelled or subject to reduction of coverage until not less than ____ days after written notice has been delivered to Landlord.

7.02 Waiver and subrogation: If either party to this Lease incurs any loss, costs, damage, or expense resulting from fire, explosion, or any other casualty or occurrence in connection with the Premises, for which the party is covered (or is required under this Lease to be covered) in whole or in part by insurance, the insured party releases the other party from any liability it may have on account of such loss, costs, damage, or expense for the amount recovered from insurance. The insured party waives any right of subrogation that might otherwise exist, provided that such release of liability, and waiver of the right to subrogation will not invalidate such insurance coverage or increase its cost thereof (provided, that in the case of increased costs, the other party shall have the right, within ____ days following written notice, to pay such increased costs, thereupon keeping such release and waiver in full force and effect). Landlord and Tenant shall use their respective best efforts to obtain such a release and waiver of subrogation from their respective insurance carriers and shall obtain any special endorsements, if required by their insurer, to evidence compliance with the aforementioned waiver.

7.03 Hold harmless: The Landlord and Landlord's agents and employees shall not be liable to any person or party for the injury or death of any persons or damage to property in or about the Premises caused by Tenant, or Tenant's employees, servants, agents, subtenants, licensees, concessionaires, or invitees, arising out of the use of the Premises by Tenant or arising out of the Tenant's failure to fulfill its obligations under this Lease. The Tenant indemnifies and holds Landlord harmless from any loss, expense (including reasonable attorney's fees), or claims arising out of such injury, death, damage, use, or default. The Landlord and Landlord's agent and employees shall not be liable to Tenant for the injury or death of any persons, damage to property sustained by Tenant, or any person claiming through the Tenant, resulting from any accident or occurrence in or about the Premises. The Landlord shall not be liable to the Tenant for any loss or damage caused by or through the acts or omissions of any other persons, excepting those instances where the Landlord, its agents, and employees have been legally judged to be negligent.

ARTICLE VIII

8.01 Casualty: If the Premises, or any portion of the Premises, is damaged by fire or another casualty covered by the insurance carried by Tenant, and the cost of repairing such damage shall not be greater than _____ percent (%) of the full replacement cost as determined by the Landlord, then, subject to the following provisions of this Article, the Tenant shall repair the Premises.

If the Premises are damaged by fire or other casualty not covered by the insurance carried by Tenant under the terms of this Lease or damaged to an extent greater than _____ percent (%) of the full replacement costs of the Premises, then the Landlord will have the option of either having the Tenant repair or reconstruct the Premises to substantially the same condition as it was in immediately before the fire or other casualty or terminating this Lease by notifying the Tenant within _____ days after the date of the fire or other casualty. In case of termination, it will be effective as of the date of such fire or other casualty. If Landlord elects, or is required, to repair or reconstruct the Premises, the Tenant will diligently support the completion of the repair or reconstruction, provided all the proceeds of the insurance are assigned to and made available to the Landlord and are adequate for the purpose.

The rent required to be paid under the terms of this Lease shall not be abated while repairs of the Premises are being carried out, but shall continue to be in effect. To cover such an eventuality, the Tenant shall carry, at Tenant's sole cost and expense, appropriate Business Interruption Insurance. The Landlord shall not be liable for any damages, compensation, or claims related to loss of the use of the whole or any part of the Premises; Tenant's personal property; or any inconvenience, loss of business, or annoyance arising from any such repair and reconstruction. The Landlord shall not be required to repair or replace any furniture, furnishings or other personal property, equipment, inventory, fixtures, or goods that Tenant is entitled to remove from the Premises.

8.02 End of term casualty: Notwithstanding anything to the contrary in this Article, when the damage resulting from any casualty covered under this Article occurs during the last _____ months of the term of this Lease or any extension of it, the Landlord shall not be under any obligation whatsoever to repair, reconstruct, or restore the Premises if the cost of repair is greater than _____ percent (%) of the cost of fully repairing the building on the Premises and such repairs cannot be completed within _____ days.

8.03 Condemnation: If more than _____ percent (%) of the premises shall be taken or appropriated by any public or quasi-public authority under the power of eminent domain or conveyed or leased in lieu of such taking or appropriation, either party to the Lease shall have the right, at its option, to terminate this Lease on the date when title or right of possession is enacted. If either party terminates the Lease, Tenant shall be entitled to a refund of all rent paid for any period beyond the date of termination; the Landlord shall be entitled to any and all income, rent, award, or any interest therein whatsoever which may be paid or made in connection with such public or quasi-public use or purpose. The Tenant shall have no claim against Landlord for the value of any unexpired term of this Lease. The Tenant shall be entitled, to the extent provided under the general law, to obtain the value of its leasehold improvements, business interruption, and moving expenses. If _____ percent (%) or less of the premises is taken, or more than _____ (%) percent of the Premises is taken, and neither party elects to terminate as herein provided, the amount of the rental will be reduced accordingly. The Landlord will repair, reconstruct, or restore the Premises to fulfill the original terms of the Lease, but will not be obligated to spend for such purposes an amount greater than the condemnation proceeds received by Landlord that are attributable to the Premises.

ARTICLE IX

9.01 Default: The occurrence of any one or more of the following events shall constitute a default under this Lease by Tenant:

a. The Tenant's failure to pay the rent or any other payment required to be made by Tenant, according to the terms of this Lease, for a period of _____ days after the date when the payment is due.

b. The material breach by the Tenant of any condition in the Lease, or the Tenant's failure to fulfill or perform, in whole or in part, any of its obligations under this Lease other than the payment of any monetary obligations, in the event that such a failure continues for a period of _____ days after the Landlord delivers written notice to the Tenant. If the nature of Tenant's default is such that more than _____ days is reasonably required for its remediation, the Tenant shall not be considered in default if the Tenant begins remediation within the ____-day period, and thereafter diligently completes the obligation.

c. The failure by Tenant to remove any lien filed against this leasehold estate or the Premises as a consequence of the Tenant's actions within _____ days after the Tenant has received written notice that the lien has been filed.

d. The initiation of bankruptcy proceedings by the Tenant, the making of any general arrangement by the Tenant for the benefit of creditors, the initiation of bankruptcy proceedings against the Tenant unless those proceedings are dismissed within _____ days, the appointment of a trustee or receiver to take possession of substantially all of the Tenant's assets located at the Premises or of Tenant's interest in this Lease where possession is not restored to Tenant within ____ days, or the attachment or other judicial seizure of substantially all of Tenant's assets located at the Premises or of Tenant's interest in this Lease, where such seizure is not discharged in _____ days.

e. The transfer, mortgage, assignment, or other encumbrance by Tenant of this leasehold estate, except as specified below.

f. Failure to occupy the Premises on or before the Commencement Date given in this Lease agreement.

g. Abandonment by Tenant under Section 10.04 below.

9.02 Rights upon default: If a default occurs and Tenant fails to take action as required by the terms of this Lease, the Landlord may at any time, with or without further notice or demand, exercise all rights and remedies available to Landlord under this Lease, at law, or in equity, including, without limitation, the termination of this Lease and the termination of the Tenant's right to possession of the Premises without terminating the Lease. If the Tenant defaults, the Landlord may, without additional notice and without court proceedings, repossess the Premises and remove all persons and property from the Premises. The Tenant agrees to surrender possession of the Premises, waives any claim arising from surrender of the Premises or by reason of issuance of any distress warrant or writ of sequestration, and to hold Landlord harmless from any such claims.

In the event that the Landlord chooses to terminate this Lease, it may treat the default as an entire breach of this Lease, and the Tenant shall immediately become liable to Landlord for damages equal to the total of:

a. The cost of recovering, reletting (including the costs of lease commissions attributable to the unexpired portion of the term of this Lease), and remodeling the Premises,

b. All unpaid Base Rent and other amounts earned or due through such termination, plus

c. The excess, if any, of the present value of the Base Rent and other amounts scheduled to be paid by Tenant under this Lease for the remainder of the full term, over the present fair market value of the Premises for the remainder of the full term. Such present value is to be computed as of the date of termination and based on a _____ percent (%) per year discount rate.

If the Landlord elects to terminate Tenant's right to possession of the Premises without terminating the Lease, Landlord may, but is not obligated to, rent the Premises, or any part thereof, on behalf of the Tenant to any person or persons under terms and conditions and for an amount that the Landlord deems appropriate. The Tenant shall be liable to the Landlord for the amount, if any, by which the rent for the unexpired balance of the term of this Lease exceeds the net amount, if any, received by Landlord from such reletting, after the costs of repossession, reletting, remodeling, and other expenses incurred by the Landlord have been deducted. Such sum shall be paid by the Tenant in monthly installments on the first day of each month of the term. In the event of default by the Tenant, the Landlord shall make a reasonable effort to relet the Premises, but, in no event, shall the Landlord be held responsible for failure to relet the premises or to collect the rent due under such reletting. In no event shall the Tenant be entitled to any excess rents received by the Landlord. All rights and remedies of the Landlord shall be cumulative and not exclusive.

9.03 Costs: The Tenant shall reimburse the Landlord on demand for all costs reasonably incurred by the Landlord in connection with a default including, but not limited to, reasonable attorney's fees, court costs, and related costs, plus interest on the amount of these costs from the date such costs are paid by Landlord until Tenant reimburses Landlord, at the rate specified in Section 9.04.

9.04 Interest: All late payments of rent, costs, or other amounts due from Tenant under the terms of this Lease shall bear interest from the date they come due, until they are paid, at the maximum non-usurious rate of interest at which Tenant may legally contract.

The acceptance by Landlord of any late payment does not constitute a waiver by Landlord of its rights to demand performance of any other obligation under this Lease.

9.05 Landlord's lien: The Landlord is granted a first and superior lien and security interest (in addition to and not in replacement of the statutory Landlord's lien) on all leasehold improvements, fixtures, equipment, and personal property (tangible and intangible) placed by Tenant in or on the Premises now or later, to secure all sums due by Tenant under this lease. This lien and security interest may be enforced by Landlord in any legal manner, including without limitation, in accordance with the Uniform Commercial Code. The provisions of this Section shall constitute a security agreement under the Uniform Commercial Code. At the Landlord's request, the Tenant shall file, where appropriate, all documents necessary to grant this security interest in accordance with the Uniform Commercial Code.

At the request of the Tenant, the Landlord shall subordinate its lien and security interest as retained in this Lease (as well as any statutory Landlord's lien), to any lien that secures bona fide financing of Tenant's movable personal property placed in the Premises.

9.06 Non-waiver: If the Landlord fails to insist upon the strict performance of, or to seek remedy for violations of any covenant or condition of this Lease, it shall not prevent a subsequent violation of this Lease from having all the force and effect of an original violation. Receipt by the Landlord of rent, with or without knowledge that the Tenant has breached any provision of this Lease, shall not be considered a waiver of such breach. Payment of rent shall not reinstate this Lease or the Tenant's right of possession of the Premises if either or both have been terminated, and shall not otherwise affect any notice, election, action, or suit by Landlord.

Nothing done by the Landlord during the term of this Lease shall be taken as an acceptance of a surrender of the Premises, and no agreement to accept a surrender of the Premises shall be valid unless made in writing and signed by the Landlord.

ARTICLE X

10.01 Assignment and subletting: The Tenant will not voluntarily, by operation of law or otherwise, assign, transfer, mortgage, pledge, hypothecate, or encumber this Lease and shall not sublet the said Premises or any part thereof or any right or privilege associated with the Premises or allow any other person except the employees, agents, servants, and invitees of the Tenant to occupy or use the Premises or any portion of the Premises without the prior written consent of Landlord. The Consent Factors are set forth in Section 10.02.

Any such assignment, transfer, mortgage, pledge, hypothecation, encumbrance, sublet, or permission to use will be collectively referred to as a "Transfer" for the purposes of this document. Consent to one Transfer shall not constitute consent to any subsequent Transfer. Any such Transfer made without consent of the Landlord shall be void and shall constitute a default under this Lease; however, the Landlord may collect rent from the assignee or sublessee without waiving any provision of the Lease or releasing Tenant from the performance of its obligations under this Lease. Any Transfer by Tenant that has been approved by Landlord does not relieve Tenant of its direct and primary liability under the covenants and obligations contained in or derived from this Lease for the full term of this lease. The Landlord shall have the right to enforce the provisions of this Lease against the Tenant or any assignee or sublessee without making any demand or proceeding in any way against any other person or entity.

10.02 Consent factors: The Landlord may consider any reasonable factor in determining whether or not to consent to a sublet of the Premises or an assignment of this Lease. The Landlord and Tenant hereby agree that any one of the following factors, or any other reasonable factor, may be reasonably considered in consenting to or denying a sublet or an assignment:

a. The financial strength of the proposed subtenant/assignee must be equal to or greater than the financial strength of Tenant on the Commencement Date of this Lease. The Landlord may require reasonably acceptable evidence of a present and future capacity to perform the financial obligations of Tenant under the Lease.

b. The business reputation of the proposed subtenant / assignee must meet generally acceptable commercial standards.

c. The nature and activities of the proposed subtenant / assignee will not violate or create any potential violation of any laws, covenants, or other agreements affecting the Premises or other leases in the adjoining shopping center development.

d. The Tenant is not in default under this Lease.

e. The sublease is for a term shorter than the remaining Lease term and / or at a rental rate less than the then current market rate for comparable premises.

10.03 Proceeds: Any sublet or assignment approved by Landlord must be submitted in writing and in a form acceptable to Landlord. In the event that the Landlord consents to a sublet or an assignment, the Tenant agrees to pay the Landlord _____ percent (%) of any lump sum received by the Tenant for such sublet or assignment, as well as _____ percent (%) of all rental payments made to Tenant by any subtenant or assignee in excess of the rent payable under the terms of this Lease. Any payments by an assignee or sublessee to the Tenant for personal property, goodwill, or the value of the business as a going concern will not be included in the amounts paid to Landlord under this Section. The Tenant shall reimburse the

Landlord for all reasonable attorney's fees and other direct costs incurred by the Landlord on account of such sublet or assignment.

10.04 Abandonment: If the Tenant vacates the Premises or otherwise ceases to operate the Premises for its intended purpose for a period of _____ or more days after the Commencement Date, the Landlord will have the right, following the ____-day period, to terminate this Lease after giving _____ days' notice. The termination notice will inform the Tenant that unless Tenant recommences operations within the ____-day period, the Lease shall automatically be terminated without further notice upon the expiration of the _____ days. The Tenant shall then vacate the Premises immediately and surrender the Premises to Landlord on the same terms set forth in this Lease for the expiration of the Lease term. If the Landlord does not provide such written notice, the Tenant may remain in possession of the Premises and not operate it for its intended purpose as long as the Tenant continues to pay the rent required under the terms and conditions of this Lease and to fulfill all other obligations under the Lease.

ARTICLE XI

11.01 Entry by landlord: The Landlord and its agents, employees, and representatives shall have the right to enter the Premises at all reasonable times provided prior notice is given to Tenant to inspect the Premises; supply any service to be provided by Landlord to Tenant under the terms of this Lease; show the Premises to prospective purchasers, mortgagees, or tenants; post notices of non-responsibility; perform alterations or repairs to the Premises; or for any other purpose that Landlord may reasonably consider necessary or desirable, without abatement of rent. At the Tenant's request, the Landlord shall utilize identification provided by the Tenant and / or consent to being accompanied by an escort during such visits. The Tenant hereby waives any claim for damages or for any injury, inconvenience to, or interference with Tenant's business; any loss of occupancy or quiet enjoyment of the Premises; and any other loss occasioned by such activities on the part of the Landlord, except for damages resulting from the Landlord's gross negligence or willful misconduct.

In an emergency, the Landlord has the right to use any and all means which the Landlord considers proper to obtain entry to the Premises without liability to Tenant, except for any failure to exercise due care for Tenant's property.

11.02 Subordination and nondisturbance: This Lease and all rights of the Tenant under this Lease are subject and subordinate to any and all mortgages or other security instruments which encumber the Premises now or in the future, any interest of Landlord in the Premises, to any and all advances made on the security of the Premises, and to any and all increases, renewals, modifications, consolidations, and extensions of any such leases, mortgages, and/or security instruments, provided that the Landlord, under any such mortgage, agrees not to disturb the Tenant's rights under this Lease if the Tenant attorns to such a Landlord under such mortgage. The Tenant agrees to execute a Subordination, Nondisturbance, and Attornment Agreement as required within ____ days after written request from Landlord, provided it contains a nondisturbance agreement customarily used in the industry. No further writing from the Tenant shall be necessary to document such subordination.

11.03 Attornment: If any mortgage is terminated or foreclosed, the Tenant shall, upon request, attorn to the mortgagee or purchaser at such foreclosure sale, as the case may be, and sign documents confirming such attornment, provided that if this Lease was approved and accepted in writing by such mortgagee, the Tenant's attornment shall be conditional upon the agreement by the successor to the Landlord's interest not to disturb the Tenant's possession under this Lease during the term as long as Tenant performs its obligations under this Lease. If such a termination or foreclosure occurs, and the Tenant attorns as described above, the

Tenant will automatically become the Tenant of the successor to Landlord's interest without any change in the terms or provisions of this Lease.

11.04 Quiet enjoyment: As long as the Tenant pays the rent required by the terms of this Lease and observes and performs all of the covenants, conditions, and provisions set forth in this Lease, the Tenant shall have quiet possession of the Premises for the entire term of this Lease, subject to all of the provisions of this Lease.

ARTICLE XII

12.01 Rules and regulations: The Tenant agrees to faithfully observe and comply with the rules and regulations promulgated from time to time by the Landlord, including, but not limited to, those set forth in Appendix "E" attached to and included in this Lease. The Landlord has the right from time to time to make reasonable additions, modifications, and deletions to these rules and regulations. These additions, modifications, and deletions shall be binding upon the Tenant as soon as a copy of same is delivered to the Tenant. The Landlord shall not be responsible to the Tenant if any of said rules and regulations are not followed by any other Tenant or person.

12.02 Holding over: The Tenant may not remain in possession of the Premises after the termination or expiration of this Lease. If the Tenant remains in possession of the Premises after the termination or expiration of this Lease, and the Landlord and the Tenant have not executed a new lease or an extension of this Lease, the Tenant shall be considered to be occupying the Premises as a tenant-at-sufferance, subject to all of the covenants and obligations of this Lease, except that a per-day Base Rent will be in effect immediately after the Lease has expired or been terminated. In addition, the Tenant will be liable for and will pay to Landlord any and all claims and / or damages (consequential or otherwise) resulting from such holding over by the Tenant. The Tenant hereby agrees to indemnify Landlord for any and all such claims, damages, and liability. It is expressly understood and agreed that the Tenant's holding over does not constitute an extension or renewal of the term of this Lease.

12.03 Estoppel certificate: The Tenant shall, at any time and from time to time upon not less than ____ days prior written notice from Landlord, execute, acknowledge, and deliver to Landlord an estoppel certificate in the form attached hereto as Appendix "F," or in such form as may be reasonably required by Landlord. Such a certificate will be made for the benefit of the Landlord, any prospective purchaser, or transferee of Landlord's interest under this Lease or of the Landlord's property, or any current or prospective mortgagee of all or any portion of the real property of which the Premises are a part.

12.04 Parking: The Tenant shall have the nonexclusive right to use the parking facilities of the Premises, subject to the rules and regulations established by the Landlord. The Landlord has the right to make reasonable alterations to these regulations at any time.

12.05 Authority of tenant's signatory: If the Tenant is a corporation or a limited partnership, the corporation or limited partnership represents and guarantees that the person signing this Lease on behalf of Tenant is duly authorized to execute and deliver this Lease on behalf of Tenant, according to a duly adopted resolution of the board of directors of this corporation, or according to the bylaws of said corporation, or as part of the limited partnership agreement. The corporation or limited partnership agrees that this Lease is binding upon it in accordance with its terms. The Landlord shall have the right to request any reasonable documentation from the Tenant to demonstrate his or her authority to execute this Lease.

12.06 Tenant's financial condition:

a. The Tenant hereby represents to Landlord, as a material condition for the acceptance of this Lease, that

i. The Tenant has the financial capability to discharge its obligations under this Lease, and

ii. The Tenant has never been declared bankrupt, taken advantage of any bankruptcy law or regulation to reorganize, made an assignment for the benefit of creditors, or been insolvent, nor is currently insolvent or involved in any proceeding or action by which any of the foregoing could occur.

b. Upon request, the Tenant shall provide copies of its most recent audited financial statements, distributed to the shareholders or filed with the Securities and Exchange Commission, to the Landlord.

c. The Tenant understands that the representations made and obligations undertaken in this Section 12.06 act as an inducement to Landlord to enter into this Lease, and that any misrepresentation or failure to provide the required documentation will constitute a default under this Lease.

12.07 Landlord's liability: The liability of the Landlord to the Tenant for any default by Landlord under the terms of this Lease shall be limited to the interest of Landlord in the Premises. It is expressly understood and agreed that the Landlord shall not be personally liable for any judgment or deficiency beyond the equity of Landlord's interest in the Premises.

12.08 Transfer and assignment by landlord: If the Landlord transfers or assigns the Premises, or the Landlord's interest in this Lease, in whole or in part, the Landlord will be entirely freed and relieved of all liability under any of its covenants and obligations under this Lease, or derived from it, arising out of any act, occurrence, or omission taking place after such a transfer of assignment has been consummated. The transferee or assignee, or any subsequent transferee or assignee, shall be considered without any further agreement between the parties or their successors in interest, or between the parties and any such transferee or assignee, to have agreed to carry out any and all of the covenants and obligations of the Landlord under this Lease.

12.09 No liens: The Tenant shall keep the Premises free from any liens arising out of any work performed, materials furnished, or obligations incurred by Tenant. If required by any of Landlord's mortgages or financing entities, the Tenant shall provide to Landlord, at Tenant's sole cost and expense, a lien and completion bond in an amount equal to _____ times the estimated costs of any improvements, additions, or alterations in the Premises, to insure Landlord against any liability for mechanics' and material men's liens, and to insure completion of the work where the amount contracted for exceeds U.S. $ _____.

12.10 Brokers: The Landlord and the Tenant each represent and guarantee to the other that they have had no dealings with any real estate broker or agents in connection with the negotiation of this Lease, and they know of no real estate broker or agent who is entitled to any commission in connection herewith. They each hereby indemnify and hold the other harmless from and against all claims of any broker(s) or similar parties claiming a commission in connection with this Lease, and of any costs of defending against and investigating such claims.

ARTICLE XIII

13.01 Notice: Except as otherwise indicated in this Lease agreement, any statement, notice, or other communication that Landlord or Tenant may desire or be required to give to the other shall be in writing. It will be considered delivered if it has been hand delivered, or if it has been sent by registered or certified mail, to the address(es) given at the beginning of this Lease document or to any other address(es) that the other party may designate from time to time by prior written notice, delivered and effective before the communication is sent. Until further notice, written communications will be sent to the following addresses:

Landlord: _____

Address: _____

City: _____ State: _____ ZIP code: _____

Tenant: _____

Permanent Address: _____

City: _____ State: _____ ZIP code: _____

13.02 Joint obligation: If there is more than one Tenant, the obligations imposed upon Tenants under the terms of this Lease shall be joint and several.

13.03 Captions: The captions in this Lease are used only as a matter of convenience and for reference, and they shall have no effect upon the construction or interpretation of any provision hereof.

13.04 Time: Time is of the essence of this Lease, including, particularly each and all of its provisions in which performance is a factor.

13.05 Parties and successors: Except for any limitations and conditions set forth elsewhere in this Lease, the terms of this Lease shall apply to the respective heirs, legal representatives, successors, and permitted assigns and/or sublessees of the Landlord and the Tenant. The term "Landlord," as used in this Lease, shall mean only the owner of the Premises at the time in question. In the event of any transfer of title to the Premises, the party making the transfer is relieved of all liability and obligations of the Landlord arising under this Lease from and after the date that the transfer is completed.

13.06 Recordation: Either Landlord or Tenant may record a short form memorandum hereof without the prior written consent of the other party as the same is shown on Appendix "F," attached to and considered a part of this Lease.

(a) Limitation on Mechanics Liens: The Landlord shall not be subject to liens for improvements made by the Tenant. The Tenant is responsible for notifying any and all contractors, subcontractors, and / or material men.

13.07 Prior agreements and amendments: This Lease contains all of the agreement between the Landlord and the Tenant with respect to any matter covered or mentioned in this Lease. No prior agreements or understandings pertaining to any of these matters shall be effective for any purpose. Any agreement made between the Landlord and the Tenant after the signing of this Lease shall not modify, release, or otherwise affect this Lease, in whole or in part, unless that agreement is made in writing and signed by the party to be bound by it.

13.08 Inability to perform: If either the Landlord or the Tenant is unable to perform any of its obligations under the terms of this Lease or is delayed in doing so because of strike, riot, labor disputes, acts of God, war, shortages of labor or materials, or any other cause whatsoever beyond the reasonable control of one or the other party, this inability or delay will not be considered a breach or default under this Lease. If non-performance occurs because of such circumstances, this Lease and the obligations of both the Tenant and the Landlord under this Lease will not be affected or impaired, and neither party shall be liable to the other.

13.09 Use of name: The Tenant shall not have the right to use the words, "_____ _____," as any portion of the name of its business located on the Premises without the consent of the Landlord and the Association.

13.10 Severability: Any provision of this Lease that shall prove to be invalid, void, or illegal shall in no way affect, impair, or invalidate any other provision hereof and such other provisions shall remain in full force and effect.

13.11 Cumulative remedies: No remedy or election under the terms of this Lease will be exclusive of all other remedies or elections, but shall, wherever possible, be cumulative with all other remedies at law and in equity.

13.12 Governing law: This Agreement, and all transactions set forth in this Lease, shall be governed by, construed, and enforced in accordance with the laws of the state of _____. The Landlord and the Tenant waive trial by jury and agree to submit to the personal jurisdiction and venue of a Court of subject matter jurisdiction located in _____ County, state of _____. Should litigation result from this Lease or from performance of the obligations set forth in this Lease, the Landlord and Tenant agree to reimburse the prevailing party for reasonable attorney's fees, Court costs, and all other expenses, whether or not taxable by the Court as costs, associated with the litigation, in addition to any other remedy to which the prevailing party may be entitled. No action shall be entertained by said Court or any Court of competent jurisdiction if filed more than one year after the date of the cause(s) of action actually accrued, regardless of whether damages could be accurately calculated at that time.

13.13 Waiver by Tenant: The Tenant hereby waives any and all right to fight any eviction action instituted by Landlord with the exception of an affirmative defense based upon payment of all amounts that the Landlord claims the Tenant has not paid. Any other matters may only be dealt with in a separate suit instituted by Tenant.

13.14 Memorandum of Adjustments: All adjustments to the terms and provisions in Sections 1.01, 2.01, 2.02, 3.01, and 4.01 of this Lease may be accomplished by a memorandum executed by Landlord and Tenant prior to the Commencement Date.

13.15 Prorations: Any monthly payment due to Landlord under the terms of this Lease that is for a period of less than _____ month shall be prorated based upon a _____-day month.

13.16 Appendices: The appendices attached to this Lease are hereby incorporated herein and made a part hereof for all purposes.

13.17 Reliance on Financial Statement: Concurrently with the execution of this lease, the Tenant shall furnish a financial statement of Tenant prepared by an accountant. The Tenant, both in corporate capacity, if applicable, and individually, hereby represents and warrants that all the information contained therein is complete, true, and correct. The Tenant understands that the Landlord is relying upon the accuracy of the information contained in this financial statement. If any inaccuracy be found to exist within the financial statement that adversely affects the Tenant's financial standing or if the Tenant's financial circumstances materially change, the Landlord may demand, as additional security, an amount equal to an additional two (2) months' rent. This additional security shall be subject to all terms and conditions of this Lease, require a fully executed guaranty by a third party acceptable to Landlord. The Landlord may elect to terminate this Lease or hold Tenant personally and individually liable hereunder.

13.18 Notice on Radon Gas: Radon is a naturally occurring radioactive gas that may present health risks to persons who are exposed to it over time, when it has accumulated in a building in sufficient quantities. Levels of radon that exceed federal and state guidelines have been found in buildings in this state. Additional information regarding radon and radon testing may be obtained from your county public health unit.

EXECUTED the day and year first above written.

LANDLORD: _____

WITNESS: _____

TENANT: _____

WITNESS: _____

APPENDIX "A": **LEGAL DESCRIPTION**

APPENDIX "B": **SITE PLAN**

APPENDIX "C": **DEVELOPMENT AGREEMENT**

APPENDIX "D": **USE OF PREMISES**

APPENDIX "E": RULES AND REGULATIONS

1. No sign, placard, picture, symbol, mark, advertisement, name, or notice shall be inscribed, displayed, printed, placed, or affixed on or to any part of the outside or inside of the Premises without the prior written consent of Landlord. Landlord has the right to remove any such sign, placard, picture, symbol, mark, advertisement, name, or notice without notice to and at the expense of Tenant. Tenant will not place anything or allow anything to be placed near the glass of any window, door, partition, or wall which is visible from outside the Premises. Tenant shall not, without the prior written consent of Landlord, cause to be covered or otherwise sunscreen any window.

2. The sidewalks, walks, corridors, passages, exits, entrances, stairways, and ramps of the Premises shall not be obstructed or used by Tenant or the employees, agents, servants, visitors, or licensees of Tenant for any purpose other than for ingress and egress to and from the Premises.

3. Only workers employed, designated, or approved by Landlord may perform repairs, installations, alterations, painting, material moving, and other similar work that may be done in or on the Premises. Nonstructural alterations and installations may be carried out by Tenant's employees or persons under their supervision.

4. The toilet rooms, urinals, wash bowls, and other apparatus shall not be used for any purpose other than that for which they are constructed, and no foreign substance of any kind whatsoever shall be thrown therein. The Tenant will be responsible for the expense caused by any breakage, stoppage, or damage resulting from the violation of this rule caused by Tenant, its employees, or invitees.

5. Tenant shall not overload the floor of the Premises or in any way deface the Premises or any part thereof. Maximum floor loading shall be _____ pounds per square foot.

6. Tenant shall not permit or suffer the Premises to be occupied or used in a manner offensive or objectionable to Landlord because of light, radiation, magnetism, noise, odors, and / or vibrations. Neither Tenant, nor the employees, agents, servants, visitors, or licensees of Tenant shall place, leave, or discard any rubbish, paper, articles, or objects of any kind whatsoever outside the doors of the Premises. No animals or birds may be brought into or kept in or about the Premises.

7. Tenant shall not use or keep in the Premises any poisonous, corrosive, caustic, explosive, inflammable, or combustible gas, fluid or substance or use any method of heating or cooling other than that approved by Landlord.

8. Landlord will direct electricians as to where and how telephone and telegraph wires are to be introduced. No boring or cutting for wires will be allowed without the consent of the Landlord. The

location of telephones, call boxes, and other office equipment affixed to the Premises shall be subject to the approval of Landlord.

9. Tenant shall not use any of the common areas of the Premises for the care or maintenance of vehicles.

10. Landlord reserves the right to exclude or expel from the Premises any person who, in the judgment of Landlord, is intoxicated, under the influence of liquor or drugs, or who shall in any manner violate any of the rules and regulations of the Premises.

11. Landlord shall have the right to prohibit any advertising by Tenant which, in Landlord's sole judgment, in any way impairs the reputation of the Premises, and upon written notice from Landlord, Tenant will refrain from or discontinue such advertising.

12. Canvassing, soliciting, peddling, and similar activities are prohibited in the Premises without the prior approval of Landlord. Tenant will cooperate to prevent same.

13. No additional locks or bolts of any kind shall be placed on any door in the Premises, and no lock on any door in the Premises shall be changed or altered in any respect. Landlord shall furnish _____ keys for each lock on exterior doors to the Premises. Tenant shall not make duplicate keys; duplicate keys can be obtained from the Landlord at Tenant's expense. All keys shall be returned to Landlord upon the expiration or termination of this Lease, and Tenant shall give to Landlord the explanations of the combinations of all safes, vaults, and combination locks remaining with the Premises. Landlord may at all times keep a passkey to the Premises. All entrance doors to the Premises shall be kept closed at all times and left locked when the Premises are not in use.

14. Tenant shall give immediate notice to Landlord in case of theft, unauthorized solicitation, or accident in the Premises; of defects in the Premises or in any fixtures or equipment; or of any known emergency in the Premises.

15. Tenant shall not use the Premises or permit the Premises to be used for photographic, multilith, or multigraph reproductions except in connection with its own business and not as a service for others without Landlord's prior permission.

16. Tenant shall not advertise for laborers giving the Premises as an address, nor pay such laborers at a location in the Premises.

17. Tenant shall at all times keep the Premises neat and orderly.

Landlord _____

Tenant _____

EXHIBIT "F": MEMORANDUM OF LEASE

THIS MEMORANDUM OF LEASE, dated _____ (date) by and between

_____ ("Landlord"), with its principal place of business located at:

_____

City: _____ State: _____ ZIP code: _____

and _____ ("Tenant"),

with its principal place of business located at:

City: _____ State: _____ ZIP code: _____

WITNESSETH

1. That by Lease ("Lease") dated _____,

2. Between Tenant and Landlord, Landlord has demised and leased to Tenant, and Tenant has leased from Landlord, the premises described on Exhibit "A" attached hereto ("Leased Premises") for a term beginning on the day of _____("Commencement Date"), and ending, unless sooner terminated, on the last day of the month during which the _____ anniversary of the Commencement Date occurs.

3. The interest of the Landlord shall not be subject to any liens or claims asserted against the Leased Premises in connection with Tenant's improvements on the Leased Premises or Tenant's use of the Leased Premises, and Tenant shall provide notice of such limitation to all contractors, subcontractors, and material men as required under Section 12.09 of this Lease.

4. This Memorandum of Lease is executed pursuant to the terms of the Lease and is not intended to vary the terms and conditions of the Lease.

IN WITNESS WHEREOF, the parties have caused this instrument to be duly executed and sealed as of the date above.

LANDLORD: _____

WITNESS: _____

TENANT: _____

WITNESS: _____

Commercial Lease Agreement

This Commercial Lease Agreement (Lease) is entered into on this ____ day of _____, 20__, between _____ (Landlord) and _____ (Tenant). Landlord is the owner of the parcel land and its improvements located at the legal address of: _____ ___. Landlord makes available for lease the portion of the Building designated as _____ and described as _____ (Leased Premises).

Landlord hereby leases the Leased Premises to Tenant, and Tenant leases the Leased Premises from Landlord for the entire term, at the rental rate described, and upon the provisions that are set forth hereunder.

THEREFORE, in consideration of the mutual promises contained herein, and for other good and valuable consideration, it is agreed:

TERM

The term of the Lease shall begin on the _____ day of _____, 20__, and end on the _____ day of _____, 20__. Landlord shall use his/her best efforts to make available to Tenant possession of the Leased Premises on the first day of the Lease term. If Landlord is unable to make timely provision of the Leased Premises, rent shall be abated for the period of delay at the rate of: _____. Tenant shall make no other claim against Landlord for delays.

Tenant will have the option to renew the Lease for one extended term of _____. If Tenant should decide to exercise such renewal option, he / she will provide written notice to Landlord not less than ninety (90) days before the expiration of the initial term. The renewal term shall be at the rental set forth below and otherwise upon the same covenants, conditions, terms, and provisions as contained in this Lease.

RENTAL

Tenant shall pay to Landlord during the initial term rent of _____ Dollars ($) per year, payable in installments of _____ Dollars ($) per month. Each installment payment shall be due in advance on the first day of each calendar month during the lease term to Landlord at the following address: _____.

The rental payment amount for any partial calendar months included in the lease term shall be prorated on a daily basis.

Tenant shall also pay to Landlord a Deposit in the amount of _____ Dollars ($). This Deposit shall be paid upon _____ date and will be held for the duration of the lease term.

The rental for any renewal lease term, if created as permitted under this Lease, shall be _____ Dollars ($) per year payable in installments of _____ Dollars ($) per month.

PROHIBITED USES

Notwithstanding the forgoing, Tenant agrees not to use the Leased Premises for the purposes of storing, manufacturing, or selling any explosives, flammables, other inherently dangerous substance, chemical, thing, or device, or for any other illegal activity.

SUBLEASE AND ASSIGNMENT

Tenant shall have the right without Landlord's consent, to assign this Lease to a business with which Tenant may merge or consolidate, to any subsidiary of Tenant, to any corporation under common control with Tenant, or to a purchaser of substantially all of Tenant's assets.

Except as set forth above, Tenant agrees not to sublease all or any part of the Leased Premises or assign this Lease, in whole or in part, without Landlord's written consent. If consent is requested, Landlord agrees to provide either consent or dissent within seven (7) days of request.

REPAIRS

During the Lease term, Tenant shall make, at Tenant's expense, all necessary repairs to the Leased Premises. Repairs include routine repairs of floors, walls, ceilings, and other parts of the Leased Premises damaged or worn through normal occupancy, and other similar items, except for major mechanical systems or the roof, subject to the obligations of the parties otherwise set forth in this Lease.

ALTERATIONS AND IMPROVEMENTS

Tenant, at Tenant's expense, shall have the right, upon obtaining Landlord's consent, to remodel, redecorate, and make additions, improvements, and replacements of and to all or any part of the Leased Premises from time to time as Tenant may deem desirable. Tenant agrees that same are to be made in a workmanlike manner and utilizing quality materials. Tenant has the right to place and install personal property, trade fixtures, equipment, and other temporary installations in and upon the Leased Premises and fasten the same to the premises. All personal property, equipment, machinery, trade fixtures, and temporary installations, whether acquired by Tenant at the commencement of the Lease term or placed or installed on the Leased Premises by Tenant after the lease has begun, shall remain Tenant's property free and clear of any claim by Landlord. Tenant shall have the right to remove the same at any time during the term of this Lease provided that Tenant repairs, at Tenant's own expense, all damages to the Leased Premises caused by such removal.

PROPERTY TAXES

Landlord shall pay, before delinquency, all real estate taxes and special assessments due before or during the Lease term on the Leased Premises and all personal property taxes with respect to Landlord's personal property, if any, on the Leased Premises. Tenant shall be responsible for paying all personal property taxes with respect to Tenant's personal property at the Leased Premises.

INSURANCE

If the Leased Premises or any other part of the Building is damaged by fire or other casualty resulting from any act of negligence by Tenant or by any of Tenant's agents, employees, or invitees, rent shall not be diminished or abated while such damages are under repair, and Tenant shall additionally be responsible for the costs of repair not covered by insurance.

Landlord agrees to maintain fire and extended coverage insurance on the Building and the Leased Premises in such amount as Landlord shall deem appropriate. Tenant shall be responsible, at his / her expense, for fire and extended coverage insurance on all of its personal property, including removable trade fixtures, located in the Leased Premises.

Tenant and Landlord shall each maintain a policy or policies of comprehensive general liability insurance with respect to the particular activities of each in the Building. Signatures below indicate that the premiums thereon are fully paid on or before due date. Such insurance policy shall be issued by and binding upon an insurance company approved by Landlord and shall afford minimum protection of not less than $1,000,000 combined single limit coverage of bodily injury, property damage, or combination thereof. Tenant shall provide Landlord with current Certificates of Insurance evidencing Tenant's compliance with this Paragraph.

UTILITIES

Tenant shall pay all charges for water, sewer, gas, electricity, telephone, and other services and utilities used by Tenant on the Leased Premises during the term of this Lease unless otherwise expressly agreed in writing by Landlord. In the event that any utility or service provided to the Leased Premises is not separately metered, Landlord shall pay the amount due and separately invoice Tenant for Tenant's pro rata share of the charges.

Tenant shall pay all such utility charges on or before the due date. Tenant acknowledges that the Leased Premises are designed to provide standard office-use electrical facilities and standard office lighting. Tenant agrees not to use any equipment or devices that utilize excessive electrical energy or that may, in Landlord's reasonable opinion, overload the wiring or otherwise interfere with electrical services to other tenants.

SIGNS

Following Landlord's consent, Tenant shall have the right to place on the Leased Premises, at locations selected by Tenant, all signage that is permitted by local zoning ordinances and private restrictions. Landlord may refuse consent to any proposed signs that are in Landlord's opinion too large, deceptive, unattractive, or otherwise inconsistent with or inappropriate to the Leased Premises or use of any other tenant. Landlord shall assist and cooperate with Tenant in obtaining any necessary permission from governmental authorities or adjoining owners and occupants for Tenant to place or construct the foregoing signs. Tenant shall, at end of lease term, repair all damage to the Leased Premises resulting from the removal of signs installed by Tenant.

ENTRY

Landlord shall have the right to enter upon the Leased Premises during reasonable hours to inspect the same provided Landlord does not thereby unreasonably interfere with Tenant's business on the Leased Premises.

PARKING

For the duration of this Lease, Tenant shall have the nonexclusive use in common with Landlord, other tenants of the Building, their guests, and invitees, of the non-reserved common parking areas, driveways, and footways, subject to rules and regulations for the use thereof as prescribed by Landlord. Landlord reserves the right to designate parking areas for Tenant and Tenant's agents and employees. Tenant shall provide Landlord with a list of all license numbers for the cars owned by Tenant, its agents, and employees.

BUILDING RULES

Tenant will comply with the rules of the Building adopted and altered by Landlord from time to time and will cause all of its agents, employees, invitees, and visitors to do so; all changes to such rules will be sent by Landlord to Tenant in writing. The initial rules for the Building are attached hereto as Exhibit "A" and incorporated herein for all purposes.

DAMAGE AND DESTRUCTION

If the Leased Premises, or any part thereof, is so damaged by fire, casualty, or structural defects, such damage or defects not being the result of any act of negligence by Tenant or by any of Tenant's agents, employees, or invitees, that the same cannot be used for Tenant's purposes, then Tenant shall have the right within ninety (90) days following damage to elect by notice to Landlord to terminate this Lease as of the date of such damage. In the event of minor damage to any part of the Leased Premises, and if such damage does not render the Leased Premises unusable for Tenant's purposes, Landlord shall promptly repair such damage at the cost of the Landlord. In making the repairs called for in this paragraph, Landlord will not be liable for any delays resulting from matters that are beyond the reasonable control of Landlord such as strikes, governmental restrictions, inability to find necessary materials or labor, or other delays. Tenant will be released from paying rent and other charges during any portion of the Lease term that the Leased Premises are inoperable or unfit for occupancy or use, in whole or in part, for Tenant's purposes. Rentals and other charges paid in advance for any such periods shall be credited on the next ensuing payments, if any. If no further payments are to be made, due to the Tenant's termination of the lease or the natural ending of the lease, then any such advance payments shall be refunded to Tenant. The provisions of this paragraph extend not only to the matters aforesaid, but also to any occurrence that is beyond Tenant's reasonable control and that renders the Leased Premises, or any appurtenance thereto, inoperable or unfit for occupancy or use, in whole or in part, for Tenant's purposes.

DEFAULT

In the event of a default made by Tenant in the payment of rent when due to Landlord, Landlord will submit written notice to Tenant. Tenant shall have fifteen (15) days after receipt of written notice thereof to resolve such default. In the event of a default made by Tenant in any of the other covenants or conditions to be kept, observed and performed by Tenant, Tenant shall have thirty (30) days after receipt of written notice thereof to resolve such default. In the event that the Tenant fails to resolve any default within the time allotted in this paragraph, Landlord may at his discretion declare the term of the Lease terminated by giving Tenant written notice of such intention. If possession of the Leased Premises is not surrendered, Landlord may reenter said premises, using any other right or remedy available to Landlord on account of any Tenant default, either in law or equity. Landlord shall use reasonable efforts to mitigate its damages.

QUIET POSSESSION

Landlord covenants and warrants that upon performance by Tenant of its obligations hereunder, Landlord will keep and maintain Tenant in exclusive, quiet, peaceable, undisturbed, and uninterrupted possession of the Leased Premises during the term of this Lease.

CONDEMNATION

If the Building is condemned by any legally constituted authority or such action thereof is made that shall render the Leased Premises unsuitable for leasing, this Lease shall cease upon the possession by public authority, and Landlord and Tenant shall account for rental as of that date. Such termination shall be without prejudice to the rights of either party to recover compensation from the condemning authority for any loss or damage caused by the condemnation. Neither party shall have rights in or to any award made to the other by the condemning authority.

SUBORDINATION

Tenant accepts this Lease subject and subordinate to any mortgage, deed of trust, or other lien currently existing or hereafter arising upon the Leased Premises, or upon the Building and to any renewals, refinancing and extensions thereof, but Tenant agrees that any mortgagee shall have the right at any time to subordinate such mortgage, deed of trust, or other lien to this Lease on such terms and subject to such conditions as such mortgagee may deem appropriate in its discretion. Landlord is hereby irrevocably vested with authority to subordinate this Lease to any mortgage, deed of trust, or other lien that now exists or is hereafter placed upon the Leased Premises of the Building. Tenant agrees that it will from time to time upon request by Landlord execute and deliver to such persons as Landlord shall request a statement in certifying that this Lease is in full force and effect. If there have been modifications, Tenant will state that the same is in full force and effect as so modified. The statement will indicate the dates to which rent and other charges payable under this Lease have been paid, will state that Landlord is not in default herewith, and further, will state such other matters as Landlord shall reasonably require.

SECURITY DEPOSIT

Landlord will hold the Security Deposit without liability for interest and as security for the performance by Tenant of Tenant's covenants and obligations under this Lease. It is expressly understood between both Landlord and Tenant that the Security Deposit is not an advance payment of rent or a measure of Landlord's damages in case of default. Unless otherwise provided by law or regulation, Landlord may commingle the Security Deposit with Landlord's other funds. Landlord may, from time to time, without prejudice to any other remedy, use the Security Deposit to the extent necessary to make good any arrearages of rent or to satisfy any other covenant or obligation of Tenant hereunder. If such action is taken with the Security Deposit, Tenant shall pay to Landlord on demand the amount to apply in order to restore the Security Deposit to its original amount. If Tenant is not in default at the termination of this Lease, Landlord agrees to return the balance of the Security Deposit remaining after any such application to Tenant.

NOTICE

Any notice required or permitted under this Lease shall be deemed sufficiently given or served if sent by United States certified mail, return receipt requested, addressed as follows:

Landlord: _____

Tenant: _____

Landlord and Tenant shall each have the right from time to time to change the place. Written notice is to be given under this paragraph to the other party.

WAIVER

No waiver of any default of either party hereunder shall be implied from any omission to take any action on account of such default if such default persists or is repeated, and no express waiver shall affect any default other than the default specified in the express waiver and that only for the time and to the extent therein stated. One or more waivers by Landlord or Tenant shall not be construed as a waiver of a subsequent breach of the same covenant, term, or condition.

MEMORANDUM OF LEASE

The parties hereby agree that this Lease shall not be filed for record, but in lieu thereof, at the request of either party, Landlord and Tenant shall execute a Memorandum of Lease to be recorded for the purpose of giving record notice of the appropriate provisions of this Lease.

HEADINGS

The headings used in this Lease are for convenience of the parties only and shall not be considered in interpreting the meaning of any provision of this Lease.

SUCCESSORS

The provisions of this Lease shall extend to and be binding upon Landlord and Tenant and their respective legal representatives, successors, and assigns.

CONSENT

Landlord shall not unreasonably withhold or delay its consent with respect to any matter for which Landlord's consent is required, requested, or desirable under this Lease.

PERFORMANCE

If default occurs with respect to any of Landlord's covenants, warranties, or representations under this Lease, and if the default continues more than fifteen (15) days after notice in writing from Tenant to Landlord specifying the default, Tenant may, at its option and without affecting any other remedy hereunder, cure such default and deduct the cost thereof from the next accruing installment or installments of rent payable hereunder until Tenant shall have been fully reimbursed for such expenditures, together with interest thereon at a rate equal to the lesser of _____ percent per annum or the then highest lawful rate. If this Lease terminates before Tenant's receiving full reimbursement, Landlord shall be required and agrees to pay the unreimbursed balance, plus accrued interest to Tenant on demand.

COMPLIANCE WITH LAW

Tenant and Landlord each agree to comply with all laws, orders, ordinances, and other public requirements now or hereafter affecting the Leased Premises.

FINAL AGREEMENT

This Agreement supersedes all prior understandings or agreements on the subject matter hereof. This Agreement may be modified only by a further writing that is duly executed by both parties.

IN WITNESS WHEREOF, the parties have executed this Lease as of the day and year first above written.

Landlord:_____ Date: _____

Tenant: _____ Date: _____

Agreement to Execute Lease

AGREEMENT is made by and between the following parties, _____ (hereinafter referred to as "Landlord") and _____ (hereinafter referred to as "Tenant"), on this _____ (Month & Day), _____ (Year).

IN CONSIDERATION OF THE PROMISES AND COVENANTS CONTAINED HEREIN, and in consideration of the amount of _____ ($_____) paid by the Tenant to the Landlord that shall be credited toward the first month's rent under a certain lease described below and receipt of which is hereby acknowledged, the parties mutually agree as follows:

1. A certain lease for the following subject premises more particularly described as: _____ _____ shall be made, signed, executed, and delivered by the parties.

2. The execution and delivery of said Lease shall take place on _____ (Month & Day), _____ (Year), at a location specifically described as: _____

Americans with Disabilities Act — Addendum

Notwithstanding anything else in this lease to the contrary, this paragraph shall apply to all issues related to compliance with both the Americans with Disabilities Act (ADA) and the _____ *(state statute)*. In the event of any conflict between the rest of the lease and this Paragraph, this Paragraph shall control:

a. Any remodeling, construction, reconstruction, installation of improvements, or other work done to the common areas or other portions of the property of which the Premises are a part (the "Property") shall be performed by Landlord, at Landlord's expense, in compliance with the requirements of the ADA and the _____ *(state statute)* and regulations promulgated pursuant to them.

b. Any remodeling, construction, reconstruction, installation of improvements, or other work done to the Premises shall be done in compliance with ADA and _____ *(state statute)* requirements, at the expense of the party who is performing the work.

c. In the event that a regulatory agency, private party, organization, or any other person or entity makes a claim under either the ADA or the _____ *(state statute)* against either (or both) parties, the party whose breach (or alleged breach) of responsibility under this lease gave rise to the claim shall promptly retain attorneys and other appropriate persons to advise the parties regarding the same and shall, in good faith and at that party's sole cost and expense, take whatever actions are necessary to bring the Premises or the Property, as the case may be, into compliance with ADA or _____ *(state statute)* requirements. That party shall defend, save, and hold harmless the other party from any and all expenses incurred in responding to such a claim, including without limitation the fees of attorneys and other advisers, court costs, and costs incurred for bringing the Property and / or the Premises into compliance. If the claim relates to an aspect of the Premises or the Property as it existed at the time of the execution of the lease, as opposed to work performed by either party after the execution of the lease, then Landlord shall be deemed to be the party whose breach of responsibility gave rise to the claim. *(Alternatives: If a claim is made, Tenant has the option of terminating the lease; the parties split the cost in an agreed-upon proportion (e.g., 50 / 50, 60 / 40, etc.); Tenant bears the cost if the claim pertains only or primarily to the Premises; while Landlord bears the cost if the claim relates only or primarily to the Property, etc.)*

d. Common-area maintenance (CAM) charges shall not include any costs or expenses incurred by Landlord in bringing the Premises or the Property into compliance with ADA or _____ *(state statute)* requirements, either voluntarily or in response to a claim of noncompliance. *(Alternatives: Only a certain dollar amount or percentage may be included; all of the cost for such items may be included; those pertaining to the Premises could be passed on in CAM charges, but not those pertaining to common areas, etc.)*

e. Tenant shall not change its use of the Premises without the prior written consent of Landlord. If the proposed change in use would, in the good faith written opinion of Landlord's advisors, trigger expenditures to comply with ADA or _____ *(state statute)* requirements not applicable to the then current use of the Premises by Tenant, Landlord may refuse the proposed change in use on that ground or condition approval of the change in use on Tenant's agreement to bear the expense of compliance with ADA and _____ *(state statute)* requirements triggered by Tenant's proposed change in use. This subparagraph shall also apply to proposed assignments or subleases that would change the use of the Premises. *(Alternatives: An outright prohibition on change of use; Landlord's options limited to approval or disapproval; Tenant bears the first $_____ of expenses, etc.)*

f. Notwithstanding the above, neither party shall be responsible for any costs or expenses relating to practices of the other that are deemed to be discriminatory under the ADA or _____ *(state statute)* and that relate solely to the conduct of such party (as opposed to physical barriers), and each party shall indemnify the other against costs or expenses relating to the other party's conduct.

g. Notwithstanding the above, Tenant shall be solely responsible for expenses necessary to comply with ADA and _____ *(state statute)* requirements triggered solely by a disability of one or more of Tenant's employees. *(Alternative: If the expense to be incurred would be for an item that would become a fixture to the real estate, the cost might be shared in some proportion.)*

h. Both parties covenant with one another to cooperate reasonably to comply with ADA and _____ *(state statute)* requirements in the least expensive reasonable manner and to create as little disruption as possible to the business operations of Landlord, Tenant, and the other tenants of the Property.

i. Any rules and regulations that would prohibit either party from complying with ADA or _____ *(state statute)* requirements are deemed by this subparagraph to be modified to the extent necessary to allow compliance.

j. Noncompliance with the provisions of this Paragraph, after written notice to the non-complying party and an opportunity to cure within a reasonable period, shall be an event of default under the lease. A reasonable period to cure shall mean cure or commencement of efforts to cure within ten days, which efforts are diligently pursued to completion.

Agreement to Cancel Lease

Date: _____ (month, day, year)

Landlord (as listed on the Lease Agreement): _____

Retailer (the successor in interest to Tenant under the Lease Agreement):

_____

The Retailer has stopped operating a business on the premises and wishes to cancel all of its obligations under the Lease Agreement; the Landlord is willing to cancel the lease providing the following terms and conditions are met.

The Landlord and the Retailer agree to the following conditions:

1. The Landlord will sign and deliver at closing to Retailer:
   a. A Surrender of Lease form (attached to this document as Exhibit "A").

   b. An Assignment of Lease and Assumption Agreements form attached to this agreement.

2. The Retailer agrees at closing to:
   a. Provide to the Landlord a check for $_____.

   b. Sign and deliver to the Landlord a "Bargain and Sale Deed with Covenant Against Grantor's Acts" form, appended to this agreement, for the property located at: Street address: _____
   City: _____ State: ____ ZIP: _____
   As of the date of closing, title to the property must be legal and insurable according to the requirements of _____ Title Insurance Company, at regular rates, free of all liens, encumbrances, and conditions, except those that might be detailed in an appendix to this document.

   c. Sign and deliver to the Landlord a form, appended to this document, assigning to Landlord all of the Retailer's right, title, and interest as Lessee in the Lease dated _____, between _____ (Lessor) and _____, (Lessee), for property located at:
   Street address: _____
   City: _____ State: ____ ZIP: _____
   as described in the Lease, a copy of which is already held by the Landlord.

   d. Sign and deliver to the Landlord an assignment of all of Retailer's right, title, and interest as Landlord in the Lease dated _____(year), between Retailer as Landlord, and _____ as Tenant, for property located at:
   Street address: _____
   City: _____ State: ____ ZIP: _____
   as described in the Lease, a copy of which is already held by the Landlord, together with the sum of $_____ representing the deposit paid by Tenant to the Retailer (as Landlord) on the making of the Lease.

3. Any adjustments, including adjustments for real estate taxes, fuel, and rents, shall be made as of the closing date.

4. The closing shall be held at_____(time) _____(date) _____(year) at the office of:

_____

Street address: _____

City: _____ State: _____ ZIP: _____

5. If the Landlord, after receiving from the Retailer all of the items required in Paragraph 2 above, fails to sign and deliver a Surrender of Lease as set forth in Paragraph 1 above, the Retailer shall nevertheless be released from all of its obligations under the Lease Agreement as of the closing date given in Paragraph 4.

6. If Retailer fails to supply all of the items required of it in Paragraph 2 above, the Landlord may (1) sue for the Retailer to provide specific legal documents and payments or (2) cancel this Agreement, in which case the Landlord and Retailer named in this Agreement will no longer be party to this Agreement.

7. The Landlord agrees to accept, in its present condition as of the date of this Agreement, the property located at:
Street address: _____
City: _____ State: _____ ZIP: _____

8. This Cancellation Agreement is subject to the approval of the Bank of _____. None of the rights or obligations set forth in this Agreement is valid until the Bank has given approval. If approval from the Bank is not obtained within ten (10) days from the date of this Agreement, the Retailer may terminate this Cancellation Agreement, after giving fifteen (15) days' notice. This Cancellation Agreement will be null and void from and after the date specified in such a termination notice.

9. This Cancellation Agreement is complete concerning the matters referred to in this document. Changes, modifications, and amendments must be requested in writing and signed by both parties.

10. This Cancellation Agreement is binding upon the parties listed in this document and their respective successors, assignees, and agents.

11. Any communications or notices required by this document shall be in writing and shall be considered delivered if sent by registered or certified U.S. mail, return receipt requested postage prepaid, either to the Landlord at the address given above, or to any other address that the Landlord may give in writing to the Retailer or to the Retailer as two copies sent separately to the attention of the President of Retailer and to the attention of the Vice President in charge of real estate at the address of Retailer given above or at any other address that the Retailer may give in writing to the Landlord. In the case of a postal strike or other interference with the mail, personal delivery of documents and notices will take the place of registered or certified mail.

Date: _____ (month, day, year)

Signature of Landlord: _____

Signature of Retailer: _____

Witnessed by: _____

Lease Assignment

Date: _____

Assignor: _____

Address: _____

City: _____ State: _____ ZIP code: _____

Assignee:_____

Permanent Address: _____

City: _____ State: _____ ZIP code: _____

_____, Assignor, in consideration of the sum of

$ _____, paid by _____, Assignee, assigns

to the Assignee the Lease, a copy of which is attached to this document as Exhibit "A", made by _____

_____(Landlord) and _____

_____ (Tenant), and dated _____, covering that

portion of the property described in the Lease as follows: _____

_____

_____

_____

_____

together with the premises described in the Lease, the buildings on the property, and all appurtenances associated with those premises and buildings, to be held by the Assignee from _____ (Date) for the remainder of the term of the attached Lease, subject to the rents, covenants, conditions, and provisions set forth in that Lease.

1. The Assignee hereby assumes the performance of all of the terms, covenants, and conditions of the Lease herein assigned by the Assignor to the Assignee and agrees to pay the rent reserved by the said Lease on the next rent day and monthly thereafter until the termination of the Lease and will perform all the terms, covenants, and conditions of the Lease herein assigned — all with full force and effect as if the Assignee had signed the Lease originally as Tenant named therein.

2. The Assignee agrees to indemnify and save harmless the Assignor from any and all suits, actions, damages, charges, and expenses, including attorney's fees and costs, arising from the Assignee's failure to pay the rent as stated in the attached Lease or from the Assignee's breach of any of the terms, covenants, and conditions of the attached Lease.

3. The Assignee agrees that the obligations assumed by the Assignee in this Agreement shall inure jointly and severally to the landlord named in the attached Lease and to the Assignor.

4. This is an assignment, and the Assignor's interest in the premises is as Lessee under a Lease made by _____(Landlord) and _____

_____ (Tenant), and dated _____, a copy of which is attached to and made a part of this document as Exhibit "A." Except for any provisions stated in this Agreement, this assignment is expressly made subject to all the terms and conditions of the underlying Lease and the Assignee agrees to use the premises in accordance with the terms of the underlying Lease and not to do or omit to do anything that will breach any of the terms of that Lease. If the underlying Lease is terminated for any reason, this assignment shall terminate simultaneously. In such an event, any unearned rent paid in advance shall be refunded to the Assignee, provided that such termination is not the result of a breach by Assignee of the terms of the Lease. The Assignee hereby agrees to assume the obligation for performance of all the Assignor's obligations under the attached Lease.

5. Governing Law. This agreement, and all transactions covered by it, shall be governed by, construed, and enforced in accordance with the laws of the state of _____. The parties to this Agreement waive trial by jury and agree to submit to the personal jurisdiction and venue of a court of subject matter jurisdiction located in _____ County, state of _____. In the event that litigation results from or arises out of this Agreement or the performance of obligations under this Agreement, the parties agree to reimburse the prevailing party's reasonable attorney's fees, court costs, and all other expenses, whether or not taxable by the court as costs, in addition to any other relief to which the prevailing party may be entitled. No action shall be entertained by said court or any court of competent jurisdiction if filed more than one year after the date when the cause(s) of action actually accrued, regardless of whether damages were calculable at that time.

6. Contractual Procedures. Unless specifically disallowed by law, should litigation arise hereunder, process will be considered served if delivered through certified mail, return receipt requested; the parties to this Agreement waive any and all rights they may have to object to the method by which process was served.

ASSIGNOR: _____

WITNESS: _____

TENANT: _____

ASSIGNEE: _____

The foregoing instrument was acknowledged before me, this

_____ day of _____, 20 _____.

_____ Notary Public

(SEAL) State of _____

My Commission Expires: _____

CONSENT OF LANDLORD IN PRIMARY LEASE

The Landlord consents to this Lease Assignment from Assignor to Assignee and agrees to look principally to Assignee and only subsequently to Assignor for the fulfillment of any outstanding debts or obligations left unsatisfied by the breach or termination of the Lease.

IN WITNESS WHEREOF, this Assignment has been duly executed by the Landlord on _____ (Date).

Signed, sealed and delivered in the presence of:

_____ Signature of Landlord

_____ Witness

Agreement for Sale of Commercial Real Estate

Date: _____

Seller: _____

Address: _____

City: _____ State: _____ ZIP code: _____

Buyer: _____

Permanent Address: _____

City: _____ State: _____ ZIP code: _____

In consideration of the mutual promises, covenants, agreements, and conditions contained herein and for other good and valuable consideration, receipt of which is hereby acknowledged, the Buyer(s) and Seller(s) agree to the following:

1. Agreement. The Sellers agree to sell to Buyers, and Buyers agree to purchase the land and buildings located in _____ Township, _____ County, and _____ State as described in Deed to Sellers recorded in _____ County Record Book ____, on Page _____. The aforementioned property contains _____ acres, more or less.

2. Purchase Price and Deposit. The agreed upon Purchase Price is $_____. The Sellers acknowledge that a Deposit in the amount of $_____ is due prior to the signing of this Agreement. Deposit will be held by _____ until closing has been completed and will then be applied towards the Purchase Price.

3. Allocations. Seller(s) and Buyer(s) agree that the allocations of the Purchase Price described below are fair and reasonable and are the result of negotiations between both parties for the terms and conditions of this sale:

Personal Property, Equipment & Fixtures	$_____
Buildings	$_____
Land	$_____
Total Purchase Price	$_____

4. Damages. Seller is responsible for all risk of any losses from fire, damages, or other casualty until closing.

5. Condition of Property. Seller(s) must remove all debris from Property before closing and must maintain the property and land in-like condition until closing.

6. Inspection. Buyer(s) may inspect Property and land before closing provided they submit a forty-eight (48)-hour written notice to the Seller's attorney.

7. Appliances. The appliances listed below are to be conveyed with the property and must be in good working order at the time of closing. Seller(s) must complete any repairs prior to closing, or the cost

of said repairs will be deducted at closing. List of Appliances: _____

_____

_____.

8. Transfer fees. Each Party agrees to pay one-half of the _____ (State) and _____ (Local) Realty Transfer Taxes due. Each side's payment amount is expected to be $_____. The real estate taxes for the dates __/__/20__ to __/__/20__ are to be prorated to the date of closing. Township and County taxes are to be prorated on a calendar-year basis, and School tax is to be prorated on a fiscal-year basis. Buyer will take possession of Property at closing.

9. Septic System. The Buyers are hereby notified that the premises described in this Agreement require an on-site septic system and are not serviced by a community sewage treatment facility. Buyers should contact the local government agency charged with wastewater disposal to learn the requirements prior to signing this Agreement.

10. Seller's Warranty. As of the date of closing, Seller(s) represent and warrant that to the best of the Seller(s)' knowledge and belief, no government agency or employee or official of a government agency has given any notice to the Seller that it considers the construction on the Property or the operation or use of the Property to be out of compliance with any law, ordinance, regulation, or order, or that any investigation has been or might be initiated respecting any possible non-compliance. There are no lawsuits involving the property and no unpaid expenses or outstanding invoices from any person, entity or authority, including, but not limited to, any tenant, lender, insurance carrier, or government authority, for the cost of repairs, restorations, or improvements to the Property.

11. Hazardous Substances. To the best of the Seller(s)' knowledge, understanding, and information, no person, firm, or entity has dumped any hazardous or toxic substance on the Property. Seller(s) also guarantee that the Deed conveying the property will contain a "hazardous waste clause."

12. Lead Disclosure. Seller(s) and Buyer(s) both agree to comply with the Federal Lead Disclosure Act and the _____ (State) Real Estate Sales Disclosure Act Laws and to execute all required disclosure statements.

13. Title. Title to the Property will be transferred by General Warranty Deed. An attorney for the Buyer(s) will determine that the title to the Property is good and marketable based on a sixty- (60) year title examination and a good and sufficient General Warranty Deed. Any exceptions and reservations for oil, gas, and / or minerals in, on, and under the property existing in favor of another party in the chain of title will not be deemed a defect in title or detrimental to an otherwise good and marketable title to the Property.

14. Property Inspection. The Buyer(s) may, at their own expense, choose to have licensed or otherwise qualified professionals inspect and / or certify the Property within _____ days of the execution of this Agreement, any property inspection of the property, as defined in the _____ (State) Home Inspection Law, must be completed by a full member in good standing of a national home inspection association or by a person supervised by a full member of a national home inspection association, in

accordance with the ethical standards and code of conduct or practice of that association. If any written report of such an inspection reveals defects in the condition of the Property, Buyer may:

a. Accept Property as is with the information stated in the given inspection report(s); or

b. Terminate this Agreement within fifteen (15) days of the inspection by written notice to Seller(s). In this event, any deposits paid toward the Purchase Price will be immediately returned to the Buyer(s), and this Agreement will be null and void; or

c. Enter into a mutually acceptable written agreement with the Seller(s) providing for any repairs or improvements to the premises and / or any credit to the Buyer(s) for the cost of such repairs at closing. Should Buyer(s) and Seller(s) fail to arrive at a mutually acceptable agreement, the Buyer(s) must then either accept Property as is or terminate this Agreement within _____ days.

15. Default. If Seller(s) fail to comply with the terms and conditions of this Agreement due to the failure of title or because a fire / casualty partially or completely destroys the premises, the Buyer(s), as their sole and exclusive remedy, may terminate this Agreement by delivering written notices to the Seller(s) at or prior to the closing. In such event, any deposit and all interest earned on the deposit will belong to the Buyer(s), this Agreement shall be dissolved and Seller(s) shall have no further obligation or liability to the Buyer(s) and the Buyer(s) shall have no further rights under this Agreement.

Signed this _____ day of _____ (Month) 20____ (Year).

Witnesseth, both parties have executed this agreement at the day and year first above written.

_____ Seller Printed   _____Seller Printed

_____Seller Signature   _____ Seller Signature

_____ Buyer Printed   _____ Buyer Printed

_____ Buyer Signature   _____Buyer Signature

Commercial or Industrial Property Real Estate Sale Contract

Date: _____

Purchaser: _____

Address: _____

City: _____ State: _____ ZIP code: _____

Seller: _____

Permanent Address: _____

City: _____ State: _____ ZIP code: _____

1. _____(Purchaser) agrees to purchase, under the terms of this agreement, for the price of _____ dollars ($_____), the real estate located at:

    Address: _____

    City: _____ County: _____ State: _____ ZIP: _____

    commonly known as _____, and

    with approximate lot dimensions of _____ × _____, together with the following property currently located on it: _____.

2. _____ (Seller) agrees to sell the real estate and the property described above, for the price and under the terms set forth in this agreement, and to convey title to it to the Purchaser or the Purchaser's agent by a recordable _____ deed with release of dower and homestead rights, if any, and a proper bill of sale. The bill of sale will be subject only to:

    a. Covenants, conditions, and restrictions of record;

    b. Private, public, and utility easements and roads and highways, if any;

    c. Party wall rights and agreements, if any;

    d. Existing leases and tenancies (as listed in Schedule A attached to this document);

    e. Special taxes or assessments for improvements not yet completed;

    f. Installments due to be paid after this date of sale of any special tax or assessment for improvements already completed;

    g. Mortgage or trust deed specified below, if any;

    h. General taxes for the year 20___ and subsequent years; and to _____.

3. Purchaser has made a down payment of $_____to be applied to the purchase price and agrees to pay or satisfy the balance of the purchase price, plus or minus prorations, at the time of closing as follows: (*Delete any of the following language which is not applicable.*)

    a. The payment of $_____.

    b. The payment of $_____ with the balance payable as follows: _____ as set forth in writing by the Purchaser (grantee) in a document granting full prepayment privileges without penalty, which shall be secured by a part-purchase money mortgage (trust deed); both of these documents shall be attached as Schedule B to this agreement, or, in the absence of this attachment, shall be identified as forms No. _____ and _____, prepared by _____. These documents shall be accompanied by a security agreement (for which the Purchaser will provide any financial statements required under the Uniform Commercial Code in order to make the lien created under them effective) and an assignment of rents. The security agreement and assignment of rents shall be appended to this agreement as Schedules C and D.

Purchaser shall furnish to seller an American Land Title Association loan policy issued by the _____ Title Insurance Company, insuring the mortgage (trust deed).

(*If no Schedule B is attached to this document, and the blanks above are not filled in, the note shall be secured by a trust deed, with both the note and trust deed in the forms used by the _____(*name of bank or trust company*).)

   c. The acceptance of the title to the real estate subject to a mortgage or trust deed of record securing a debt (which the Purchaser *(agrees) (does not agree)* to assume) of $_____ bearing interest at the rate of _____% a year. The Purchaser will pay an amount equal to the difference between the amount due on the debt at the time of closing and the balance of the purchase price.

4. At his or her own expense, the Seller will furnish Purchaser with a current plat of survey of the above real estate made and certified by the surveyor as having been carried out in compliance with the _____ Land Survey Standards.

5. The closing will take place at _____ (time) on _____ (date), or on the date, if any, to which such time is extended if the conditions in Paragraph 2 of the Conditions and Stipulations are in effect (whichever date is later), unless subsequently mutually agreed otherwise, at the office of _____ at _____ _____ (address) or of the mortgage lender, if any, provided title is shown to be good or is accepted by the Purchaser.

6. Seller agrees to pay a broker's commission to _____ in the amount set forth in the broker's listing contract or as follows: _____.

7. The deposit shall be held by _____ on behalf of both parties.

8. The Seller warrants that it and its beneficiaries, agents of the Seller, or of Seller's beneficiaries, have received no notices associated with this real estate from any city, village, or other governmental authority of zoning, building, fire, or health code violations that have not been corrected.

9. A duplicate original of this contract, duly executed by the Seller and his or her spouse, if any, shall be delivered to the Purchaser within _____ days from the date of this contract, otherwise, at the Purchaser's option, this contract shall become null and void and the deposit shall be refunded to the Purchaser.

This contract is subject to the conditions and stipulations set forth on the back page of it, which conditions and stipulations are made a part of this contract.

Date: _____

Signature of Purchaser: _____

Purchaser: _____

Address: _____

City: _____ State: _____ ZIP code: _____

Signature of Purchaser: _____

Purchaser: _____

Address: _____

City: _____ State: _____ ZIP code: _____

Signature of Seller: _____

Seller: _____

Address: _____

City: _____ State: _____ ZIP code: _____

CONDITIONS AND STIPULATIONS

1. **Seller** shall provide to **Purchaser** or **Purchaser's** agent, no less than five days before the closing date, the plat of survey (if required under the terms of this contract) and a title commitment for an owner's title insurance policy issued by the _____ Title Insurance Company in the amount of the purchase price, covering title to the real estate on or after the date of this contract, showing title in the property subject only to:

    a. The general exceptions contained in the policy;

    b. The title exceptions set forth above;

    c. Title exceptions associated with liens or encumbrances of an ascertainable amount that may be discharged by the payment of money at the time of closing and that the **Seller** may discharge by using the funds to be paid upon the delivery of the deed (all of these must be permitted exceptions under the terms of this contract). The title commitment shall be conclusive evidence of good title in reference to all matters insured by the policy, subject only to the exceptions as stated in the policy. **Seller** also shall furnish **Purchaser** an affidavit of title in customary form, valid at the date of closing and demonstrating that the **Seller** holds title subject only to the permitted exceptions as set forth in items (b) and (c), and unpermitted exceptions or survey defects, if any, for which the title insurer commits to extend insurance coverage as specified in Paragraph 2 below.

2. If the title commitment or plat of survey (if required under the terms of this contract) reveals either unpermitted exceptions or survey defects that render the title unmarketable, the **Seller** will have 30 days from the date of its delivery to correct these survey defects, have the exceptions removed from the commitment, or to obtain a commitment from the title insurer to insure against any loss or damage resulting from these exceptions or survey defects. In such a case, the closing will take place 35 days after delivery of the commitment or on the date expressly specified in Paragraph 5 on the front page of this contract, whichever is later. If the **Seller** fails to have the exceptions removed, correct the survey

defects, or to obtain the commitment for title insurance described above within the specified time, the **Purchaser** has two options: to terminate this contract, or after delivering notice to Seller within 10 days after the expiration of the 30-day period, to take title as it then is, with the right to deduct liens or encumbrances of a definite or ascertainable amount from the purchase price. If **Purchaser** does not choose to take title, this contract shall automatically become null and void.

3. Rents, premiums under assignable insurance policies, water and other utility charges, fuels, prepaid service contracts, general taxes, accrued interest on mortgage indebtedness, if any, and other similar items shall be adjusted according to current rates as of the time of closing. If the amount of the current general taxes is not available, the adjustment for taxes will be based on the amount of the most recent available tax figures. All prorations are final unless otherwise provided in this contract. Existing leases and assignable insurance policies, if any, will then be assigned to the **Purchaser**. **Seller** will pay any stamp tax imposed by law on the transfer of the title and will furnish a completed real estate transfer declaration signed by the **Seller** or the **Seller's** agent according to the requirements of the Real Estate Transfer Tax Act of the state of _____.

4. The provisions of the Uniform Vendor and Purchaser Risk Act of the state of _____ shall be applicable to this contract.

5. If this contract is terminated through no fault of the **Purchaser**, the deposit will be returned to the **Purchaser**. If the termination is caused by the **Purchaser,** at the **Seller's** option, after and notifying the **Purchaser**, the deposit will be forfeited to the **Seller** and used to pay the **Seller's** expenses and the broker's commission; the balance, if any, may be retained by the Seller as liquidated damages.

6. If the **Seller** or **Purchaser** so chooses and notifies the other party in writing not less than 5 days before the closing date, this sale can be closed through an escrow with _____ _____*(bank or trust company)*, in accordance with the usual deed and money escrow agreement used by _____*(bank or trust company)*, with any special provisions required by this contract inserted in the escrow agreement. Upon the creation of such an escrow, anything in this contract to the contrary notwithstanding, payment of the purchase price and delivery of the deed shall be made through the escrow, and this contract and the earnest money shall be deposited in the escrow. The cost of the escrow shall be divided equally between **Seller** and **Purchaser**. *(Strike paragraph if inapplicable.)*

7. Time is of the essence of this contract.

8. All payments required in this contract to be made at the time of closing shall be by certified check or cashier's check, payable to **Seller.**

9. All notices required in this contract shall be in writing and shall be delivered to the addresses following the signatures on the contract. The mailing of a notice by registered or certified mail, return receipt requested, shall constitute delivery.

Mortgage Form

Date: _____

Mortgagor: _____

Address: _____

City: _____ State: _____ ZIP code: _____

Mortgagee: _____

Permanent Address: _____

City: _____ State: _____ ZIP code: _____

AMOUNT OF LIEN: "NOTE"

Mortgagor is justly indebted to Mortgagee in the sum of $_____ (U.S. Dollars) and has agreed to pay this amount, plus interest, according to the terms of a certain note (the "Note") given by Mortgagor to Mortgagee, dated _____ (Date).

DESCRIPTION OF PROPERTY SUBJECT TO LIEN: "PREMISES"

To secure the payment of the Secured Indebtedness defined in this mortgage agreement, Mortgagor grants, sells, and conveys to the Mortgagee the property located in _____ County, in the state of _____, described in detail in Exhibit "A" attached to and made a part of this document,

Together with all buildings, structures, and other improvements now located, or to be located in the future, on, above or below the surface of the property described in this agreement, or on any part and parcel of this property; and,

Together with all and any of the tenements, hereditaments, easements, riparian and littoral rights, and appurtenances belonging to or associated in any way with the property, whether now owned or acquired by Mortgagor in the future, and including all rights of ingress and egress to and from adjoining property (currently existing or arising in the future) together with the reversion or reversions, remainder and remainders, rents, issues, and profits from them; and also all the estate, right, title, interest, claim, and demand of any kind of Mortgagor in respect to the property and every part and parcel thereof; and,

Together with all machinery, apparatus, equipment, fittings, fixtures, whether actually or constructively attached to the property specified in this mortgage agreement, and including all trade, domestic, and ornamental fixtures, and articles of personal property of every kind and nature ("Equipment") now owned or acquired in the future by Mortgagor and located now or in the future in, upon or under said property or any part of the property, and used or usable in connection with any present or future operation of the property; and,

Together with all the common elements appurtenant to any parcel, unit, or lot which is all or part of the property;

ALL the foregoing encumbered by this Mortgage will be collectively referred to as the "Premises" for the purpose of this agreement.

The Premises are hereby granted to the Mortgagee to have and to hold, for the use and benefit of the Mortgagee, forever.

U.C.C. SECURITY AGREEMENT

It is agreed that if any of the property mortgaged in this agreement is of a nature so that a security interest in it can be realized under the Uniform Commercial Code, this instrument shall constitute a Security Agreement, and Mortgagor agrees to join with the Mortgagee in the execution of any financing statements and to execute any and all other instruments that may be required for the perfection or renewal of such security interest under the Uniform Commercial Code.

EQUITY OF REDEMPTION

This agreement is made on the condition that if Mortgagor promptly pays or causes to be paid to Mortgagee, at its address listed in the Note, or at any other place which may be designated by Mortgagee, its or their successors or assigns, with interest, the principal sum of _____DOLLARS ($_____) when the note reaches maturity, as stated in said Note, if not sooner, unless amended or extended according to the terms of the Note executed by Mortgagor and payable to the order of Mortgagee, then the lien on the property shall cease and be void; otherwise, the lien shall remain in full force and effect.

ARTICLE ONE: COVENANTS OF MORTGAGOR

Mortgagor covenants and agrees with Mortgagee as follows:

1.01 Secured Indebtedness

This Mortgage is given as security for the Note and also as security for any and all other sums, debts, obligations, and liabilities of any and every kind arising under the Note or this Mortgage, any amendments, modifications, or supplements to the Note or Mortgage, and any renewals, modifications, or extensions of any or all of the foregoing obligations and liabilities (all of which are collectively referred to as the "Secured Indebtedness"). The entire Secured Indebtedness is equally secured with and has the same priority as any amounts owed at the date of this agreement.

1.02 Performance of Note, Mortgage, Etc.

Mortgagor shall observe and comply with all provisions of this agreement and of the Note and shall promptly pay to Mortgagee, in U.S. dollars, the Secured Indebtedness with interest as set forth in the Note. This Mortgage and all other documents constitute the Secured Indebtedness.

1.03 Extent of Payment Other Than Principal and Interest

Mortgagor shall pay, when due and payable, (1) all taxes, assessments, general or special, and other charges levied on, or assessed against the Premises, this instrument or the Secured Indebtedness or any interest of the Mortgagee in the Premises or associated obligations; (2) premiums on insurance policies covering the Premises against fire and other hazards, as required by this agreement; (3) ground rents or other lease rentals; (4) any other sums related to the Premises or the indebtedness secured hereby, for which Mortgagor is responsible.

1.04 Insurance

Mortgagor shall, at its sole cost and expense, keep the Premises insured against all hazards as is customary and reasonable for properties of a similar type and nature located in _____County, _____.

1.05 Care of Property

Mortgagor shall maintain the Premises in good condition and repair and shall not commit or allow any material damage to the Premises.

1.06 Prior Mortgage

With regard to the Prior Mortgage, Mortgagor hereby agrees to:

a. Pay promptly, when due, all installments of principal and interest and all other sums and charges payable according to the Prior Mortgage;

b. Promptly perform and observe all of the terms, covenants, and conditions required by Mortgagor under the Prior Mortgage, within the period provided in the Prior Mortgage;

c. Promptly notify Mortgagee of any default, or any notice claiming any event of default by Mortgagor in the performance or observance of any term, covenant, or condition required under any such Prior Mortgage.

d. Mortgagor will not request or accept any voluntary future advances under the Prior Mortgage without Mortgagee's prior written consent, which consent shall not be unreasonably withheld.

ARTICLE TWO: DEFAULTS

2.01 Event of Default

The occurrence of any one of the following events, if it is not resolved within_____ days after written notice of the occurrence of the event for a monetary default, or _____days after written notice from Mortgagee for non-monetary defaults, shall constitute an "Event of Default":

a. Mortgagor fails to pay the Secured Indebtedness, or any part of the Secured Indebtedness, or the taxes, insurance, and other charges, as set forth in this agreement, when these become due and payable;

b. Any material statement of Mortgagor contained in this agreement, or contained in the Note, proves to be untrue or misleading in any material respect;

c. Mortgagor materially fails to keep, observe, carry out, and execute the covenants, agreements, obligations, and conditions set out in this Mortgage or in the Note;

d. Foreclosure proceedings (whether judicial or otherwise) are instituted on any mortgage or any lien of any kind secured by any portion of the Premises and affecting the priority of this Mortgage.

2.02 Options of Mortgagee Upon Default

Upon the occurrence of any Event of Default, the Mortgagee may immediately do any one or more of the following:

a. Declare the total Secured Indebtedness, including without limitation all payments for taxes, assessments, insurance premiums, liens, costs, expenses, and attorney's fees as set forth in this agreement, to be due and collectible at once, by foreclosure or otherwise, without notice to Mortgagor. The right to receive such notice is hereby expressly waived.

b. Pursue any and all remedies available under the Uniform Commercial Code. It is hereby agreed that ten (10) days' notice of to the time, date, and place of any proposed sale shall be reasonable.

c. In the event that Mortgagee elects to accelerate the maturity of the Secured Indebtedness and declares the Secured Indebtedness to be due and payable in full at once as provided for in Paragraph

2.02(a) above, or as may be provided for in the Note or any other provision of this Mortgage, the Mortgagee shall have the right to pursue all rights and remedies for the collection of such Secured Indebtedness, whether such rights and remedies are granted by this Mortgage, any other agreement, law, equity, or otherwise, to include, without limitation, the institution of foreclosure proceedings against the Premises under the terms of this Mortgage and any applicable state or federal law.

ARTICLE THREE: MISCELLANEOUS PROVISIONS

3.01 Prior Liens

Mortgagor shall keep the Premises free from all prior liens (except for those consented to by Mortgagee).

3.02 Notice, Demand, and Request

A written notice and demand or request, delivered in accordance with the provisions of the Note relating to that notice, shall constitute fulfillment of those provisions.

3.03 Meaning of Words.

The words "Mortgagor" and "Mortgagee," whenever used in this agreement, include all individuals, corporations (and if a corporation, its officers, employees, or agents), trusts, and any and all other persons or entities, and the respective heirs, executors, administrators, legal representatives, successors, and assigns of the parties hereto, and all those holding under either of them.

The pronouns used in this notice refer to either gender and both singular and plural, where appropriate. The word "Note" may also refer to one or more notes.

3.04 Severability

If any provision of this Mortgage or any other Loan Document or the application of such an agreement is, for any reason and to any extent, invalid or unenforceable, neither the remainder of the document in which that provision is contained, nor the application of that provision to other persons, entities, or circumstances, nor any other instrument referred to in this agreement shall be affected, but instead shall be enforced to the maximum extent permitted by law.

3.05 Governing Law

The terms and provisions of this Mortgage are governed by the laws of the state of _____. No payment of interest, or payment in the nature of interest for any debt secured in part by this Mortgage, shall exceed the maximum amount permitted by law. Any payment in excess of the maximum amount shall be applied to the Secured Indebtedness or disbursed to Mortgagor as set forth in the Note

3.06 Descriptive Headings

The descriptive headings used in this document are for convenience of reference only, and are not intended to have any effect whatsoever in determining the rights or obligations of the Mortgagor or Mortgagee; they shall not be used in the interpretation or construction of this agreement.

3.07 Attorney's Fees

For purposes of this Mortgage, attorney's fees include, but are not limited to, fees incurred in all matters of collection and enforcement, construction, and interpretation, before, during, and after suit, trial, proceedings, and appeals. Attorney's fees may also include hourly charges for paralegals, law clerks, and other staff members operating under the supervision of an attorney.

IN WITNESS WHEREOF, the Mortgagor has caused this instrument to be duly executed as of the day and year first above written.

Signature of Mortgagor: _____

Date: _____

Signature of Mortgagee: _____

Date: _____

STATE OF _____, COUNTY OF _____

The foregoing instrument was acknowledged before me, this

_____ day of _____, 20 _____.

_____ Notary Public

(SEAL) State of _____

My Commission Expires: _____

Balloon Mortgage Note Form

Date: _____

Holder: _____

Address: _____

City: _____ State: _____ ZIP: _____

Maker: _____

Address: _____

City: _____ State: _____ ZIP: _____

Payee: _____

Address: _____

City: _____ State: _____ ZIP: _____

For the value received, the Maker promised to pay to the Payee listed above the principal amount of $_____ at an interest rate of _____ % annually on the unpaid balance. Payment must be tendered in U.S. currency and be paid in the United States. Maker agrees to the following payment terms:

Monthly Payment of $_____ payment of Principal and Interest

Payment due date: _____

Beginning date of payments: _____

Number of Payments due at this amount: _____

After the number of payments above have been reached, on _____(date), along with the monthly payment listed above, the entire unpaid principal balance, as well as any accrued interest, will then balloon and become due without delay.

This Note and the interest associated with it is secured by a mortgage on the real estate property and was made by the aforementioned Maker to the Payee and is to be enforced according to the laws of the state of _____.

Should the Maker default on any payment as described above or within the mortgage, then the entire balance of the mortgage will be due and payable immediately to the Holder. The unpaid balance will accrue interest at the highest rate allowed under the state laws of _____. Should the Holder fail to implement this option, it will not represent a waiver of his/her right to implement it in the event of any subsequent default by the Maker.

Maker or Endorser or any person liable for this shall hereby waive any objection or protest and hereby agrees that to pay any costs and reasonable legal fees should any legal action be taken in order to collect on this Note or to protect the security of the Mortgage herein mentioned.

_____

Signed Maker

Promissory Note A

$ _____

DATE: _____

This note is given a "Good Faith Deposit" as outlined in the attached Contract to Purchase Real Estate between _____ and _____ _____ dated _____ relating to the property listed as _____ _____ _____ _____.

When requested the undersigned, hereinafter called the Payer, promises to pay the amount of $_____ without interest, to _____ or his assigns, hereinafter call the Payee.

This note is to be payable immediately once the Payee and Payer agree to the conditions, contingencies, and inspections outlined in the said contract are met.

In the event that this note goes unpaid for any length of time and collection action is taken, the undersigning Payer agrees to pay the Payee of this note all legal fees associated with the collections efforts. These fees include, but are not limited to, cost of suit, including attorney's fees.

_____   _____

Buyer   Witness

_____   _____

Seller   Witness

Buyer-Broker Agency Agreement

Date: _____

Buyer: _____

Broker: _____

Length of Agreement (in months): _____

Ending Date of Agreement: _____

The broker shall be employed by the buyer to find and obtain specific property for the buyer. The broker shall be thorough and diligent in all attempts at locating satisfactory property for the buyer.

Both parties are in agreement in regard to the following:

The broker is a properly licensed real estate broker in the state of _____ and maintains an office capable of performing the agreed-upon task.

The buyer wishes to acquire property located in

County: _____

State: _____

The desires for and intended uses of the property are clearly explained in attached Exhibit A.

The buyer affirms availability of the necessary finances to purchase the property in accordance with the terms and conditions laid out in attached Exhibit B.

The broker is hereby given the right to find and buy property in accordance with the terms of this agreement and the attached exhibits.

The broker shall inspect any potential property and provide thorough information to the buyer prior to showing the property to the buyer.

The buyer shall purchase no property until a detailed, written account of such transaction has been supplied to the broker.

In the event that the broker's efforts lead to a purchase, either during or within _____ days of the termination of this agreement, the buyer shall pay the broker a commission of _____% of the property's purchase price upon closing. The broker is hereby granted the right to obtain commission from both the buyer and the seller of the property.

The buyer is free to enter into a purchase agreement independent of the broker, with no obligation to pay the broker commission. In such an event, the buyer shall reimburse the broker for any expenses incurred during the course of this contract on behalf of the buyer. The buyer also agrees to notify the broker within 24 hours of contact with such a prospective seller and to provide the broker with the property description and address, seller's name and contact information, and a detailed description of how the buyer located the property.

Either party may terminate this contract at any time by providing notice to the other party. Upon termination by the buyer, the buyer shall reimburse the broker for any expenses incurred during the course of the contract. In the event that a property that was presented to the buyer by the broker is purchased by the buyer at any time after cancellation of the contract, the buyer shall pay the broker the aforementioned commission.

Any monies paid by the buyer as a binder or deposit to the broker may be accepted and held by the broker or an authorized escrow agent according to the state laws of _____. If a prospective seller forfeits, all such monies shall be returned to the buyer at once.

While this agreement is not a guarantee of the location or purchase or property, it does imply a guarantee that the broker's best efforts shall be put forth.

The buyer's name *(may)* / *(may not)* be used in the broker's course of action in locating property on the buyer's behalf.

The finding of any portion of this agreement to be invalid shall in no way limit the validity of any remaining portions of the agreement.

This agreement is all-inclusive and can only be modified if both parties do so in writing. This agreement shall be unaffected by any previous oral or written agreements.

The laws of the state of _____ shall govern and enforce this agreement and all related transactions. Jury trial is hereby waived by both parties in favor of personal jurisdiction and venue and a subject matter jurisdiction court in _____ County, state of _____. In the case that this agreement results in such litigation, both parties agree that the losing party shall reimburse the prevailing party's reasonable expenses arising from said litigation. No action shall be pursued by the court if filed more than one year after the said violation took place.

This is a legally binding agreement for parties, as well as their assigns, heirs, legal representatives, and successors. Furthermore, this agreement shall not, in any way, be recorded in any public records.

_____   _____
Buyer   Witness

_____   _____
Broker   Witness

Building Inspection Checklist

The following checklist in NOT intended to replace a full-blown inspection by a professional building inspector. Those inspections are detailed (or should be); seasoned inspectors can spot evidence of problems you might otherwise overlook. The purpose of this checklist is to remove as much of the euphoric glaze from your eyes as possible as you walk through your potential dream house. Take your time and write down the answers to your questions. Once the owner or Realtor® sees you writing down answers, they will give crisp responses to your questions.

Exterior

1. Driveway Condition:

    ☐ Very Good ☐ Fair ☐ Poor

2. Sidewalk and Patio:

    ☐ Very Good ☐ Fair ☐ Poor

3. Topography:
    ☐ Flat ☐ Sloping ☐ Steep Hillside

4. Exterior Drainage:

    ☐ Water drains toward ☐ away from ☐ ponds ☐ at edges / sides of house.

5. Trees/Landscaping:

    ☐ Very Good ☐ Fair ☐ Poor

6. Fencing

    ☐ Very Good ☐ Fair ☐ Poor ☐ None

7. Detached Buildings:

    ☐ Very Good ☐ Fair ☐ Poor

8. Gutters/Downspouts:

    ☐ Very Good ☐ Fair ☐ Poor

9. Siding Condition:

    ☐ Very Good ☐ Fair ☐ Poor

Basement / Crawlspace

10. Wall Cracks/Defects:

    ☐ Very Good ☐ Fair ☐ Poor

11. Evidence of Seepage (water marks on walls / floors):

    ☐ Yes ☐ No ☐ Possible

12. Crawlspace Vapor Barrier:

    ☐ Very Good   ☐ Fair   ☐ Poor

13. Floor Slab:

    ☐ Very Good   ☐ Fair   ☐ Poor

14. Staircase / Handrail:

    ☐ Very Good   ☐ Fair   ☐ Poor

15. Lighting:

    ☐ Very Good   ☐ Fair   ☐ Poor

Furnace / Air Conditioning

16. Equipment Cleanliness:

    ☐ Very Good   ☐ Fair   ☐ Poor

17. Vent Pipe Condition:

    ☐ Very Good   ☐ Fair   ☐ Poor

18. Furnace Filter (ask to see):

    ☐ Clean   ☐ Fair   ☐ Dirty

19. Air Conditioner Unit Paint:

    ☐ Looks New   ☐ Looks Old

Plumbing System

20. Water Heater Age (from serial number) _____

21. Faucets Dripping:

    ☐ Yes   ☐ No

22. Noisy Drain Pipes when Toilets Flushed:

    ☐ Yes   ☐ No

23. Visible Corrosion on Pipes:

    ☐ Yes   ☐ No

24. Sinks and Tub Drainage:

    ☐ Slow   ☐ Normal   ☐ Fast

Electrical System

25. Main Service Cable:

    ☐ Very Good   ☐ Fair   ☐ Poor

26. Extra Circuit Breaker Space:

    ☐ Yes   ☐ No

27. GFCI Outlets at Wet / Sink Locations:

    ☐ Yes   ☐ No

28. Outdoor Outlets:

    ☐ Yes   ☐ No

29. Adequate Room Receptacles:

    ☐ Yes   ☐ No

Kitchen/Break Room

30. Cabinets / Tops:

    ☐ Very Good   ☐ Fair   ☐ Poor

31. Appliances:

    ☐ Very Good   ☐ Fair   ☐ Poor

32. Flooring:

    ☐ Very Good   ☐ Fair   ☐ Poor

Bathrooms

33. Fixtures:

    ☐ Very Good   ☐ Fair   ☐ Poor

34. Flooring:

    ☐ Very Good   ☐ Fair   ☐ Poor

Windows

35. Do Windows Operate?

    ☐ Yes   ☐ No

36. Insulated Glass — Windows Fogged?

    ☐ Yes   ☐ No

37. Drapes / Shades:

    ☐ Very Good   ☐ Fair   ☐ Poor

Doors

38. Operation:

    ☐ Smooth   ☐ Rub against Frame

39. Lock Operation:

    ☐ Very Good   ☐ Fair   ☐ Poor

Roof

40. Appearance:

    ☐ Looks Worn   ☐ Looks New

41. Metal Flashings:

    ☐ Rusty   ☐ Painted   ☐ Poor

Attic

42. Minimum 14 to 18 Inches Insulation:

    ☐ Yes   ☐ No

43. Visible Mildew or Damaged Wood:

    ☐ Yes   ☐ No

44. Visible Soffit and Ridge Ventilation:

    ☐ Yes   ☐ No

45. Visible Water Leaks:

    ☐ Yes   ☐ No

46. Functioning Storage Space:

    ☐ Yes   ☐ No

57. Access:

    ☐ Very Good   ☐ Fair   ☐ Poor

CHAPTER

6

Financial Reports, Accounting and Money Management

A well-organized accounting system is crucial to any business. Whether you hire an accountant or do your own bookkeeping, familiarize yourself with the many aspects of keeping financial records and creating reports. In order to price your goods and services profitably, you must have an accurate understanding of your income and your cost of doing business.

The checklists, forms, and sample documents in this chapter serve as guides to help you establish and maintain an accounting system for your business.

Forms and checklists in this chapter include:

Banking Checklists and Forms

Questions to Ask When Researching a Bank Account

The services offered for small businesses vary from bank to bank. Open your business account with a bank that can accommodate your needs. When looking for a bank, ask these questions:

1. Is online banking for small businesses available?_____

    _____

    _____

2. Does the bank offer telephone banking? _____

    _____

3. Can you access important information online, such as your account balance, paid expenses, and whether checks have cleared? (Some banks allow customers to view canceled checks online.)

    _____

4. Does the bank have branches nationwide or in other cities where you do business?_____

    _____

5. What, if any, fees are there for opening a small-business account?

6. What are the fees associated with maintaining a small-business account?

7. How long must you have an account with the bank before you can apply for loans or overdraft protection? _____

    _____

8. Does the bank offer small-business credit cards? If so, how long must you be a customer to be eligible? What are the terms of the credit card? _____

    _____

9. If you need a loan in the future, how much does the bank generally lend to small-business owners?

    _____

    _____

10. What is the typical interest rate and repayment schedule? _____

    _____

11. Will you get a business debit card? _____

    _____

12. Can you obtain merchant services to process credit-card purchases online from this bank?_____

    _____

    _____

Questions to Ask Before Setting Up Your Merchant Account

A merchant account is used to accept and process credit-card transactions. Here are some questions to ask yourself before you set up an account:

1. What kind of transactions will you be processing? For most retail and service businesses, you will be processing credit cards face-to-face, with the customer handing you a card and you swiping it, inputting the amount, having the customer sign, and waiting for the transaction to be approved. If you plan to sell products, this process works the same way. _____

    _____

    _____

2. How many transactions will you process each month? This amount will grow as you gain new customers, so look toward the largest number you think you will process each month.

    _____

    _____

3. What gateway and merchant will you use? If you already have a relationship with one bank, talk with it first. Processing and recording transactions is much easier if you use the same bank for all your transactions. Your bank probably will have a preferred "gateway" — a company that receives the credit-card payments online through card-processing units and transmits the information and funds to the bank. Compare costs, however, before you sign up with your bank. Some banks charge high fees, and it might make sense for you to go elsewhere for these services. You can use an online service instead._____

    _____

4. What kind of card-processing unit (POS terminal) will you need? For in-person transactions, find a relatively inexpensive terminal that will produce a paper receipt and copy. If you are processing debit transactions, you will need a keypad so people can input their PINs. _____

    _____

    _____

5. Will you need an additional phone line? If you are going to process in-person transactions with a dial-up POS terminal, you might need a separate, dedicated phone line. Although this may seem like an unnecessary expense, consider that having one phone line for both phone calls and Internet transactions means that a phone call in one part of your office might interrupt a transaction, or that you might need to keep customers waiting to process a credit-card transaction until the phone line is not tied up. Having two lines will save time and improve customer service._____

    _____

    _____

6. What cards will you take? You probably will need to accept the most common credit cards, but you also may have customers who want to use others. Each company has different policies regarding how fast they disburse your money, the fees they charge, and the way they handle cases of credit-card fraud and identity theft. The major credit-card companies in the U.S. are: Visa, MasterCard, American Express, Diner's Club, and Discover. _____

    _____

    _____

Questions to Ask Before Seeking Outside Financing

The U.S. Small Business Administration suggests asking yourself these questions before seeking outside financing:

1. Do you need more capital, or can you manage existing cash flow more effectively?

   _____

   _____

2. How do you define your need? Do you need money to expand or as a cushion against risk?

   _____

   _____

3. How urgent is your need? You can obtain the best terms when you anticipate your needs rather than looking for money under pressure. _____

   _____

4. How great are your risks? All businesses carry risks, and the degree of risk will affect cost and available financing alternatives. _____

   _____

5. In what state of development is the business? Needs are most critical during transitional stages.

   _____

   _____

6. For what purposes will the capital be used? Any lender will require that you request capital for very specific needs. _____

   _____

7. What is the state of your industry? Depressed, stable, or growth conditions require different approaches to money needs and sources. Businesses that prosper while others are in decline will often receive better funding terms. _____

   _____

8. Is your business seasonal or cyclical? Seasonal needs for financing generally are short term.

   _____

   _____

9. How strong is your management team? Management is the most important element assessed by money sources._____

   _____

10. How does your need for financing mesh with your business plan? _____

   _____

   _____

When you approach a bank to obtain a small-business loan, you will be asked to submit a personal financial statement like the one below.

Personal Financial Statement of: (NAME), mm/dd/yyyy

Assets	Amount in Dollars
Cash — checking accounts	$
Cash — savings accounts	$
Certificates of deposit	$
Securities — stocks / bonds / mutual funds	$
Notes & contracts receivable	$
Life insurance (cash surrender value)	$
Personal property (autos, jewelry, etc.)	$
Retirement funds (e.g. IRAs, 401k)	$
Real estate (market value)	$
Other assets (specify)	$
Other assets (specify)	$
Total Assets	**$**

Liabilities	Amount in Dollars
Current debt (credit cards, accounts)	$
Notes payable (describe below)	$
Taxes payable	$
Real estate mortgages (describe)	$
Other liabilities (specify)	$
Total Liabilities	**$**
Net Worth (assets minus liabilities)	*$*

Signature: Date:

1. ASSETS — Details

Notes and Contracts you hold

From Whom	Balance Owed	Original Amount	Original Date	Monthly Payment	Maturity Date	History / Purpose
	$	$		$		
Total	$	$		$		

Securities: stocks / bonds / mutual funds

Name of Security	Number of Shares	Cost	Market Value	Date of Acquisition
		$	$	
Total		$	$	

Stock in Privately Held Companies

Company Name	Number of shares	$ Invested	Market Value
		$	$
Total		$	$

Real Estate

Description / Location	Market Value	Amount Owing	Original Cost	Purchase Date
	$	$	$	
Total	$	$	$	

Your Credit Card and Charge Card Debt

Name of Card / Creditor	Amount Due
	$
Total	$

Notes Payable (excluding monthly bills)

Name of Creditor	Amount Due	Original Amount	Monthly Payment	Interest Rate	Secured by:
	$	$	$		
Total	$	$	$		

Mortgage / Real Estate Loans Payable

Name of Creditor	Amount Due	Original Amount	Monthly Payment	Interest Rate	Secured by:
	$	$	$		
Total	$	$	$		

Financial Statements

Use the templates in this section to gather information from your accounts and prepare the financial reports that allow you to evaluate your business activity.

End-Of-The-Year Financial Assessment

Use this informal worksheet to assess your financial situation:

What is the current financial status of your company? _____

_____.

Income and Expenses

Record what the annual expenses were for the first year in the following categories: (Fill in the amounts if the category applies to your company. Draw these figures from your records.)

- Advertising expenses: $ _____
- Auto expenses: $_____
- Cleaning and maintenance expenses: $ _____
- Dues and publications: $_____
- Office equipment expenses: $_____
- Business insurance expenses: $ _____
- Legal and accounting expenses: $ _____
- Business meals and lodging: $ _____
- Miscellaneous expenses: $ _____
- Postage expenses: $ _____
- Office rent / mortgage expenses: $_____
- Repair expenses: $ _____
- Office supplies: $ _____
- Federal unemployment taxes: $ _____
- State unemployment taxes: $ _____
- Telephone / Internet expenses: $_____
- Utility expenses: $ _____
- Wages and commissions: $_____

Record the first year's annual income from the following sources:

- Service income: $ _____

- Miscellaneous income: $ _____

What types of debts does your company currently have?

Fill in all of the types of debts applicable to your company. Draw these amounts from your records.

- Current liabilities: $ _____

- Taxes due: $ _____

- Accounts payable: $ _____

- Short-term loans / notes payable: $ _____

- Payroll accrued: $ _____

- Miscellaneous: $ _____

- Long-term liabilities: $ _____

- Other loans / notes payable: $ _____

Financial Needs

Based on the estimated profits and losses of your company, what finances will you need to keep the company going?

- Second year: $_____

- Third year: $ _____

- Fourth year: $ _____

- Fifth year: $_____

Estimate the cash flow for the business for the next four years:

- Second year: $_____

- Third year: $ _____

- Fourth year: $ _____

- Fifth year: $_____

From what sources do you expect to raise the necessary funds?

- Cash on hand: $ _____

- Personal funds: $_____

- Family: $_____

- Friends: $_____

- Conventional bank financing: $ _____

- Finance companies: $ _____

- U.S. Small Business Administration: $ _____

Record the cost of doing business for the first year:

- Assets and liabilities: $_____

- What forms of credit have already been used by your company?_____

- What is the cash flow of your company? $ _____

- What are the sources of that cash flow? $ _____

- What types of bank accounts are in place for the business, and what are the current balances? $ _____

What types of assets are currently owned by the business? (Fill in the amounts applicable to your company. Calculate these based upon your records from the past year.)

- Current assets: $ _____

- Cash in bank: $ _____

- Cash on hand: $ _____

- Accounts receivable: $ _____

- Autos / trucks: $ _____

- Equipment: $_____

- Amount of depreciation taken on above: $_____

- Fixed non-depreciable: $ _____

- Miscellaneous: $_____

Balance Sheet

A balance sheet lists assets (cash, receivables, inventory, and property) in the left-hand column and liabilities (debts, accounts payable, and other financial obligations) in the right-hand column. The "bottom line," which shows your total assets alongside your total liabilities, is a succinct expression of your business's financial health.

Balance Sheet As of: (date)	
Assets	*Liabilities*
Current Assets	Current Liabilities
Cash and Equivalents	Accounts Payable
Petty Cash	Accrued Liabilities
Receivables	Accrued Income Taxes
Inventory	Long-Term Debt, due within one year
Prepaid Expenses	Capital Lease Obligations, due within one year
Other Assets	
Total Current Assets	*Total Current Liabilities*
Property and Equipment	
Buildings, Improvements	Long-Term Debt
Fixtures, Equipment	Long-Term Capital Lease Obligations
Transportation Equipment	Deferred Income Tax
Total Property and Equipment, at cost	Other
Less Depreciation	
Net Property And Equipment	
Property Under Capital Lease	
Less Amortization	
Net Property Under Capital Lease	*Owner's Equity*
Goodwill	
Other Assets	
Total Assets	*Total Liabilities*

Profit and Loss Statement

Starting Date:	Ending Date:
Income	
a. Income From Sales	
b. Beginning inventory	
c. Purchases (on starting date)	
d. C.O.G. available sale (b+c)	
e. Ending inventory (on ending date)	
Cost of Goods Sold (d – e)	
Gross Profit on Sales (IFS – COGS)	
Expenses	
f. Advertising / marketing	
g. Freight	
h. Order fulfillment	
i. Packaging	
j. Wages	
k. Travel	
l. Depreciation (product assets)	
m. Other variable (not fixed) expenses	
Total Variable Expenses (add f though m)	
n. Insurance	
o. Salaries	
p. Licenses	
q. Rent	
r. Utilities	
s. Administrative costs	
t. Depreciation (equipment)	
u. Other fixed expenses	
Total Fixed Expenses (add n through u)	
Total Operating Expenses (TVE + TFE)	

Net Operational Income (GPS – TOE)	
aa. Interest income	
bb. Interest expense	
Net Profit Before Tax (NOI + aa – bb)	
cc. Federal taxes	
dd. State taxes	
ee. Local taxes	
Total Taxes (cc + dd + ee)	
Net Profit / Loss After Taxes (NPBT – TT)	

Income Statement

Income Statement				
Period/Month:	**Month 1**	**Month 2**	**Month 3**	**Totals**
Income				
Proceeds from Business				$0.00
Other				$0.00
Total Sales	**$0.00**	**$0.00**	**$0.00**	**$0.00**
Operating Expenses				
Salaries and wages				$0.00
Employee benefits				$0.00
Payroll taxes				$0.00
Rent				$0.00
Utilities				$0.00
Repairs and maintenance				$0.00
Insurance				$0.00
Travel				$0.00
Telephone				$0.00
Postage				$0.00
Office supplies				$0.00
Advertising/Marketing				$0.00
Professional fees				$0.00
Training and development				$0.00
Bank charges				$0.00
Depreciation				$0.00
Miscellaneous				$0.00
Other				$0.00
Total Operating Expenses	**$0.00**	**$0.00**	**$0.00**	**$0.00**
Operating Income	**$0.00**	**$0.00**	**$0.00**	**$0.00**
Interest income (expense)				$0.00
Other income (expense)				$0.00
Total Nonoperating Income (Expens	**$0.00**	**$0.00**	**$0.00**	**$0.00**
Income (Loss) Before Taxes	0	0	0	0
Income Taxes				0
Net Income (Loss)	0	0	0	0
Cumulative Net Income (Loss)	0	0	0	0

Sample Startup Funding Financial Statement

Startup Sources and Uses of Funds Statement

Uses of Funds	
Startup assets: equipment	$ 196,176
Startup assets: supplies / advertising	$ 1,144
Startup facilities costs	$ 34,325
Other startup costs	$ 8,585
Term loan amount:	$ 240,230
Working capital line of credit	$ 123,166
Total funds required	$ 363,396

Sources of Funds	
Owner-provided funds:	
Owner-provided cash for term loan:	$ 20,047
Startup equipment, supplies, etc.	$ 13,047
Personal savings	$ 7,000
Bank financing — term loan	$ 207,136
Bank financing — working capital	$ 123,166
Total sources of funds	$ 363,396

Bookkeeping System

Before you can record transactions, you need to set up a bookkeeping system. To begin, set up a "Chart of Accounts" by designating specific accounts to be used for recording transactions. These accounts are set up in five categories:

- **Assets**, which are items your business owns that have value. Assets are listed in order of liquidity, which relates to how quickly you can turn them into cash.

- **Liabilities**, which are amounts you owe to others either on a long-term or short-term basis. Liabilities are listed according to how quickly you must pay them off.

- **Income**, which is listed by the types of products and services you sell. This category also includes accounts for returns and adjustments to sales, which reduce total sales. If you are selling products, this category will include "Cost of Goods Sold," which is either the wholesale price you paid for the product or the cost of the items you used to make the product.

- **Expenses**, or the amounts you owe to others on a continual basis. This category comprises the largest number of accounts. You will need to make the most decisions about how many accounts to include in this area.

- **Owner's Equity** shows the net amount you own of the business. Owner's equity is determined by calculating the company's net worth, which is its total assets less its total liabilities.

For example, if a business has $500,000 in assets and $300,000 in liabilities, its net worth is $200,000. Net worth also takes into account the profits of the business over the preceding periods, so it represents the increasing or decreasing value of the owner's equity (ownership) in the business.

Determining which accounts to include in the Chart of Accounts is an important decision because what you record is shown on your reports at the end of each month, each quarter, and each year. If you do not record something, you will not have the full information about your business for your personal use or for tax purposes.

Consider how much detail you want to know about your business before you begin. For example, do you want to know the amount you spend on each utility (e.g., gas, electric, phone, water, and sewage) separately, or can you list them all together? The more detail you include, in the form of separate accounts, the more information you have at your disposal.

This is a list of all the accounts you might need in order to keep track of financial records:

1. **Assets**

   a. Cash

      i. In your business checking account

      ii. In your payroll account if you are paying employees

      iii. In business savings or money market accounts

      iv. On hand in your office for paying small amounts ("petty cash")

   b. Receivables, which are amounts owed to your business by others

   c. Inventories, if you are selling products

      i. Finished goods for sale

      ii. Work in process

      iii. Raw materials

   d. Prepaid expenses. These are amounts you have paid before they are due.

      i. The most common prepaid expenses are for insurance and advertising, which you may pay in advance for several months at a time. There is a value in these amounts because you can get a refund if you cancel the policy or the advertising.

      ii. You may also have prepaid rent, usually in the form of a security deposit on which you can get a refund if you leave.

   e. Property and equipment

      i. Land, which has a separate value from the building

      ii. Buildings, listed at purchase price

      iii. Allowance for depreciation, which reduces the building's asset value

    iv. Automobiles and trucks, if these are the property of the business and are used for business purposes. These assets are listed at purchase price.

    v. Allowance for depreciation on autos and trucks

    vi. Furniture and office equipment, listed at purchase price

    vii. Allowance for depreciation on each item of furniture and office equipment

    viii. Leasehold improvements (sometimes called "build-out" by real estate people), which are improvements you have made to an office or building to make it usable for your business. These improvements may include constructing walls, adding lighting fixtures and outlets, renovating restrooms, and other construction.

    ix. Allowance for depreciation on leasehold improvements

2. Liabilities

a. Notes and accounts payable to others. These liabilities, listed as "payables," are short-term amounts representing bills you have received, but not paid, at the time the report is produced.

b. Current payables on long-term debts. These are amounts payable within the next year on long-term debts, such as loans and mortgages.

3. Owner's Equity

a. An equity account for each owner or partner. Amounts are held separately for each individual who is eligible to receive a share of the business's profits. If you are a sole proprietor, you receive the entire net income of the business. If you are in a partnership, a shareholder of a corporation, or a member of an LLC, your share of the net income is distributed to your equity account according to the written terms of the agreement in place.

b. A draw account for each owner or partner. Draw accounts represent amounts taken out from the business by owners or partners for personal use. Draws reduce the amount of equity (ownership) of the individual. For example, if your equity account as a sole proprietor as of the date of the report is $50,000, and you have drawn out $5,000 for personal use, your net equity is $45,000.

For a business that is organized as a corporation, this section is listed as "Shareholder's Equity" and the section includes an account for "Retained Earnings." The retained earnings are income amounts held by the company for growth and development, rather than paying these amounts to the shareholders in the form of dividends. A corporation does not have a draw account because amounts are paid out only in the form of pay to employees or dividends to shareholders.

4. Income

a. Sales of merchandise and services. You may have several different accounts in this section, representing various products and / or services you sell. For example, if you are selling several categories of products, you may want to list each specifically. A wine vendor may want to record sales of domestic wines separately from foreign wines and may even want to break down wine sales by vineyard or distributor. The possibilities for recording sales are limited only by your interest in knowing where your sales are coming from.

b. Sales returns and allowance. Record returns and allowances as negative totals in this section. Reductions to sales will reduce your tax liability.

c. Cash discounts allowed to customers. In the same way as sales returns, record discounts as reductions to sales. If you do not record these reductions, your sales figures will be higher than actual sales.

d. Cost of goods sold. If your business is selling products, keep track of the amounts spent on buying the products from a wholesaler or for the materials and supplies used to create the products. A quilt shop, for example, records its cost for bolts of fabric that it sells to customers and records the cost of time and materials in producing quilts for resale. Recording everything that goes into a product you sell can be tedious, but the IRS requires that you go through this exercise so you can include "Cost of Goods Sold" on your business tax return each year. If you are selling a product, you will need an accountant to help you set up a process for determining costs of goods sold.

5. **Expenses**

a. Operating expenses

   i. Wages and salaries paid to employees (gross amounts)

   ii. Supplies. Depending on the type of business you have, you will want to keep separate categories for different kinds of supplies, such as office supplies, production supplies, and maintenance supplies.

   iii. Equipment rental. If you are renting both office equipment and equipment related to making a product, keep them in separate categories.

   iv. Repairs and maintenance on equipment.

b. Selling expenses

   i. Advertising expenses

   ii. Expenses relating to salespeople, such as travel expenses

   iii. Commissions on sales

   iv. Entertainment of clients

c. Administrative expenses. This category includes everything you need to run your office.

   i. Office supplies, if these are kept separate from other supplies

   ii. Postage

   iii. Phones

   iv. Dues and subscriptions to trade publications or professional journals

   v. Insurance

vi. Professional services for your attorney, CPA, and any other professionals who work as independent contractors and provide specific services to your business, such as a virtual assistant or business coach.

vii. Automobile expenses, if you are using your car for business purposes. It is important that you separate expenses for driving back and forth to work (which are not considered business expenses) from legitimate business use of your car, such as for calls on clients or to professional meetings.

viii. Bad debts. This category is set up to allow you to delete any uncollected accounts receivable at the end of each year. Work with your accountant to determine whether there are any clients you expect will never pay you; the amounts these clients owe can be legitimately deducted from your profits each year before you pay taxes.

ix. Building expenses

   I. Rent on your office space or building

   II. Utilities, including gas, electric, water, and sewage

   III. Maintenance expenses, such as snow removal, landscaping services, and lawn-mowing services

   IV. Building repairs

x. Depreciation, including decreases in the value of buildings and other assets over time

xi. Taxes paid

   I. Payroll taxes, such as FICA (social security and Medicare), federal and state unemployment, and workers' compensation taxes

   II. Real estate taxes on any buildings owned by your business

   III. Federal income taxes paid on behalf of the business

   IV. State income taxes paid on behalf of the business

Chart of Accounts

Assets	

Liabilities	

Income	

Expenses	

Owner's Equity	

Pricing Strategy Worksheet

A pricing strategy will guide you in choosing the right prices for your product, based on your marketing research.

Cost per item

Materials _____

Labor _____

Other _____

Total: _____

Overhead of production

Utilities _____

Machine depreciation _____

Automobile _____

Other _____

Total: _____

Overhead of business

Advertising _____

Promotion _____

Professional services _____

Other _____

Total: _____

Shipping/Handling

Packaging _____

Insurance _____

Postage _____

Other _____

Total: _____

Grand Total (Wholesale): _____

(Now you must either double or triple your wholesale price in order to get your retail price. This is the market price you will want to charge for your product to cover the expense of the product and still make a profit. If you are offering a service, break down your hours into units: What is the cost per hour? This is the hourly rate you want to achieve.)

Accounting Forms and Checklists

Expense Reimbursement Form

Date of Expense	Item or Service Purchased	Reason for Expense	Cost	Receipt Attached

Employee's Signature   Date Submitted   Employee's Name (Print)

Supervisor's Signature   Date Approved   Supervisor's Name (Print)

Expense Report

EMPLOYEE: _____ DATE: _____

LOCATIONS VISITED: _____ PURPOSE OF TRIP: _____

ITEM	MON	TUES	WED	THURS	FRI	SAT	SUN	TOTAL
Airfare								
Breakfast								
Lunch								
Dinner								
Lodging								
Parking/Toll								
Transportation								
Postage								
Supplies								
Telephone								
Other								
Other								
TOTAL								

	MON	TUES	WED	THURS	FRI	SAT	SUN	TOTAL
Mileage ($. per mile)								

ADDITIONAL EXPENSES	DETAILS	AMOUNT

TOTAL EXPENSES: _____ (- Any Advance) _____ TOTAL DUE EMPLOYEE: $ _____

Sample Delinquent Account Notice

Date: _____

Dear (**Client Name**):

Upon reviewing our records, I have found a delinquent account on your balance in the amount of $_____.
This balance is for pet-sitting services provided by (**Sitter Name**) of (**Company Name**) from (**dates of service**). While this may just be an oversight on your part, we appreciate your prompt attention to this matter. We enjoy caring for your pets and would like to continue providing our services to you. For this reason, we ask that you remit payment to us within five (5) days.

Best Regards,

_____

(**Company Name**)

Business Credit Application

Use this format for customers who wish to apply for credit with your business.

Business Name_____ Date_____

Address_____City_____State_____Zip_____

Owner/Manager_____ Tel. No._____

How long in business_____ D & B Rated_____

Trade References:

Name_____Address_____

Name_____Address_____

Name_____Address_____

Name_____Address_____

Bank Information:

Bank Name_____

Bank Account #_____

Bank References:

Name_____Address_____

Name_____Address_____

Credit line requested $_____

The undersigned authorizes inquiry as to credit information. We further acknowledge that credit privileges, if granted, may be withdrawn at any time.

Signed_____

Checklist of Tax Records

☐ Income records (including self-employed income). If you are self-employed and use your home as an office, you will need to provide your mortgage payments, electric, phone, and other home expenses. See a CPA about these needs.

☐ Reports of stock purchases and sales

☐ Statements sent to you by your brokerage company, mutual funds company, or any other investment company

☐ Records of acquired securities

☐ Dividends for dividend reinvestment plans

☐ Records of IRA or other retirement fund contributions

☐ Documentation for worthless securities

☐ Interest expense documentation

☐ Travel and meal expense documentation

☐ Home improvement records

☐ Home-selling expenses

☐ Charitable donation records

☐ Records of stock given away

☐ Records of tax help and legal counsel

Payroll Forms and Checklists

Payroll Budget Estimate

DATE PREPARED: _____ WEEK OF: _____

PREPARED BY: _____

HOURLY EMPLOYEES

EMPLOYEE NAME	POSITION	PAY RATE	HOURS	OVERTIME	TOTAL EARNED
TOTAL					

Allowance for Social Security, Medicare, Federal & State Unemployment Taxes:

Total Hourly Wages _____ x Rate _____ = _____

Payroll Cost Report

DATE PREPARED: _____ WEEK OF: _____

PREPARED BY: _____

TOTAL PAYROLL COST

Total Gross Wages **$** _____

(+) Total Employee Meals **$** _____

(=) Total Payroll Cost **$** _____

PAYROLL COST PERCENTAGE

Total Payroll Cost **$** _____

(÷) Total Gross Sales **$** _____

(_____ x 100 =) Payroll Cost **%** _____

SALES PER PERSON PER HOUR

Total Gross Sales **$** _____

(÷) Total Hours Worked **$** _____

(=) Sales Per Person Per Hour **$** _____

Daily Payroll Form

DATE _____ MONTH _____ YEAR _____

H = HOURS   G = GROSS

EMPLOYEE	RATE	H	G	H	G	H	G	H	G	H	G	H	G	H	G	H	G	TOTAL

TOTAL

Employee Turnover Rate Worksheet

PREPARED BY: _____

DATE: _____

EMPLOYEE TURNOVER RATE

Number of Completed W-2s   _____

(-)

Current Number of Employees   _____

(=)

Number of Past Employees   _____

Number of Past Employees   _____

(÷)

Average Number of Employees Employed   _____

(x 100)

Employee Turnover Rate Percentage   _____%

COST OF EMPLOYEE TURNOVER

Number of Past Employees   _____

(x)

Cost to Hire Each Employee $ _____

(=)

Cost of Employee Turnover $ _____

Checklist for Accounting Fraud

Use this checklist to review your accounting system for possible weaknesses or signs of fraud:

Cash Receipts

___ How are checks and cash protected and secured?

___ Who prepares the deposits? Who takes them to the bank?

___ Who posts cash receipts to the accounting system?

___ Who supervises the processing of cash receipts?

___ Are there missing or altered bank deposit slips?

___ Are there large numbers of voided transactions?

___ How often are bank deposits prepared? When are they taken to the bank?

Bank Statements

___ Are deposits made on a regular basis?

___ Are there large, recurring fluctuations in the bank balance? If so, why?

___ Are bank reconciliations done in a timely manner?

Accounts Receivable

___ Who receives incoming payments?

___ Who posts them to the accounting system?

___ What is the policy for write-offs?

___ Who reviews and approves write-offs?

___ Are there any unapproved write-offs or adjustments in accounts receivable?

Accounts Payable

___ How are vendor records created and updated?

___ Who prepares checks for payments to vendors?

___ Who posts these payments to the accounts?

___ Are there multiple vendors with similar names?

___ Is there a recurring amount paid to the same vendor?

___ Is there a vendor whose invoices have sequential numbers?

___ Have payments to one vendor increased significantly? Why?

___ Are payments to vendors posted directly to an expense account instead of accounts payable?

___ Is there a noticeable pattern of adjustments for goods returned to vendors?

Checklist for Payroll Procedures Analysis

This checklist incorporates many of the recommended procedures and controls for maintaining the integrity of the payroll process. Separation of duties is the most important safeguard against payroll fraud. If this checklist reveals the same person is handling multiple responsibilities related to the payroll, examine the situation closely.

Human Resources

____   Are reference and background checks done for all new employees? Who does this, and how is the information recorded?

____   Is there a social security number and tax-withholding form for every employee?

____   Are forms for tax-withholding and payroll deductions completed, signed, and on file for each employee?

____   Who authorizes wage and salary rates for employees? Is a signed wage authorization on file for each employee?

____   What is the procedure for making changes to an employee's wage rate or salary?

____   Are bonuses, overtime, and commissions in line with company policies?

____   Who approves bonuses, overtime, and commissions? Are they approved in advance?

____   Are sick leave, personal leave, and vacation time approved, verified, and checked to see whether they comply with company policies?

____   How are work hours verified? Is there a time clock?

____   Is the time clock secure? Does someone supervise the punching of time cards?

____   Are time cards or time sheets reviewed and signed by a supervisor at the end of each pay period?

____   Are employee time sheets and production reports compared to production schedules and employee schedules?

Accounting

____ Are personnel records maintained by the same person who verifies time sheets and prepares the payroll?

____ Is payroll accounting done by the same person who makes entries to the general ledger?

____ Are payroll registers reviewed for employee names, hours worked, deductions, salary and wage rates, and agreement with paychecks, and approved before paychecks are disbursed? Who does this?

____ Who distributes payroll checks?

____ Is the payroll paid out of a separate bank account?

____ Who has access to blank paychecks, signature plates, and computer programs that issue checks?

____ Are bank statements for the payroll bank account reconciled regularly? Are canceled checks compared to the payroll register, and are the endorsements examined?

____ Who does this bank reconciliation?

____ Are payroll registers reconciled with the general ledger?

____ What procedures are followed for filing tax returns and paying payroll taxes?

____ Are records kept of vacation and sick pay owed to employees? Are these amounts reconciled to the general ledger control accounts?

____ Are payroll amounts periodically compared to budgets and estimated costs? Are variations investigated?

Checklist for Bank Reconciliation

Use this checklist to test bank reconciliations for signs of fraud. Get copies of statements and bank reconciliations for all bank accounts, including checking, savings, money market accounts, CDs, and investment accounts:

____ Who does the bank reconciliations?

____ How are bank statements received (by mail or electronically)? Who receives (or downloads) them?

____ Are reconciliations done in a regular, timely manner?

____ Are there any signs that the bank statements have been altered?

____ Are the bank reconciliations mathematically accurate?

____ Trace the balance on the bank statements back to the cut-off date or compare with online bank statements.

____ Compare the balance with the company's ledger.

____ Trace pending transactions and d.i.t.s (deposits in transit) on the statement to see whether they were recorded for the proper accounting period.

____ Look at canceled checks closely. Compare them with a list of outstanding company checks.

____ Look at invoices and documentation associated with outstanding checks for large amounts.

____ Examine invoices and receipts associated with checks written for large amounts.

____ Look at current activity for investment accounts, CDs, savings accounts, and money market accounts. Verify balances, interest rates, maturity dates, and the institution where each account is held.

____ Is interest accrued for investment accounts, CDs, savings accounts, and money market accounts recorded in the company books?

Checklist for Cash Receipts Analysis

Use this checklist to analyze the processes used to receive and record incoming payments:

At what points do cash payments enter the company?

Cash register

___ Are the cash registers in a secure location?

___ How is security maintained?

___ Do employees have individual log-ins?

___ Are cash registers ever left unattended? When?

___ Who counts the cash in the register at the beginning and end of each shift?

___ Does cash counting take place in a secure environment?

___ Is the person doing the cash count different from the person operating the register?

___ What is the policy for handling discrepancies and errors?

___ What is the procedure for authorizing voids and returns?

___ Do register tapes reconcile with the cash counts in register drawers?

___ Do register tapes show signs of being altered or damaged?

___ Are employees visually monitored at the cash registers?

___ Are there security cameras filming the registers?

___ What happens to merchandise when it is returned or rejected?

___ What are the procedures for opening and closing the store and registers?

___ Has anyone reported suspicious activity related to cash registers?

Mail

___ Is the mail secure after it enters the building?

___ Who sorts the mail, and how is it distributed?

___ Who opens the mail?

___ What is done when a payment by check is received?

___ Is there a log for incoming checks?

___ Are checks kept in a secure place?

___ What is the procedure for recording and processing an incoming payment?

Electronic

___ What is the process for recording an electronic payment in the accounts?

___ If the payment is made online, is the connection secure?

___ Are there any software glitches that could cause or allow a duplicate payment?

___ How is information such as address, e-mail, and credit-card number verified?

___ If the payment is made over the telephone, who enters the information and how?

___ Is there a confidentiality policy for employees to follow?

___ Who has access to the data for electronic payments?

___ Does anyone have the ability to alter or update the data?

___ How are cancellations and returns for online payments handled?

___ Do security logs show that employees' activity in the computer network coincides with their work schedules?

___ Is the database password protected?

___ Who has access to these passwords?

___ Has anyone every hacked into this system? What were the circumstances?

Preparation of Deposits

___ Is cash handled in a secure environment?

___ Is there legitimate documentation for each cash receipt (such as a cash register entry or invoice)?

___ Is an independent list of cash receipts prepared before receipts are submitted to the bookkeeper?

___ Are deposits complete and equal to each day's total cash receipts?

___ Are the total cash receipts verified against the deposit slip by an independent person?

___ Are bank deposits prepared and taken to the bank by separate people?

___ Who prepares the deposits?

___ Who takes deposits to the bank?

___ How soon are deposits made after cash has been received?

___ Are authenticated deposit slips kept and reconciled to the amounts in the cash receipt records?

___ Does an independent person check the authenticated bank receipts and deposits listed in the bank statement against the amounts in the cash receipts journal?

___ Are there any times when someone else might have access to the deposit before it reaches the bank?

Checklist for Check Tampering

Check tampering is the diversion of company funds through altering or otherwise interfering with checks issued by the business or received from customers. This checklist will help identify weaknesses in financial controls that could create an opportunity for check tampering:

___ What is the procedure for requesting checks?

___ What is the procedure for preparing checks?

___ Who prepares checks?

___ Who signs checks? How are they signed?

___ Does the person signing checks review them before signing?

___ Is the same person preparing checks and signing them?

___ What happens to a check immediately after it is signed?

___ Are bank statements and checks regularly reviewed?

___ Who reviews them?

___ Are bank reconciliations done immediately after the bank statement cut-off date?

___ Who does bank reconciliations?

___ Are bank reconciliations done by the same person who prepares or signs checks?

___ Who reviews bank reconciliations?

___ Who registers checks and assigns them to expense categories?

___ Are canceled checks stored and filed in a secure place?

___ Are blank checks stored in a secure place?

___ Who has the keys or access to the place where blank checks are stored?

___ If checks are printed or signed electronically, who knows the password to access the check printing function?

___ Does someone review and approve the printed checks before they are sent out?

___ Are paper checks used for large payments to vendors?

___ Are old checks and checkbooks destroyed?

___ Are inactive bank accounts regularly reviewed?

___ Are computer network security procedures carefully observed, passwords guarded, and activity logs scrutinized or tagged for unusual activity?

___ Are the persons responsible for handling checks routinely rotated?

___ What happens to a check that is returned in the mail?

___ Is a list of outstanding checks maintained?

Personal Finance

As a business owner, you must keep your personal, as well as your business financial records, organized and up-to-date. You will need these records each year when you prepare your personal income tax returns. If you rely on income from your business for personal expenses, you need to know what those expenses are. These records are also important if you suddenly become incapacitated because of an accident or illness; they will make it possible for someone else to take over your responsibilities and continue running the business in your absence.

Budget Worksheet

This worksheet will guide you in listing all of your income and expenses:

Category	Budget Amount
Income (After Taxes):	
Wages and bonuses	
Interest income	
Investment income	
Miscellaneous income	
Income Total	
Expenses:	
Home (Fixed):	
Mortgage or rent	
Homeowners / renters insurance	
Property taxes	
HOA dues	
Home (Variable):	
Home repairs	
Maintenance	
Utilities (variable):	
Electricity	
Water and sewer	
Natural gas or oil	
Telephone (land line, cell)	
Food (variable):	
Groceries	
Family obligations (fixed):	
Child support / alimony	
Day care, babysitting	
Church tithing	
Health and medical (fixed):	
Insurance (medical, dental, vision)	

Health and medical (variable):

Out-of-pocket medical expenses

Transportation (fixed):

Car payments

Auto insurance

Transportation (variable):

Auto repairs / maintenance / fees

Gasoline / oil

Other (tolls, bus, subway, taxi)

Debt payments (fixed):

Student loans

Other loans

Debt payments (variable):

Credit cards

Investments and savings (fixed):

401(k) or IRA

Stocks / bonds / mutual funds

College fund

Savings

Emergency fund

Miscellaneous (variable):

Toiletries, household products

Grooming (hair, makeup, other)

Total Monthly Expenses

Discretionary Funds (Spendable Income Minus Expenses)

Home improvements

Fitness (yoga, massage, gym)

Cable TV / videos / movies

Computer expense

Hobbies

Subscriptions and dues

Vacations

Eating out

Pet food

Pet grooming, boarding, vet

New clothing

Gifts

Miscellaneous expense

Record of Personal Assets

Asset	Fair Market Value	Liens	Exemption	Net Worth	How Titled
Personal					
Home					
Vehicles					
Stocks and shares					
Bank accounts and CDs					
Commodities, such as gold or other precious metals, owned					
Personal property					
Retirement and benefits — pensions, Individual Retirement Accounts (IRAs), simplified employee pension plans					
Life insurance cash value / face value					
Long-term care insurance					
Other items					
Business					
Furniture and office furnishing					
Current assets — accounts and notes receivable					
Tools of the trade, inventory					
Ownership interests, limited partnerships, unrealized investments					
Other items					

Personal Business Worksheet

Current Business Interests

These are businesses I currently own or have interest in:

Name and Location

Name of Business	Location and Telephone of Business	Where to Find Documents Related to Business

Ownership

Who Owns the Business	Address and Phone Number of Owner	Owner's Job Title or Position	What Percentage They Own

Disposition

This section describes what should be done with my business should I become incapacitated, or upon my death.

Disposition	
Directions concerning disposition of entire business	
Directions concerning my interest	

Contact Information for Key Individuals

Name	Position	Contact Information	Their Role in Business

Disposition Documents	
Tax ID Number	
State ID Number	

Employees

This section deals with the people who are key in keeping the business running.

Employee Name	Type of Agreement They Have with the Company	Benefits	Contact Information

Business Taxes

Tax Record Information

Current-Year Records	Location of documents
	Who is responsible for documents

Prior-year records	Location of documents
	Who is responsible for documents

Assets and Liabilities

This section lists assets and liabilities. This information is intended to help manage, transfer, or sell the business.

Assets

Description of Particular Asset	Current Location of Asset	Value of Asset	Contact Name and Information	Location of Asset Documents

Liabilities

Description of Liability	Value of Liability	Contact Name and Information	Location of Documents

Employer Retirement and Pension Plans

I am listing my retirement accounts and where they can be located:

Company That Has the Account	Description of the Retirement Plan	Account Number	Amount Vested in the Plan

Property I Own

I have listed all the real estate I own or rent. I have designated whether I own the property as a sole owner or as a co-owner.

Where the Property Is Located	Type of Ownership	Beneficiary	How Often It Is Occupied	Company That Property Is Financed With	Who Currently Occupies the Property	Estimated Value of the Property

Instructions for Care of Property I Own

In this section, I have provided you with information concerning who is responsible for upkeep of the property. Following are special instructions to help you care for the property listed above. I have listed service providers' information in that section of my portfolio with their contact information:

Location of Property	Maintenance Needs	Cost of Maintenance

Properties I Rent or Lease

I have listed the properties that I own, but have rented or leased to others:

Location of the Property	How Often It Is Occupied	Contact Information for Leasing Agent	Terms and Conditions of the Lease	Rental Income

Instructions for Care of Leased or Rented Property

This section has special instructions concerning the upkeep and maintenance of my rented properties. The list and contact information of the services providers can be found in that section of my portfolio:

Location of Property	Maintenance Needs	Cost of Maintenance

IRS Forms and Publications

At the end of each year, you must file tax returns for your business, and you must report each employee's earnings to the IRS on a Form W-2 (for an employee) or a Form 1099-MISC (for an independent contractor). You will find forms and instructions on the IRS website (**www.irs.gov**). These forms and publications are included on the companion CD-ROM:

- Form 1099 MISC — Miscellaneous Income

- Form 2290 — Heavy Highway Vehicle Use Tax Return

- Form 4562 — Depreciation and Amortization (Including Information on Listed Property)

- Form 720 — Quarterly Federal Excise Tax Return

- Form 941 — Employer's Quarterly Federal Tax Return

- Form 1040SS — U.S. Self-Employment Tax Return

- Form W-9 — Request for Taxpayer Identification Number and Certification

- Publication 15A — 2010 Employer's Supplemental Tax Guide

- Publication 334 — Tax Guide for Small Businesses

- Publication 505 — Tax Withholding and Estimated Tax

- Publication 583 — Starting a Business and Keeping Records

- Publication 946 — How to Depreciate Property

- Schedule E — Supplemental Income and Loss

- W-2 Form — Wage and Tax Statement

- W-4 Form — Employee's Withholding Allowance Certificate

Commercial tax preparation software and online tax services walk you step-by-step through the process of filling out tax forms. If your business is small, and you are self-employed, you can report your business income on your personal tax return. If your situation is complicated, consult a tax accountant or tax lawyer. You can also contact the IRS directly by phone, but note that in 2009, the IRS was only able to answer 70 percent of its incoming calls.

CHAPTER 7

Purchasing and Managing Supplies and Inventory

The amount you pay for merchandise, cleaning supplies, equipment, food and liquor for a restaurant, construction materials, or supplies and furnishings for your office ultimately will determine whether your business makes a profit. Your success depends on buying the right goods at the best possible prices, protecting them from damage and theft, and making sure you have items on hand when you need them. Large companies use highly sophisticated inventory control systems and expensive technology to track everything they buy and sell. Every step of the inventory process — screening prospective vendors, ordering, shipping, storage, controlling what leaves the stock room or warehouse, verifying prices, and paying invoices — is subject to constant review and improvement. Your small business may not require such stringent controls, but you need to be able to assess your costs and your inventory at any time. You also must take measures to prevent theft by customers and employees and confirm that your suppliers are charging a fair price for their goods and services. The worksheets, checklists, and forms in this section will guide you in setting up an organized inventory and purchasing system.

Purchasing

Always research at least three vendors before making a final decision. In addition to price, ask about shipping costs and arrangements, return policies, minimum orders, payment terms, and the time it takes the vendor to fill an order. Ask for references. Keep records of all the vendors you contact in case the vendor you select raises its prices or is unable to supply all your needs. Keep a file on each vendor and a list for your employees of your preferred vendors for all the products your business purchases.

Supplier Contact Sheet

Company name

Website

Phone number

Fax

Contact name

Contact phone

Contact e-mail

Product lines

Minimum order

Payment terms

Warranties

Return policy

Notes

Supplier name

Reference name

Reference phone number

Reference fax

Reference e-mail

Reference comments about:

Quality of supplier's products:

Selection:

Speed of shipping:

Handling of returns:

Other comments:

Purveyor Information

Prepared By: _____   Date: _____

PURVEYOR	PHONE NUMBER	PRODUCTS SUPPLIED	SALES REP.	DELIVERY DAYS

Purveyor Order Schedule

Prepared By: _____ Date: _____

PURVEYOR	SUN	MON	TUE	WED	THUR	FRI	SAT	PH #

Inventory

Document each step of the ordering process in a way that is appropriate for the type and quantity of goods being ordered. For example, employees might be required to fill out a requisition form stating why they need an item. After a supervisor approves the requisition, the accounting department issues a numbered purchase order, and a copy is sent to the vendor. When the goods are delivered, the packing slip and invoice must be submitted to the accounting department with another copy of the purchase order. As items are delivered, they should be logged into inventory, stored in a secure location, and logged out when they are taken for use. Many companies do not require approval for purchases under a certain amount. The purchasing system should not be so cumbersome that it takes up excessive time and impedes production, but it must be adequate to account for the money being spent and prevent vendors or dishonest employees from abusing the system.

Employee Order Request Log

Use this log to keep track of purchases requested by employees:

ITEM	EMPLOYEE	APPROVED	ORDERED ON	RECEIVED

Perpetual Inventory Form

A perpetual inventory is a daily tally of the units added to and taken out of inventory, broken down by item. By comparing monthly inventories and matching inventory activity to sales figures, you can detect regular patterns and anticipate when you will need additional inventory. You can also see which items are in greatest demand. Abnormal activity could be a sign inventory is being stolen.

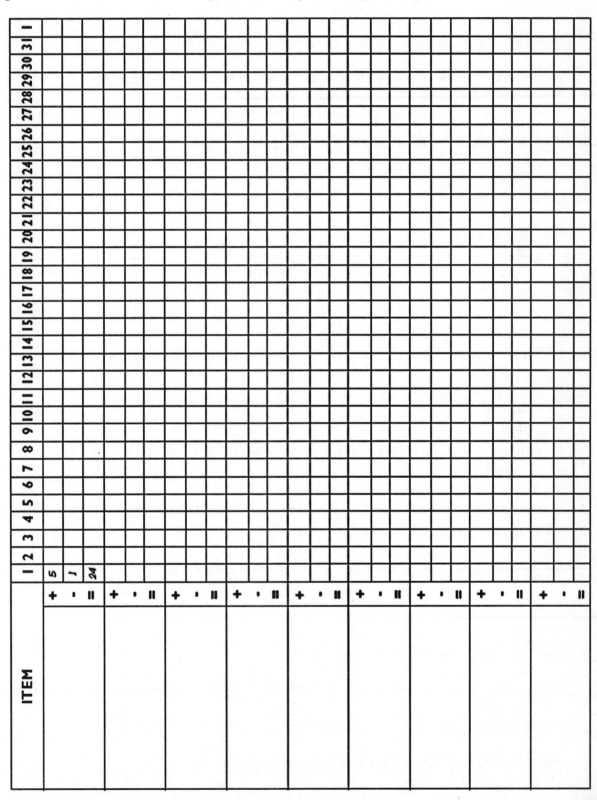

Storeroom Requisition Log Checklist for Examination of Purchasing Process

This checklist can help expose weaknesses in the purchasing system and identify individuals who might have the opportunity to commit billing fraud. If a single individual performs multiple functions, examine the situation closely.

____   Does the company have a purchasing department? If not, who does the purchasing?

____   Is the purchasing department independent of the accounting and receiving departments?

____   Are purchasing and receiving duties done by different employees than those who handle invoice processing, general ledger, and accounts payable?

____   How are purchases initiated? Are purchases made only after purchase requisitions have been authorized?

____   Who authorizes purchases?

____   Does the company use a budget system? Are purchases checked against the budgeted amounts?

Receiving

____   Who receives incoming purchases?

____   Is a log kept of received goods?

____   Are incoming purchases checked against the invoice and purchase order, and are goods examined to verify they are in good condition and are the same quantity and quality that was ordered and invoiced? Who does this work?

____   Where are incoming goods stored, and how are they secured? What happens to goods after they have been received?

____   What procedure is followed when only partial shipments are received?

Purchase Orders

____   Does the company use purchase orders?

____   Are purchase orders sent to vendors for all purchases or just for those above a certain amount?

____   How does an employee obtain a purchase order?

____   Are purchase orders logged when they are given to employees?

____ Are purchase orders numbered sequentially with printed numbers?

____ Is a list kept of outstanding purchase orders and regularly reviewed and updated?

____ Does the business maintain any blanket purchase orders (standing orders that maintain inventory at a specified level)?

____ Are quantities received under blanket purchase orders monitored, and are excess amounts returned to the vendor?

____ Who gets copies of receiving reports and where are they filed?

Vendors

____ What process is used to select vendors? Who selects vendors?

____ Does the company maintain an approved vendor list? What are the requirements for approved vendors? Are certifications and references checked?

____ Is vendor information (physical address, contact information) complete and up-to-date?

____ How often is vendor information reviewed, verified, and updated?

____ Is vendor information checked against employee addresses, phone numbers, and initials?

____ Is there a bidding process? Are items purchased only after bids have been obtained and reviewed?

____ How are vendors notified that the company is seeking bids for goods or services? How are they notified when a winning bid is selected?

____ What procedures are in place to ensure that the company gets the lowest price?

____ Is there a procedure to ensure that any available discounts or special offers are taken advantage of?

____ Is there an unusually close relationship between a company employee and a vendor?

____ Is there a policy regarding the types of thank-you gifts and favors that company employees may accept from vendors?

____ Is purchasing staff rotated periodically?

Checklist for Red Flags for Bribery in the Bidding Process

This checklist will help identify problems in the bidding and contract process that may indicate a vendor is bribing an employee. Obtain a detailed description of company policies regarding the process of soliciting, evaluating, and selecting bids from contractors and suppliers. This includes copies of bid packages — the information package given to vendors who want to submit a bid for a particular project or commodity.

Vendors

____ Are vendors required to register with the company before submitting bids?

____ How is this registration done? How long does it take?

____ Does the company assign a portion of its purchases to vendors owned by minorities, women, and disabled veterans? If so, how do vendors qualify? Are their qualifications verified? How often? By whom?

____ How often is the vendor list updated and reviewed?

Bid Solicitation

____ For what types and amounts of purchases are bids solicited? Is there another purchasing process for smaller amounts?

____ How are bid solicitations advertised? Are they posted on the company website? When are they posted? Who updates this area of the website?

____ How are bid packets sent to vendors? Who does this?

Bid Submission

____ How are bids submitted?

____ What happens to a bid after it has been submitted?

____ What is the policy regarding deadlines and late submissions?

____ What is the process for altering a bid after it has been submitted?

Vendor Selection

____ How is the winning bid selected? Who makes the decision? What are the criteria?

____ Are company policies strictly adhered to? Why or why not?

____ How is the vendor notified?

____ If the first choice falls through, how is a replacement made?

____ What is the procedure for verifying that a vendor charges prices as promised in the contract?

Electronic Bid Submission

___ Does the electronic bid submission system work smoothly, or does it exclude some types of contractors?

___ Are vendor registrations approved in a timely manner?

___ Are electronically submitted bids acknowledged and reviewed in a timely manner?

___ What procedure is followed to review electronically submitted bids?

___ Is there both an electronic submission and a manual submission process? Are manual submissions treated differently?

___ Who has access to electronically submitted bids? What kind of access?

___ Is there any way an employee might alter an electronically submitted bid, intercept it, or prevent it from being included in the bidding process?

Red Flags

___ Requirements that eliminate competition are included in the initial documents preparing the bid solicitation, such as:

- Specifications that exactly fit the product or work of a specific contractor.
- Specifications that were not included on previous similar solicitations.
- Requiring prequalification or preregistration that automatically eliminates competitors.
- Using specifications prepared by a contractor who is participating in the bidding.
- Unnecessary or falsified documents justifying noncompetitive bidding.

___ Irregular sharing of information with some potential bidders and not others:

- Permitting consultants who helped prepare the specifications or design to become subcontractors or consultants under the winning contract.
- Splitting up requirements among several contracts, so contractors can "share" the job.
- Sharing information from design or engineering firms that prepared the plans with certain contractors.

___ A major contract is split up into several smaller jobs to avoid review, when contracts over a certain amount must be reviewed and authorized by management.

___ Deadlines for submitting bids are so short that only vendors with advance knowledge have time to prepare and submit a bid.

___ Bid solicitations are posted in obscure publications, during holiday periods, or in such a way that they are difficult to find on the company website, so that only a few vendors see them.

___ The instructions and deadlines for submitting a bid are vaguely worded so that they are difficult to understand.

___ Bid solicitations are not updated when the company makes changes that affect the bid.

___ Bid packages are not sent out according to a regular procedure.

___ "Bid conferences" are held in such a way that competitors have the opportunity to communicate with each other and potentially engage in bid rigging.

___ Purchasing agents have improper contact with contractors or their representatives at trade shows, professional meetings, or social events.

___ Purchasing agents have a financial interest in a vendor company.

___ Purchasing agents assist contractors in preparing bids or refer them to specific suppliers or sub-contractors.

___ Purchasing agent has received a job offer from a vendor.

___ Documents have been falsified to allow the submission of a late bid.

___ A low bidder withdraws and becomes a subcontractor for another bidder.

___ Contractor's qualifications to do the job are misrepresented, or certifications are false.

___ A late bid is accepted against company policy.

___ Changes are made to a bid after other bidders' prices are known.

___ One bidder's price is revealed to another.

CHAPTER

8

Human Resources: Hiring and Managing Employees

I n a small business, the owner must often take on all the responsibilities of a human resources department, including tasks such as evaluating the need for employees, finding local sources of labor, recruiting and training, developing an employee handbook, developing a process for evaluating employees, and establishing criteria for hiring and firing. Contracts, information sheets, staffing schedules, time sheets, performance evaluations, and signed agreements are invaluable tools for managing employees.

This section contains a variety of forms, checklists, and contracts to guide you through the process of hiring and managing employees. Additional samples and copies of federal forms can be found on the companion CD-ROM.

Forms and Contracts for Interviewing and Hiring

Checklist for the Hiring Process

___ **Create an employment ad.**

Before you place an employment ad, write down exactly what you want this employee to do, what experience he or she will need before starting, and what software or equipment skills the person will need to have. Read your description several times, and picture the kind of person you would feel comfortable with. If you want an assistant who can become the "face and voice" of your business, the person you choose should be able to get along with the public, in person and especially on the phone. Perhaps you want someone who can do cold-calling to solicit business or a bookkeeper to take over data-entry responsibilities.

Write an ad specifying the type of work, the hours, and the qualifications needed. You may or may not give the hourly or monthly pay rate or the annual salary — some ads simply say "competitive hourly wage." Use the employment ads placed by your competitors as a guide. State in your ad that applicants must be currently eligible to work in the United States for any employer. Keep in mind that it is illegal to place an ad that discriminates against anyone because of race, sex, age, religion, and other factors. List your telephone number and/or e-mail address in the ad, rather than a physical address or post office box number, unless you want applicants coming directly to your place of business. Using a post office box will delay response time, so it is not practical if you are in a hurry.

___ **Place employment ads in newspapers and on the Internet.**

If you live in a large metropolitan area, you may get better results from community papers than from the large dailies that cover areas of 100 or more miles. Online classifieds, such as Craigslist.com and its local competitors, are a cost-effective form of advertising. Specialized sites, such as SoloGig.com, VirtualVocations.com, and JournalismJobs.com, are effective if you are looking for part-time workers or candidates with particular skills.

___ **Interview job candidates.**

Select the most suitable applicants before you schedule face-to-face meetings. The interview process begins with your first contact over the telephone as you are setting an appointment for a personal meeting. Is the attitude of the person on the other end friendly? Do not confuse nervousness or an inability to articulate with a bad attitude. What is the overall demeanor of the person you are talking to on the telephone? Does this sound like a person you would like to spend time around?

During the personal interview, apply the same standards you would expect your customers to use. How is this person presenting himself or herself? Is the person clean and well groomed? Does he or she look you in the eye? If the prospective employee claims to have experience, casually ask them two or three questions that require some knowledge of the business. You might want to present a scenario and ask how the applicant would start, perform, and finish the task you describe.

Review the applicant's résumé and ask questions about gaps in work history or lack of recommendations or past employers. Someone who tries to falsify his or her work history might not be desirable as an employee. Ideally, you will find a candidate who has knowledge and experience in your area of business. If you come across that kind of individual, find out why he or she is not employed. Experience alone is not a good indicator of a satisfactory employee; the person might have been fired for not being dependable or competent. If you sense that your candidate is lying, be cautious about hiring him or her. It is easier not to hire someone in the first place than to fire that person later.

Discuss the job with the applicant, describing in detail what you would want that person to do. Watch the person's reactions. If the candidate responds in a way that is completely unreasonable, smile, thank him for his time, and end the interview. Be wary of an applicant whose interview style is to present a list of demands he or she expects you to meet.

___ **Check references.**

Once you have narrowed your list and found the person or persons you would like to hire, call former employers to inquire about work histories and performance. Be aware that many former employers will be reluctant to say anything negative about the person. Ask specific questions such as whether the employee was punctual, did what he was supposed to do, or caused any problems. Be alert for what the former employer is not telling you. If a former employer is distant or does not seem to have much to say about the person, this may be a warning sign.

___ **Inform the candidate that he or she has been selected.**

When you have made a decision, call the candidate and set a date for beginning work. Explain clearly that there is a 60- or 90-day probationary period (your choice) during which the new employee can quit, or you can let him or her go with no hard feelings and no obligation on either side. Send a confirmation letter outlining your work policies and what is expected of the employee. Put all requirements and expectations in writing. Contact everyone else you have interviewed and explain that you have made a decision to hire someone else. Wish everyone well and thank them for their time. Keep the other appropriate résumés and contact information for when you need to hire another employee.

___ **New employee paperwork and personnel file.**

When you hire a new employee, you have to fill out and send in or retain certain government documents. These include W-4 forms, the Employee's Withholding Allowance Certificate, and the W-5 for employees with children, if they qualify for advance payment of earned income credit. Check the IRS website, **www.irs.gov**, or **http://business.gov/business-law/forms** to download forms. If you are not sure what is required, consult your accountant, your state tax officer, or your local chamber of commerce. Ask the employee to review and sign any new-hire paperwork, such as emergency contact information, code of conduct, nondisclosure or confidentiality agreements, and insurance applications. (See other documents and forms in this section for details.) Make your policies clear from the beginning so there will be no misunderstandings if you fire someone.

___ **New employee training.**

Take time right away to teach your new employee how you want the job done. Do not allow time for bad habits to develop. Closely monitor the employee at first and quickly correct any problem behavior, such as habitual tardiness. Create a standardized training checklist and schedule to use with every new employee.

___ **Cost analysis.**

You hired an employee because you wanted to decrease your own workload or because you wanted to increase revenue. After a period of time, do a cost analysis to see whether the new employee is increasing your income or costing you more money than you expected.

Questions to Ask Before Hiring Your First Employee

If you are starting your business and decide you need to hire an employee, first determine the position's requirements in terms of duties, education, training, and experience. The clearer you are about these requirements, the easier it will be to find the right person for the position.

Begin your hiring plan with a checklist, considering both the job itself and the needs of your business. Answer these questions:

1. What specific tasks will be involved with this job?_____

   _____

2. What skills will the employee need in order to perform these tasks? _____

   _____

3. What experience will be required in order to have these skills? _____

   _____

4. Will a certain level of education be required? _____

5. What personal characteristics will this person need? Will he or she deal with people in a customer service capacity, or will the job require attention to detail, as in bookkeeping or billing?

   _____

   _____

6. What physical requirements will be needed? Will this person have to stand for long periods? Will he or she need to lift heavy objects (specify how heavy these objects might be)? Will the person need to drive? _____

   _____

7. What kinds of machines or equipment will the person need to operate? _____

   _____

8. What amount of pay will you provide? Will the person be paid weekly? Monthly? Hourly?

   _____

9. Will this position be classified as exempt from overtime and minimum wage regulations or nonexempt? Salaried positions are often exempt, while hourly positions are nonexempt, but there are exceptions. Refer to federal and state labor regulations to determine how the position should be classified. The U.S. Department of Labor designates certain classes of workers including executives, administrative personnel, outside salespeople, highly skilled computer-related employees, and licensed professionals, such as doctors, lawyers, architects, engineers, and certified public accountants, as exempt._____

   _____

10. What are the hours for this position? What days will the person be required to work? Is weekend or evening work required? _____

    _____

11. What benefits will you provide? _____

    _____

What Not to Ask Prospective Employees

Anti-discrimination laws prohibit employers from asking questions about a person's religion, politics, or sexual preference during a job interview. Your questions should track the qualifications for the job, not outside interests or qualities the prospect has no control over.

Even the unintentional introduction of elements of bias and discrimination can cause problems for you, so make sure your employment application form does not ask for unnecessary information that might be cause for a biased or discriminatory rejection. Here are some guidelines:

- You may not ask an applicant's age. It is not appropriate or necessary to ask an applicant's age. You may ask whether the applicant is above 18, if that is the age of majority in your state.

- You may not ask about arrest records. You may only ask about convictions and the subject of the conviction.

- You may not ask about height or weight, unless these are requirements of the position. For example, some airlines have height and weight restrictions for flight attendants.

- You may not ask the applicant's country of origin, citizenship, race, parentage, or nationality. You may ask whether the person is legally able to work in the country, and you may ask the person to provide proof of legal work status after hire.

- You may not ask about marital status or children.

- You may ask whether the applicant has been in the military, but you may not ask about the type of discharge.

- You may not ask about the national origin of an applicant's name, but you may ask whether the applicant has worked under a different name.

- You may not ask whether an applicant is pregnant.

In an interview, here are some topics to avoid:

- You may not ask about children or babysitters, but you may ask whether the applicant can meet the job requirements, including overtime, if it may be required.

- You may not ask about religious affiliations or organizations, but you may ask about any civic organizations or volunteer work done by the applicant.

- You may not ask whether the applicant speaks other languages, unless speaking another language is a specific requirement of the job.

In general, consider these two rules of thumb when interviewing and hiring applicants:

1. Everything you ask an applicant and everything you consider about an applicant should be a "bona fide occupational qualification" (BFOQ), meaning it must be directly related to the job duties and qualifications you require for the position. You cannot ask other questions or requirements that are not related to the job.

2. You can only require something, such as an intelligence test or a typing or bookkeeping test, of one applicant if you require it of all applicants (at least those you choose to interview).

In your interviewing and hiring practices, avoid the appearance of bias and prejudice against an applicant. Treating all job applicants the same way, requiring the same things of all applicants, and avoiding questions that could be considered biased will help you avoid a possible discrimination lawsuit.

New Hire Application

Application Date_____

Position Applying For_____

Full Name_____

Address_____City_____State_____ZIP_____

Home Phone_____ Cell_____ Work_____

Are you currently employed Yes____ No_____ If so, where? _____

Address of Employer_____ City_____ State_____ ZIP_____

What is your position? _____

Current Wage_____ Current worked hours_____

How long have you worked at this place? _____

May we contact your employer? Yes____ No ___

Previous Employer_____ Phone Number _____

Dates of Employment from___/___/___ to ___/___/___ Why did you leave this place? _____

_____

_____

May we contact this employer? Yes____ No____

Previous Employer_____ Phone Number_____

Dates of Employment from___/___/___ to ___/___/___ Why did you leave this place? _____

_____

_____

May we contact this employer? Yes___/ No___

EDUCATION BACKGROUND

School_____ Dates Attended_____

School_____ Dates Attended_____

School_____ Dates Attended_____

What skills do you have that would help or qualify you for this position? _____

_____

_____

_____

Have you ever worked here before? _____ If so, please explain previous experience: _____

_____

_____

_____

Do you have any family members who work here or have ever worked here? Yes_____ No_____, If yes please explain: _____

_____

_____

Do you belong to any special groups, clubs, or organizations?_____ If so, please describe them:_____

_____

_____

_____

REFERENCES

Name_____Address_____Phone_____Relationship_____

Name_____Address_____Phone_____Relationship_____

Name_____Address_____Phone_____Relationship_____

Name_____Address_____Phone_____Relationship_____

Have you ever been convicted of a crime?_____ If so, please explain: _____

_____

_____

_____

_____

Please tell us about your hobbies: _____

_____

_____

_____

Why do you think you would be good for the above position? _____

_____

_____

_____

_____

Are you willing to take a drug test? Yes____ No _____

Note: You may be subject to drug testing at any time. Do you agree? Yes_____ No_____

I certify that the above information is true to the best of my knowledge. I understand that this is not a guarantee I will receive the above position, and if I am considered for a volunteer position, I do agree to follow all policies and procedures for that position. I do give *[Organization / Business Name]* permission to check my current and previous employers, references, and do background checks.

Print Name_____Date_____

Signature_____Date_____

Supervisor's Name_____ Date_____

Sample Employee Hiring Letter / Agreement

Date

Name of Employee

Address

City, State, ZIP

Dear *[Name of Employee]*:

This letter confirms that *[Name of Company]* ("The Company") has hired you as its *[specify title]*. In consideration thereto, you agree to be employed under the following terms and conditions:

1. You agree to work full time and use your best efforts while rendering services for the Company. As our *[specify title]*, you will be responsible for: *[specify in detail]*

2. You will make no representations, warranties, or commitments binding the Company without our prior consent nor do you have any authority to sign any documents or incur any indebtedness on the Company's behalf.

3. You shall assume responsibility for all samples, sales literature, and other materials delivered to you, and you shall return same immediately upon the direction of the Company.

4. The company employs you at will and may terminate your employment at any time, without prior notice, with or without cause. Likewise, you are free to resign at any time, with or without notice.

5. The Company shall pay you a salary of *[specify $X]* per *[specify interval]* as consideration for all services to be rendered pursuant to this Agreement. In addition, the Company shall provide you *[enter any health, illness, vacation, holiday, or stock benefits here]*.

6. You agree and represent that you owe the Company the highest duty of loyalty. This means you will never make secret profits at the Company's expense, will not accept kickbacks or special favors from Customers or Manufacturers, and will protect Company property.

7. While acting as an employee for the Company, you will not directly or indirectly own an interest in, operate, control, or be connected as an employee, agent, independent contractor, partner, shareholder, or principal in any company that markets products, goods, or services that directly or indirectly compete with the business of the Company.

8. All lists, keys, and other records relating to the clients of the Company, whether prepared by you or given to you by the Company during the term of this Agreement, are the property of the Company and shall be returned immediately upon termination or resignation of your employment.

9. You further agree that for a period of six (6) months following the termination or resignation of your employment, you shall not work for, own an interest in, or be connected with as an employee, stockholder, or partner any company that directly or indirectly competes with the business of the Company.

10. There shall be no change, amendment, or modification of this Agreement unless it is reduced to writing and signed by both parties. This Agreement cancels and supersedes all prior agreements and understandings.

11. If any provision of this Agreement is held by a court of competent jurisdiction to be invalid or unenforceable, the remainder of the Agreement shall remain in full force and shall in no way be impaired.

Your signature in the lower left corner of this Agreement will indicate the acceptance of the terms and conditions herein stated.

Sincerely yours,

_____

[Specify Name and Title]

[NAME OF COMPANY]

("The Company")

I, *[Name of Employee]*, the Employee stated herein, have read the above Agreement, understand and agree with its terms, and have received a copy.

_____

[NAME OF EMPLOYEE]

Agreement for Hiring an Independent Contractor

This Agreement is entered into as of the ___ day of _____, 20__, between _____ *[company name]* ("the Company") and _____ *[service provider's name]* ("the Contractor").

1. **Independent Contractor.** The Company engages the Contractor as an independent contractor to perform the services set forth as described in this agreement, and the Contractor hereby accepts all the terms and conditions of this Agreement.

2. **Duties, Term of Contract, and Compensation.** The Contractor has previously submitted an estimate, attached as Exhibit A, which details the Contractor's duties, term of engagement, compensation, and provisions for payment of compensation. Changes to this agreement can be made only in writing. The agreement may also be supplemented with estimates for services to be rendered by the Contractor and agreed to by the Company. All amendments and supplements will be made a part of this document to be used for reference. All amendments and supplements are to be initialed by both parties.

3. **Expenses.** During the term of this Agreement, the Company will reimburse Contractor for all reasonable and approved out-of-pocket expenses incurred in connection with the performance of the Contractor's duties under this Agreement. The Contractor shall be promptly reimbursed upon submission of a bill detailing these expenses. Contractor will not be compensated for time and expenses for traveling to and from Company facilities under this agreement.

4. **Progress Reports.** Contractor may be required to provide, on a monthly basis, project plans, progress reports, and / or a final report. When project is completed, Contractor will submit a final report to the Company in a form and containing the information and data that are reasonably requested by the Company.

5. **Confidentiality.** The Contractor acknowledges that in carrying out the responsibilities required by this Agreement, he / she may have access to various trade secrets, inventions, innovations, processes, information, records, and specifications owned, used, or licensed by the Company and / or used by the Company in connection with the operation of its business. These include, without limitation, the Company's business and product processes, methods, customer lists, accounts, and procedures. The Contractor agrees not to disclose any of these either directly or indirectly, or to use any of them in any manner, either during the term of this Agreement or at any time after the end of this Agreement, except as required in the course of this engagement with the Company. All files, records, documents, blueprints, specifications, information, letters, notes, media lists, original artwork / creative, notebooks, and similar items relating to the business of the Company, whether prepared by the Contractor or otherwise coming into his or her possession, are the exclusive property of the Company. The Contractor agrees not to keep any copies of the foregoing without the Company's prior written permission. Upon the expiration or termination of this Agreement, or at any time requested by the Company, the

Contractor shall immediately turn over to the Company all such files, records, documents, specifications, information, and other items in his or her possession or under his / her control. The Contractor further agrees not to disclose information about his/her retention as an independent contractor or the terms of this Agreement to any person without the prior written consent of the Company and shall, at all times, preserve the confidential nature of his/her relationship to the Company and of the services he provides.

6. **Conflicts of Interest; Non-hire Provision.** The Contractor warranties that he / she is free to enter into this Agreement. The Contractor's signature below represents that this engagement does not violate the terms of any agreement between the Contractor and any third party. During the entire term of this agreement, the Contractor agrees to devote his/her productive time, energy, and abilities to the performance of his / her duties under this Agreement at the level required to complete the Contractor's duties under this Agreement successfully and on time.

7. **Right to Contractual Employment.** The Contractor is expressly free to perform services for other parties while performing services for the Company under this Agreement. The Contractor agrees that for a period of six months following any termination, the Contractor shall not directly or indirectly hire, solicit, or encourage any employee, consultant, or contractor of the Company to leave the Company's employment. Within one year of his / her leaving Company's employment or contractual engagement, the Contractor will not hire any employee, consultant, or contractor who has left the company.

8. **Right to Injunction.** All parties to this Agreement acknowledge that the services rendered by the Contractor under this Agreement and the rights and privileges granted to the Company under the Agreement are of a special, unique, unusual, and extraordinary character that gives them a peculiar value, the loss of which cannot be reasonably or adequately compensated by damages in any action at law. It is further acknowledged that the breach by the Contractor of any of the provisions of this Agreement will cause the Company irreparable injury and damage. The Contractor expressly agrees that the Company is entitled to injunctive and other equitable relief to prevent or correct a breach of any provision of this Agreement by the Contractor. Resort to such equitable relief, however, shall not be considered a waiver of any other rights or remedies granted to the Company under this Agreement for damages or under law. The various rights and remedies of the Company under this Agreement or under law shall be construed to be cumulative, and no one of them shall be exclusive of any other or of any right or remedy allowed by law.

9. **Merger.** The merger or consolidation of the Company into or with any other entity, or the merger of the Contractor with another company shall not terminate this Agreement.

10. **Termination.** The Company may terminate this Agreement at any time by providing 10 working days' written notice to the Contractor. If the Contractor materially breaches provisions of this Agreement, is convicted of a crime, fails or refuses to comply with the written policies or reasonable directive of the Company, or performs acts of serious misconduct in connection with performance of this Agreement,

the Company at any time may terminate the engagement of the Contractor immediately and without prior written notice to the Contractor.

11. **Independent Contractor.** The Contractor is and will remain an independent contractor in his or her relationship to the Company and is not an employee, partner, or agent of the Company for any purpose. The Company shall not be responsible for withholding taxes from the Contractor's compensation, and the Contractor has no claim against the Company for vacation pay, sick leave, retirement benefits, social security, workers' compensation, health or disability benefits, unemployment insurance benefits, or employee benefits of any kind.

12. **Insurance.** The Contractor will carry liability insurance, including malpractice insurance, if required for any service that he or she performs for the Company, and will provide insurance policy information upon request.

13. **Successors and Assigns.** All of the provisions of this Agreement are binding upon and for the benefit of the parties to this Agreement and their respective heirs, successors, legal representatives, and assigns.

14. **Choice of Law.** This Agreement, the construction of its terms and the interpretation of the rights and duties of the parties to it are subject to the laws of the state of _____.

15. **Arbitration.** Any controversies that arise out of the terms of this Agreement or its interpretation shall be settled in _____ (location) in accordance with the rules of the American Arbitration Association, and the judgment upon award may be entered in any court having jurisdiction thereof.

16. **Waiver.** A one-time waiver by one party of breach of any provision of this Agreement by the other shall not be construed as a continuing waiver.

17. **Assignment.** The Contractor shall not assign any of his or her rights or delegate the performance of any of his or her duties under this Agreement without first obtaining the written consent of the Company.

18. **Notices.** All notices and communications required by this Agreement shall be made in writing and shall be delivered to each party's address as listed on this contract. The mailing of a notice by registered or certified United States mail, certified or return receipt requested, postage prepaid, shall constitute delivery. A notice or demand shall be deemed constructively made at the time it is personally delivered. If a communication is given by mail, it shall be conclusively deemed given five days after its deposit in the United States mail addressed to the party at the address given below:

Contractor: _____

Address: _____

City/State/ZIP: _____

Company: _____

Address: _____

City/State/ZIP: _____

DUTIES: The Contractor will perform the following duties: _____

_____

_____

TERM: The term of this contract shall begin with the execution of this Agreement and shall continue in full force and effect through _____ (date) or the earlier satisfactory completion of the Contractor's duties under this Agreement. The Agreement may be extended only by a written agreement signed by both parties.

COMPENSATION: (choose A or B)

A. As full compensation for the services rendered under this Agreement, the Company shall pay the Contractor at the hourly rate of $_____ per hour, with total payment not to exceed $_____ without prior written approval by an authorized representative of the Company. Compensation is payable within 30 days of receipt of Contractor's monthly invoice for services rendered, supported by reasonable documentation.

OR

B. As full compensation for the services rendered pursuant to this Agreement, the Company shall pay the Contractor the sum of $_____, to be paid as follows:

_____

19. **Modification or Amendment.** No modification, amendment, or change of this Agreement shall be valid unless made in writing and signed by both parties.

20. **Unenforceability of Provisions.** If any provision of this Agreement, or any portion thereof, is determined to be invalid and unenforceable under state or local law, the remainder of this Agreement shall nevertheless remain in full force and effect.

IN WITNESS WHEREOF, the undersigned have executed this Agreement as of the day and year first written above. The parties agree that facsimile signatures shall be as effective as if originals.

Company: _____

By: _____

Title: _____

Contractor: _____

By: _____

Title: _____

General Employment Contract

This Contract is made on _____, 20 ____, between _____, Employer, of _____, City of _____, State of _____, and _____, Employee, of _____, City of _____, State of _____.

In order for both parties to work together as a team, the Employer and Employee agree as follows:

1. The Employee agrees to perform the following duties and job description: *(Write down every aspect of the job the person is to do. If you add items later, add and initial them on this form or create a new form.)*
   This is considered a full/part-time position. *(Circle one.)*

2. The Employee will begin work on _____, 20 ____. This position shall continue for a period of _____. *(Either a time frame or until a specific date.)*

3. The Employee will be paid the following:
   Weekly salary: *(This may be hourly, monthly, or per event.)*
   The Employee will also be given the following benefits: *(This may not be applicable, but follow state and federal guidelines concerning benefits.)*

   Sick Pay:

   Vacations:

   Bonuses:

   Retirement Benefits:

   Insurance Benefits:

4. The Employee agrees to abide by all rules and regulations of the Employer at all times while employed. In addition, they will read and agree to the company's business plan, vision statement, and value statement.

5. This Contract may be terminated by:

   (a) Breach of this Contract by the Employee

   (b) The expiration of this Contract without renewal

   (c) Death of the Employee

   (d) Incapacitation of the Employee for more than _____ days in any one year. *(You may choose to add, delete, or modify anything you choose in this section.)*

6. The Employee agrees to sign the following additional documents as a condition of obtaining employment: *(You can add other documents, such as a noncompete agreement and an agreement not to divulge anything about the company and how it operates to any outside entity.)*

7. Any dispute between the Employer and Employee related to this Contract will be settled by voluntary mediation. If mediation is unsuccessful, the dispute will be settled by binding arbitration using an arbitrator of the American Arbitration Association. *(This professional organization can help settle disputes outside of court for a fee. More information can be found at **www.adr.org**.)*

8. Any additional terms of this Contract: _____

9. No modification of this Contract will be effective unless it is in writing and is signed by both the Employer and Employee. This Contract binds and benefits both parties and any successors. Time is of the essence of this Contract. This document is the entire agreement between the parties. This Contract is governed by the laws of the state of _____.

Dated: _____

_____   _____

Signature of Employer   Signature of Employee

_____   _____

Printed name of Employer   Printed name of Employee

(You may want to have a notary notarize your agreement.)

Application of Federal Law to Employers

Factors that may cause an employer to be covered by a federal employment law include the number of employees the employer has; whether an employer is a private entity, or a branch of federal, state, or local government; and the type of industry an employer is in.

This chart shows how the number of workers employed by a company determines whether a specific federal statute applies to the business:

Number of employees	Applicable statute
100	WARN — Worker Adjustment and Retraining Notification Act
50	FMLA — Family Medical Leave Act
20	ADEA — Age Discrimination in Employment Act
20	COBRA — Consolidated Omnibus Benefits Reconciliation Act
20	OWBPA — Older Workers Benefit Protection Act
15	ADA — American with Disabilities Act
15	GINA — Genetic Information Nondiscrimination Act
15	Title VII of the Civil Rights Act of 1964
15	PDA — Pregnancy Discrimination Act
10	OSHA workplace standards
1	EPPA — Employee Polygraph Protection Act
1	EPA — Equal Pay Act
1	FCRA — Fair Credit Reporting Act
1	FLSA — Fair Labor Standards Act
1	IRCA — Immigration Reform and Control Act
1	OSHA — Occupational Safety and Health Act (general responsibility)
1	PRWORA — Personal Responsibility and Work Opportunity Reconciliation Act
1	USERRA — Uniform Services Employment and Reemployment Rights Act

Direct Deposit Authorization Form

I hereby authorize [company name] to initiate automatic deposits to my account at the financial institution named below. I also authorize [company name] to make withdrawals from this account in the event that a credit entry is made in error.

Further, I agree not to hold [company name] responsible for any delay or loss of funds due to incorrect or incomplete information supplied by me or by my financial institution or due to an error on the part of my financial institution in depositing funds to my account.

Account Information: _____

Financial Institution:_____

Routing Number: _____

Account Number: _____

Account Type: Checking / Savings (circle one)

Signature: _____

Authorized Signature (Primary): _____

Date: _____

Authorized Signature (Joint): _____

Date: _____

Please attach a voided check or deposit slip and return this form to the Payroll Department.

Nondiscrimination Notice

Under Title VII, the Americans with Disabilities Act, and the Age Discrimination in Employment Act, it is illegal to discriminate in any aspect of employment, including:

- Hiring and firing

- Compensation, assignment, or classification of employees

- Transfer, promotion, layoff, or recall

- Job advertisements

- Recruitment

- Testing

- Use of company facilities

- Training and apprenticeship programs

- Fringe benefits

- Pay, retirement plans, and disability leave

- Other terms and conditions of employment

Discriminatory practices under these laws also include:

- Harassment based on race, color, religion, sex, national origin, disability, or age.

- Retaliation against an individual for filing a charge of discrimination, participating in an investigation, or opposing discriminatory practices.

- Employment decisions based on stereotypes or assumptions about the abilities, traits, or performance of individuals of a certain sex, race, age, religion, or ethnic group, or individuals with disabilities.

- Denying employment opportunities to a person because of marriage to, or association with, an individual of a particular race, religion, national origin, or an individual with a disability. Title VII also prohibits discrimination because of participation in schools or places of worship associated with a particular racial, ethnic, or religious group.

Employers are required to post notices to all employees advising them of their rights under the laws that the Equal Employment Opportunity Commission (EEOC) enforces and their right to be free from retaliation. Such notices must be accessible to persons with visual or other disabilities that affect reading.

Checklist for Employee File

After you have hired a candidate, immediately create an individual employee file that contains the following information:

- ☐ A W-4 form

- ☐ Current and previous performance evaluations

- ☐ Date employment has commenced

- ☐ Emergency phone number(s) for the employee

- ☐ Job title

- ☐ Rate of pay

- ☐ Signed and dated statement acknowledging the employee has read and accepts the terms of the employee handbook / policy manual

- ☐ Termination date, if the employee leaves, and a detailed reason why the employee has been terminated

- ☐ The employee's application

- ☐ The employee's legal name, address, and phone number

- ☐ The employee's social security number

Initial Employee Information Sheet

Employee Name:

Social Security Number:

Beginning Date:

Job Title:

Pay Rate:

Trained By:

Date Training Completed:

Notes:

Employee Contact Sheet

Employee Contact Sheet

Employee Name:

Social Security Number:

Address:

Telephone Number:

Cell Phone:

E-mail Address:

Emergency Contact
Name:

Telephone Number:

Acknowledgment of Drug-Free Policy

We Are a Drug-free Employer

At *[insert company name]*, we pride ourselves on a safe work environment. In doing so, it is our belief that we cannot provide employees with safe surroundings if we have an employee who is under the influence of narcotics or other mind-altering drugs. Occasionally, without warning, we will perform random drug testing. In addition, if an employee appears to be under the influence by exhibiting irrational behavior or slurring of speech, the employee may be asked to undergo a drug screening. Please indicate by signing below that you understand and fully accept the policy as a condition of employment.

Printed Name _____

Employee's Signature _____ Date_____

Technology Policy

Purpose

To remain competitive, serve our customers well, and provide our employees with the best tools to do their jobs, *[name of business or owner of computer system]* makes available to our workforce access to one or more forms of electronic media and services, including computers, e-mail, telephones, voice mail, fax machines, external electronic bulletin boards, wire services, online services, intranet, Internet, and the World Wide Web.

Voice Mail

Voice mail should be used as a customer service tool. Employees who have voice mail service are expected to keep their greeting current, retrieve messages frequently, return calls promptly, and not use it as a means of avoiding answering the telephone.

Cell Phones

Company-issued cell phones should be used for essential business-related calls and never when other phones are readily available. Managers / supervisors will review monthly cell-phone billings. If your cell phone is lost or stolen, report it immediately to your manager / supervisor. Cell-phone usage is prohibited while driving a company vehicle. You must pull off the road and park before making or receiving cell-phone calls.

Pagers

Pagers may be assigned to certain employees for company business.

Guidelines for E-mail and Internet Use

[Name of business or owner of computer system] encourages the use of these media and associated services because they can make communication more efficient and effective and because they are valuable sources of information about vendors, customers, technology, and new products and services. However, all employees and everyone connected with the organization should remember that electronic media and services provided by the company are company property and their purpose is to facilitate and support company business. All computer users have the responsibility to use these resources in a professional, ethical, and lawful manner.

To ensure that all employees are responsible, the following guidelines have been established for using e-mail and the Internet. No policy can lay down rules to cover every possible situation. Instead, it is designed to express *[name of business or owner of computer system's]* philosophy and set forth general principles when using electronic media and services.

Prohibited Communications

Electronic media cannot be used for knowingly transmitting, retrieving, or storing any communication that is:

- Discriminatory or harassing; derogatory to any individual or group;

- Obscene, sexually explicit, or pornographic; defamatory or threatening;

- In violation of any license governing the use of software or engaged in for any purpose that is illegal or contrary to *[name of business or owner of computer system's]* policy or business interests.

Personal Use

The computers, electronic media, and services provided by *[name of business or owner of computer system]* are primarily for business use to assist employees in the performance of their jobs. Limited, occasional, or incidental use of electronic media (sending or receiving) for personal, non-business purposes is understandable and acceptable, and all such use should be done in a manner that does not negatively affect the systems' use for business purposes. However, employees are expected to demonstrate a sense of responsibility and not abuse this privilege.

Access to Employee Communications

Generally, electronic information created or communicated by an employee using e-mail, word processing, utility programs, spreadsheets, voice e-mail, telephones, Internet and bulletin board system access, and similar electronic media is not reviewed by the company. However, the following conditions should be noted:

[Name of business or owner of computer system] does routinely gather logs for most electronic activities or monitor employee communications directly, e.g., telephone numbers dialed, sites accessed, call length, and time calls are made, for the following purposes:

- Cost analysis;

- Resource allocation;

- Optimum technical management of information resources; and

- Detecting patterns of use that indicate employees are violating company policies or engaging in illegal activity.

[Name of business or owner of computer system] reserves the right, at its discretion, to review any employee's electronic files and messages to the extent necessary to ensure electronic media and services are being used in compliance with the law, this policy, and other company policies. Employees should not assume electronic communications are completely private. Accordingly, if they have sensitive information to transmit, they should use other means.

Software

To prevent viruses from being transmitted through the company's computer system, downloading of any unauthorized software is strictly prohibited. Only software registered through *[name of business or owner of computer system]* may be downloaded. Employees should contact the system administrator if they have any questions.

Security / Appropriate Use

Employees must respect the confidentiality of other individuals' electronic communications. Except when explicit authorization has been granted by company management, employees are prohibited from engaging in, or attempting to engage in:

- Monitoring or intercepting the files or electronic communications of other employees or third parties;

- Hacking or obtaining access to systems or accounts they are not authorized to use;

- Using other people's log-ins or passwords; and

- Breaching, testing, or monitoring computer or network security measures.

No e-mail or other electronic communication can be sent that attempts to hide the identity of the sender or represent the sender as someone else.

Electronic media and services should not be used in a manner likely to cause network congestion or significantly hamper the ability of other people to access and use the system.

Anyone obtaining electronic access to other companies' or individuals' materials must respect all copyrights and cannot copy, retrieve, modify, or forward copyrighted materials except as permitted by the copyright owner.

Encryption

Employees can use encryption software supplied to them by the system administrator for purposes of safeguarding sensitive or confidential business information. Employees who use encryption on files stored on a company computer must provide their supervisor with a sealed, hard-copy record (to be retained in a secure location) of all of the passwords and encryption keys necessary to access the files.

Participation in Online Forums

Any messages or information sent on company-provided facilities to one or more individuals via an electronic network — for example, Internet mailing lists, bulletin boards, and online services — are statements identifiable and attributable to *[name of business or owner of computer system]*.

[Name of business or owner of computer system] recognizes that participation in some forums might be important to the performance of an employee's job. For instance, an employee might find the answer to a technical problem by consulting members of a news group devoted to the technical area.

Violations

Any employee who abuses the privilege of their access to e-mail or the Internet in violation of this policy will be subject to corrective action, including possible discharge of employment, legal action, and criminal liability.

Employee Agreement on Use of E-mail and the Internet

I have read, understand, and agree to comply with the foregoing policies, rules, and conditions governing the use of the company's computer and telecommunications equipment and services. I understand that I have no expectation of privacy when I use any of the telecommunication equipment or services. I am aware that violations of this guideline on appropriate use of the e-mail and Internet systems may subject me to disciplinary action, including discharge from employment, legal action, and criminal liability. I further understand that my use of the e-mail and Internet may reflect on the image of *[name of business or owner of computer system]* to our customers, competitors, and suppliers and that I have responsibility to maintain a positive representation of the company. Furthermore, I understand that this policy can be amended at any time.

Signed _____

Confidentiality and Nondisclosure Agreement

WHEREAS, [_____], hereafter referred to as "the Client," agrees to furnish [_____], hereafter referred to as "the Service Provider," certain confidential information relating to ideas, inventions, or products for the purposes of determining an interest in developing, manufacturing, selling, and / or joint venturing;

WHEREAS, the Service Provider agrees to review, examine, inspect, or obtain such confidential information only for the purposes described above and to otherwise hold such information confidential pursuant to the terms of this Agreement.

BE IT KNOWN, the client has or shall furnish to the Service Provider certain confidential information and may further allow the Service Provider the right to discuss or interview representatives of the Client on the following conditions:

1. The Service Provider agrees to hold confidential or proprietary information or trade secrets ("confidential information") in trust and confidence and agrees that it shall be used only for the contemplated purposes and shall not be used for any other purpose or disclosed to any third party.

2. No copies will be made or retained of any written information or prototypes supplied without the permission of the Client.

3. At the conclusion of any discussions, or upon demand by the Client, all confidential information, including prototypes, written notes, photographs, sketches, models, memoranda, or notes taken shall be returned to the Client.

4. Confidential information shall not be disclosed to any third party unless they agree to execute and be bound by the terms of this Agreement and have been approved by the Client.

AGREED AND ACCEPTED BY:

Date: _____

By: _____

Date: _____

By: _____

Taxation Forms for Employees

When you hire new employees, you must have them fill out a Form I-9, Verification of Eligibility for Employment (available on companion CD-ROM) and keep it on file. The employee must submit a social security card, work permit, or other documentation proving he or she is eligible to work in the U.S. More detailed information is found in the U.S. Citizenship and Immigration Services Form 274, *Handbook for Employers* (**www.uscis.gov/files/nativedocuments/m-274.pdf**), or you can order a copy by phone at 800-870-3636.

New employees also must fill out an IRS Form W-4 (available on companion CD-ROM). If your employees qualify for and want to receive advanced earned income credit payments, they must give you a completed Form W-5 (available on companion CD-ROM).

Checklist for Employee or Independent Contractor Determination

Employees and independent contractors are treated differently according to labor laws. For taxation purposes, the IRS uses these 20 questions to determine whether a worker is an employee or an independent contractor (the answers favorable to the contractor are in parentheses):

____ Are you required to comply with instructions about when, where, and how the work is to be done? (No) _____

____ Does your client provide you with training to enable you to perform a job in a particular method or manner? (No) _____

____ Are the services you provide integrated into your client's business operation? (No)_____

____ Must the services be rendered by you personally? (No) _____

____ Do you have the capability to hire, supervise, or pay assistants to help you in performing the services under contract? (Yes) _____

____ Is the relationship between you and the person or company you perform services for a continuing relationship? (No)_____

____ Who sets the hours of work? (You do) _____

____ Are you required to devote your full time to the person or company you perform services for? (No)

_____

____ Is the work performed at the place of business of the potential employer? (No) _____

____ Who directs the order or sequence in which the work must be done? (You do) _____

___ Are you required to provide regular written or oral reports to your client? (No)_____

___ What is the method of payment — hourly, commission, or by the job? (Contingency or project milestone-based payments are ideal.) _____

___ Are your business and / or traveling expenses reimbursed? (No)_____

___ Who furnishes tools and materials used in providing services? (You do) _____

___ Do you have a significant investment in facilities used to perform services? (Yes. The more substantial your investment, the better.) _____

___ Can you realize both a profit and a loss? (Yes)_____

___ Can you work for a number of firms at the same time? (Yes) _____

___ Do you make your services available to the general public? (Yes. It is a good idea to have a business listing in the phone book, for example.) _____

___ Are you subject to dismissal for reasons other than nonperformance of contract specifications? (No. Also, your client should provide at least a week's notice. At will termination makes you look like an employee.) _____

___ Can you terminate your relationship without incurring a liability for failure to complete a job? (Yes, assuming you are working on a time-and-materials basis. If you are working on a project, or milestone, basis, you are obligated to deliver on your commitments if you wish to be paid for your efforts.) If you have a question about the status of a particular employee, request a determination from the IRS by filing a Form SS-8, *Determination of Worker Status for Purposes of Federal Employment Taxes and Income Tax Withholding* (available on companion CD-ROM).

_____

_____

_____

Time Sheet / Time Card

Company Name: _____

Company Address: _____

Company Telephone Number: _____

Company Fax Number: _____

Employee Name: _____

Employee Title: _____

Employee Number: _____

Department: _____

Supervisor: _____

All employee time cards are to be turned in no later than *[time]* on *[day]*. Employee time cards can be faxed to *[company name]* or mailed to the address listed above. If you have any questions about how to fill out your time card, please contact your supervisor or the Human Resources Department.

Date	Day Of Week	Start	Finish	Hours Worked
Total Hours Worked				

Five-Level Systems

This rating system is the most common form organizations use. Five-level systems provide employees with the greatest detail about their performance. They also enable managers to distinguish between exceptional performance, good performance, average performance, and so on. Employees typically fall into three or four rating levels, with only a small percentage ranked in the highest or lowest categories. One downside of a five-level performance system is that managers may have a tendency to rank too many candidates in the middle or neutral position. Here is an example of a basic five-tier rating system:

1. Exceeds Expectations

2. Above Average

3. Average

4. Below Average

5. Needs Improvement

The specific qualities of each category can be fleshed out to provide the employee with greater detail about his or her performance.

1. **Exceeds Expectations —** Employee consistently exceeds expectations or performs well above expected levels:

   - Contributes to team and individual efforts.

   - Encourages new and innovative thought processes and significantly contributes to the productivity or profitability of the organization.

2. **Above Average —** The employee consistently performs above average:

   - Contributes to team and individual efforts and almost always completes work on time and in order.

   - Displays effective communication skills and contributes to the productivity of the organization.

3. **Average —** The employee consistently performs at the level of similarly assigned peers:

   - Completes most assignments in a timely and efficient time frame.

   - Often participates in team development activities and occasionally contributes to the productivity of the organization.

4. **Below Average —** The employee sometimes performs consistently, but often fails to meet work goals or objectives:

   - Some improvements needed in fulfilling work roles.

   - Sometimes communicates effectively, but needs to improve communication and participation in team and individual activities in the organization.

5. **Needs Improvement —** The employee is not performing at an acceptable level.

   - Needs additional skills training and more effective communication with peers and team members.

   - Employee's work is often incomplete or contains errors.

Performance Appraisal Form

Employee's Name: _____

Title: _____

Review Date: _____

Supervisor's Name: _____

Job Skills and Responsibilities	Comments	Rating
Example: Conflict Management	Resolves conflict frequently.	4
	Stays emotionally neutral and does not escalate situations.	3
	Keeps relationships strong despite disagreements.	
	Additional Comments:	5
[Insert skills]		

MAJOR ACCOMPLISHMENTS _____

AREAS FOR IMPROVEMENT _____

TRAINING AND DEVELOPMENT PLAN _____

EMPLOYEE COMMENTS _____

Signatures

Employee: _____

Supervisor: _____

Human Resources: _____

Employee Self-Evaluation Form

Employee Name:

Date:

Rate how often the following statements apply to you.

A=always, S=sometimes, N=never

I show up to my assigned shifts promptly.	A	S	N
I understand the responsibilities associated with my position.	A	S	N
I work well with other members of the team.	A	S	N
I do not let personal problems affect my job performance.	A	S	N
I fulfill the responsibilities of my position.	A	S	N
I treat all customers with respect.	A	S	N
I treat my coworkers with respect.	A	S	N
I do tasks outside of my job description if asked.	A	S	N
I keep information and issues about customers confidential.	A	S	N
I keep information and issues about coworkers confidential.	A	S	N
I have a good attitude while working.	A	S	N
I follow service and operational procedures.	A	S	N
I show initiative.	A	S	N
I follow through on assigned tasks.	A	S	N

Notes:

Employee Signature:

Date:

Performance Evaluation Form

Employee Name:

Evaluator's Name:

Date:

Rate how often the following statements apply to the employee.

A=always, S=sometimes, N=never

Employee shows up to assigned shifts promptly.	A	S	N
Employee understands the responsibilities associated with position.	A	S	N
Employee works well with other members of the team.	A	S	N
Employee does not let personal problems affect job performance.	A	S	N
Employee fulfills the responsibilities of position.	A	S	N
Employee treats all customers with respect.	A	S	N
Employee treats coworkers with respect.	A	S	N
Employee does tasks outside of job description if asked.	A	S	N
Employee keeps information and issues about customers confidential.	A	S	N
Employee keeps information and issues about coworkers confidential.	A	S	N
Employee has a good attitude while working.	A	S	N
Employee follows service and operational procedures.	A	S	N
Employee shows initiative.	A	S	N
Employee follows through with assigned tasks.	A	S	N

Notes:

Evaluator's Signature:

Date:

Employee's Signature:

Date:

Employee Satisfaction Survey

Current Recognition Practices and Employee Satisfaction Survey

Answer the survey questions using the following scale:

Always	Frequently	Occasionally	Seldom	Never

Recognition Activity	A	F	O	S	N
Employees are given verbal praise.					
Employees are given written praise (thank-you notes, cards, etc.).					
Employees are given praise through e-mail.					
Employees are given praise in public (at meetings, special events, informal groups, etc.).					
Employees are given certificates for specific accomplishments or achievements.					
Employees are given small monetary rewards for achievement (gift certificates, coupons, dinner, flowers, etc.).					
Employees are rewarded with paid time off from work.					
Employees are offered flexible work schedules.					
Employees are offered choice of work/assignments where appropriate.					

Recognition Effectiveness	A	F	O	S	N
Employees are given recognition in a genuine manner.					
Employee recognition is given in a timely manner.					
Employees appreciate the type of recognition they receive.					
Attempts are made to individualize the recognition provided.					
Employees feel more valued after a recognition activity.					
Employees have equal opportunity to receive recognition within our organization.					

Feedback Activity	A	F	O	S	N
Employees are given useful and constructive feedback.					
Employees are given adequate feedback about their performance.					
Employees receive feedback that helps them improve their performance.					
Employee feedback is given in a timely manner.					
Employees have an opportunity to participate in the goal-setting process.					
Employee performance evaluations are fair and appropriate.					
When employees do a good job, they receive the praise and recognition they deserve.					

Degree of Teamwork	A	F	O	S	N
Our organization practices and encourages teamwork.					
There is a strong feeling of teamwork and cooperation in our organization.					

Degree of Customer Focus	A	F	O	S	N
Letters from customers are circulated or posted for all employees to see.					

Employees are held accountable for the quality of work they produce.

Our organization maintains a very high standard of quality.

Our organization understands its customers' needs.

Awareness of Mission and Purpose	A	F	O	S	N

Employees have a good understanding of the mission and the goals of our organization.

Employees understand how their work directly contributes to the overall success of our organization.

Employees are provided with regular updates and information about the mission and the goals of our organization.

Employees understand the organization's strategic goals.

Employees derive personal satisfaction from achieving organization goals.

Compensation	A	F	O	S	N

Employees are paid fairly for the work they do.

Employees' salaries are competitive with similar jobs.

Employees' benefits are comparable to those offered by other organizations.

Employees understand and use their benefit plan for optimum results.

Employees are satisfied with their benefit package.

Workplace Resources	A	F	O	S	N

Employees are given the resources required to do their job well.

The requisite information systems are in place and accessible for employees to accomplish their tasks.

The workplace is well maintained.

The workplace is a physically comfortable place to work.

The workplace is safe.

Opportunities for Growth	A	F	O	S	N

Employees are given adequate opportunities for professional growth in our organization.

Employees receive the training they need to do their job well.

Managers are actively involved in the professional development and advancement of their employees.

Managers encourage and support employee development.

Employees are encouraged to learn from their mistakes.

Employees have mentors or coaches at work from whom they can learn.

Employees consider their work challenging.

Employees consider their work stimulating.

Employees consider their work rewarding.

Work / Life Balance	A	F	O	S	N

The environment in our organization supports a balance between work and personal life.

Managers encourage employees to maintain a balance between work and personal life.					
Employees are able to satisfy both their job and family responsibilities.					
Employees are provided a work pace that is conducive to good work.					
Employee workloads are reasonable.					
Expectations placed on employees are reasonable.					
Employees do not suffer unreasonable stress due to the functions of their jobs and their position within our organization.					
Fairness and Consistency	A	F	O	S	N
Employees are treated fairly within our organization.					
Policies are administered as consistently as possible within our organization.					
Employees are awarded raises, promotions, special assignments, etc., in accordance with stated policies.					
Favoritism or other workplace relationships are not used as factors when dealing with workplace issues.					
Respect for Employees	A	F	O	S	N
Employees are always treated with respect.					
Employees are listened to within our organization.					
The culture of our organization fosters respect for employees.					
Employees' special skills, abilities, and talents are valued within our organization.					
Managers and coworkers care about each other as people.					
Communication	A	F	O	S	N
Information and knowledge are shared openly within our organization.					
Communication is encouraged within our organization.					
Managers do a good job of sharing information.					
Senior management communicates well with the rest of the organization.					
Personal Expression	A	F	O	S	N
Employees are allowed to challenge or question current practices or decisions.					
Employees can disagree with their manager without fear of reprisal.					
Employees can express their opinions openly at work.					
Employees in our organization have diverse backgrounds.					

Employee Handbook

You should cover these topics in your employee handbook:

- Standards of Conduct
- Employee Conduct
- Bonus Plans
- Absenteeism
- Punctuality
- Work Performance
- Performance Reviews
- Work-area Neatness
- Availability for Work
- Personal Mail and E-mail
- Personal Telephone Calls
- Benefits Program
- Eligibility for Benefits
- Mandatory Meetings
- Communication
- Problem Resolution
- Disciplinary Guidelines
- Employee Relations
- Insurance and Insurance Continuation
- Company Vehicles
- Personal Appearance
- Confidentiality
- Safety
- Weapons Policy
- Violence

- Severe Weather
- Holidays
- Vacation
- Bereavement Leave
- Workplace Monitoring
- Orientation
- Suggestions
- Criminal Convictions
- Harassment
- Employment References
- Personnel Files
- Social Security
- Employment of Relatives
- Outside Employment
- Social Security
- Pre-tax Deductions
- Military Leave
- Searches
- Rehiring Employees
- Medical Leave of Absence
- Solicitation
- Substance Abuse
- Contributions
- Company Property
- Office Equipment
- Family Leave of Absence

- Tools and Equipment
- Employee Discounts, if applicable
- Hours of Work
- Workers' Compensation
- Employment Classification
- Recording Time
- Jury Duty
- Break Policy
- Overtime
- Payroll
- Educational Assistance
- Reimbursable Expenses
- Travel Expenses
- Salary and/or Wage Increases
- Job Abandonment
- Voluntary Resignation
- Performance-based Release
- Termination Procedures
- Acts of Misconduct
- Other Forms of Separation
- Equal Employment Opportunity
- Affidavit of Receipt
- Unemployment Compensation

Sample Employee Handbook

Table of Contents

WELCOME TO THE COMPANY

We have always stressed that outstanding people, unified in a group effort, are the key to our success. Through the efforts of our employees, *[COMPANY]* has become a recognized leader in the *[type of business]* in this community.

In order to continue our consistent success and growth, it is important that all employees understand our policies and subscribed methods. This employee handbook will accustom you with the many policies of *[COMPANY]*. We hope you will use it as a valuable resource and reference for understanding the company. Certain policies will change from time to time; please check with the manager for any changes. Invariably questions will arise; please do not hesitate to discuss them with your supervisor or any member of management.

Please keep in mind that your employment is with the mutual consent of both you and the company. Both have the right to terminate employment and the employment relationship. This employment-at-will relationship will be in effect throughout employment with *[COMPANY]*, unless it is changed by an agreement signed by you and the *[owner, president]* of *[COMPANY]*.

One more important thought: We all talk about working hard — and we all do — but it takes more than talk. It takes energy and effort to be the best. However, we all believe in having fun as we work. The attitude and atmosphere of our *[type of operation]* lends itself to this. We will expect a lot from you, but feel you will receive much in return.

_____ (Signed, President/Owner)

GENERAL INFORMATION ABOUT *[COMPANY]*

[COMPANY] was founded in *[year]*. The present ownership is *[insert information]*. We believe *[describe some basic philosophy about your company, etc.]*.

HOURS OF OPERATION

Describe the basic hours of operation and the seasonal changes, if any.

JOB RESPONSIBILITIES

We simply cannot stress how important it is to come to work with the proper working attitude. Leave your personal problems outside the door. No one needs them — it only hurts the effectiveness of each individual and the service and efficiency of the whole operation. If you do have problems you feel are hurting your performance, please discuss them with the manager. Communication can often remedy problems.

It is important to try to be at work at least 15 minutes ahead of your scheduled shift. Please be punctual and be sure of your schedule. Despite the enjoyable environment in which we work, it is a job — not a game. Schedule your day so you can be on time and effective while you work. Be aware that being late or misreading your schedule and not coming to work causes a hardship on your fellow workers as well as the *[type of operation]*. Excuses might make you feel better, but they do not lessen the load for the other people covering for you.

GROOMING STANDARDS

Your personal hygiene is critical. Excessively long or sloppy hair is unacceptable. You should be neatly groomed each time you come to work. Baths, deodorants, mouthwashes, and colognes are all known to be protective measures. Your hands and fingernails are especially noticeable and should be clean at all times. Open sores must always be bandaged.

UNIFORMS

Each employee will be instructed as to the designated uniform to be worn for his or her department. This uniform must be worn at all times and with all of the accessories issued. Please regard the uniforms as if they were your own, and return them in good condition when you do leave the company. Questions regarding your uniform should be addressed to *[person or position]*. Employees should not carry cash, wallets, or purses at any time while they are at their workstations.

Consider describing uniforms in detail here specific to each position.

SCHEDULING

The work schedule is posted *[insert information]*. Please check the schedule when you arrive for your shift — there may be changes. If for some uncontrollable reason you find you are going to be late for your shift, call the manager as early as possible and explain your problem. These problems can then be anticipated and solutions found. Employees who are late or excessively absent might be considered for disciplinary action, which could include termination. *[COMPANY]* will consider that you have voluntarily quit if you do not arrive for *[insert information]* scheduled shifts.

As you can imagine, it is very difficult to schedule a business around the needs of its employees. If it is important that you have a certain day or days off, note the day or days requested in advance on the schedule request sheet posted next to the schedule or *[insert information]*, and mention your request to the person doing the scheduling. Every effort will be made to change the schedule. However, just requesting a change on the sheet does not mean it will be approved. Management must approve all schedule changes.

TIME CLOCK

The time clock is located *[insert information]*. You must punch in your time card when you are scheduled to start your shift and punch out your time card when your shift is scheduled to end, except when instructed otherwise by the manager. Under no circumstances are you to punch or mark on any other employee's time card.

NON-WORKING STATUS

When you come into the building on a non-working status (on a day off), present yourself as a customer and act accordingly. Do not wander through the different working areas. It is not fair to the other employees trying to do their job, nor is it fair to the customers who have paid for a unique experience.

YOUR FRIENDS

[COMPANY] is a place of business and you, as an employee, should keep this in mind at all times. While *[COMPANY]* is a unique and fun place to work, a mature understanding on the part of each employee is necessary, especially with regard to problems that might be created by friends. Please follow these rules to prevent embarrassing situations from occurring:

- No one is permitted in the building after closing except employees (friends cannot wait for you to finish with work).

- Employees may not receive unnecessary calls at work.

- Individuals are not permitted to distract you while you are working.

CREDIT CARDS

[COMPANY] accepts Visa, MasterCard, and American Express credit cards for those customers who would like to use them.

CHECK-CASHING POLICY

We are happy to accept a *[insert information]* check with proper identification and the manager's approval for the amount of the bill. No check will be cashed that exceeds the amount of the bill and the indicated gratuity.

CUSTOMER SERVICE

Our customers are the most responsive bosses in the world. Satisfy them, and they are all smiles. Disappoint them, and they will probably go elsewhere and not tell you why. We expect all of our employees to be friendly and considerate. Our performance is evaluated every day by each customer on the following criteria:

1. Are we honest in our desire to serve the customer?

2. Do we take pride in our job?

3. Do we consistently provide quality service and products to our customer?

4. Do we realize and appreciate the fact that each customer is our true boss?

Following the philosophy that the customer is treated as a guest, we have adopted the "never say no" policy in handling customer requests. All employees, including management, have a responsibility to the customer, to recognize him or her as the basis of our business. Without the customer, nothing happens. The customer must be accorded the same respect and courtesy that each of our employees is entitled to and demands. Above all, the customer should be entitled to anything we can do to make him or her feel at ease, wanted, and needed.

CUSTOMER COMPLAINTS

We want every employee to orient his or her thinking to the policy that we will put forth our total effort to ensure customer satisfaction of the best product and service available. It is equally important the management be made aware of any complaint or dissatisfaction immediately so that corrective measures can be taken to remove the risk of similar complaints and to properly reinforce in the customers' eyes our dedication to satisfy.

TELEPHONE ANSWERING PROCEDURES

Telephone calls are to be answered with a friendly "Good evening," or "Good afternoon, *[name of business]*. This is (your name), may I help you?" Record all messages, and make sure they are received. If customers ask for directions on how to get to our location, be prepared to tell them not only our location, but also how to get here. *[Insert directions here.]*

BREAK TIMES

Since break periods are varied due to state and even local regulations, please consult with your state department of labor and / or a competent attorney who specializes in labor / employee relations.

MEETINGS

Employee meetings are an important part of your job. Make sure you regard them that way. Be prompt and, if appropriate, have a pencil and paper to jot down notes.

FAULTY EQUIPMENT

Mention any faulty equipment to the management. Do not wait until a handle falls off before telling the manager it is loose.

EMPLOYEE PARKING

There is a specific parking area for all employees. Please park *[insert information]*.

MANAGEMENT'S OPEN-DOOR POLICY

You are always welcome to meet with any member of the management team at a time that is mutually agreeable. We are very interested in your input, suggestions, or work-related problems. This communication will help us become a better company, for both employees and our customers.

SUGGESTIONS

We are very interested in your suggestions. We need constant feedback from you in order to improve the operation for everyone. We cannot meet and talk with every customer as you do. Please let us know what we can do to improve employee relations, cut costs, or anything you can think of. Drop your suggestions in the box located *[insert information]*, or see one of the managers. Suggestions that are selected for use are rewarded with *[insert information]*.

EMPLOYMENT OF MINORS

All minors (under the age of 18 years of age) are required by law to provide a valid work permit, high school diploma, or acceptable equivalency prior to them being employed. The company will be restricted by the terms and conditions of the work permit and all federal, state, and local laws and regulations.

IMMIGRATION REFORM AND CONTROL ACT OF 1986

This company is committed to complying fully with the Federal Immigration Reform and Control Act of 1986, as well as any changes or alterations to the law. This company will not knowingly employ or hire any individual who does not have the legal right to be employed in the United States. As an employee, you will be required to provide adequate documentation proving your legal identity and legal right to work in the United States.

Should you have questions about the Immigration Reform And Control Act, need I-9 forms, or the "Handbook for Employers," contact your local Immigration and Customs Enforcement office. Direct your letter or call to the "employer and labor relations officer," or consult a competent attorney who specializes in this area.

EQUAL EMPLOYMENT POLICY

This company is committed to a strong policy of equal employment opportunity. We ensure an equal employment opportunity for all employees and applicants for employment without regard to race, color, religion, sex, sexual orientation, marital status, pregnancy, national origin, ancestry, age, physical disability, mental disability, or medical condition. Our equal employment opportunity philosophy applies to all aspects of employment with *[COMPANY]*, including recruiting, hiring, training, transfer, promotion, job benefits, disciplinary action, and social and recreational activities.

All employees are expected to demonstrate respect and courtesy toward every employee, customer, and supplier, as well as uphold our commitment towards our equal opportunity objectives.

Questions about equal employment laws and/or the American With Disabilities Act (ADA) should be directed to the Equal Opportunity Commission at 800-669-4000 and the Department of Justice, Civil Rights Division, at 202-514-0301. You can receive a free copy of the ADA requirements by calling 800-USA-ABLE. The National Restaurant Association has numerous publications available on these subjects. Their address is 1200 Seventh St. NW, Washington, D.C. 20036, or you can consult a competent attorney who specializes in this area.

SEXUAL HARASSMENT

All sexual, racial, or other forms of harassment are prohibited by *[COMPANY]*, as well as by state and federal law. We are committed to providing a workplace that is free of discrimination of any kind. Any person making unwelcome sexual advances, unwelcome sexual flirtations, graphic sexual comments about another, requests for sexual favors, unnecessary touching of an individual, and other such verbal or physical conduct creating an intimidating, hostile, or offensive working environment by such conduct may be terminated immediately.

Any employee who believes he or she is being, or has been, subjected to a form of harassment prohibited by this policy, should notify their supervisor immediately.

COMPENSATION

Pay period: The standard pay period is *[insert information]*. Should a payday fall on a weekend or holiday, paychecks will be distributed on the last working day prior to the holiday. The company does not cash payroll checks for employees.

Payroll deductions: Your earnings and payroll deductions will be indicated on the paycheck stub. Most people are familiar with the standard federal income tax, state income tax, social security taxes, etc. Please keep a record of your paycheck stubs for tax purposes. Any questions about your paycheck should be directed to your manager or supervisor.

Wage review: Employees are generally reviewed *[insert information] for possible* wage increases. All increases are based on merit. A review does not imply a wage increase. Should a wage increase be awarded, it will take effect at the beginning of the next pay period.

Overtime: Occasionally, you may be asked to work overtime. Overtime is sometimes necessary during busy periods or to cover absent employees. When asked to work overtime, you will be paid a premium pay rate, if applicable, that is subject to state and federal laws. Your supervisor or manager must approve all overtime work. Certain employees may be exempt from the overtime provisions of state and federal law.

Your tip reporting: Federal law requires any employee who receives $20 or more in any calendar month to report to the company on or before the tenth (10th) day of the following month the total amount of tips received. The Internal Revenue Service requires you to keep daily records of the amount of tip income you receive. Be sure to maintain accurate and complete records of your tip income. Follow the company's established tip income reporting procedures. Pay attention to the posted notices *[insert location]*, as these regulations and procedures do change.

INTRODUCTORY TIME PERIOD

New employees are subject to a 90-day introductory period to learn procedures and assess their capabilities and suitability to their job. This also allows new employees the same opportunity to evaluate *[COMPANY]* as a place to work. This time frame does not obligate the company to retain the employee until the end of this period.

EMPLOYMENT OF RELATIVES

Relatives of current employees of *[COMPANY]* will be given consideration for employment. We have no restriction against hiring family members. However, family members will not be hired into positions or departments where they supervise or are supervised by another family member, except where indicated or modified by either state or federal law.

GENERAL COMPANY RULES

Detailed below are basic policy examples that were implemented to enhance our business for everyone involved. This list does not encompass every policy or rule. Failure to fully comply with the intent of these basic policies may result in termination of your employment with the company:

- All employees must enter and exit *[insert information]*.

- Please arrive on time and ready to work. Do not arrive at work combing your hair or fixing your uniform. Make an effort to be thoughtful and considerate to your fellow workers and customers. Remember, we are in the "people" business.

- Disorderly conduct, including, but not limited, to fighting or creating a disturbance, use of profanity and / or threatening action or language to others, theft and / or abuse of company property, disregard to prescribed safety procedures, blatant insubordination, or possession of weapons or illegal drugs will not be tolerated and may be cause for immediate termination. Items that are lost or left behind by either fellow employees or customers must be brought to the manager immediately.

- Not arriving for work on *[insert information]* consecutively scheduled workdays, without prior authorization, may be cause for immediate termination.

- Employees are expected to conduct themselves in a safe manner. Use common sense when using equipment, knives, hot water, etc. Some equipment may have posted safety rules. If you do not know how to use something or have not had the proper instruction in its use, please ask for assistance from the manager or supervisor. Never run anywhere in the establishment.

- *[COMPANY]* will not tolerate any abuse of legal or illegal substances. Any employee reporting for work or on the company premises under the influence of alcohol or non-prescription drugs will be asked to leave immediately. Should this occur, we will attempt to provide help to ensure the employee arrives home safely. Violations of this policy may result in an employee's immediate termination.

- Do not smoke in designated nonsmoking areas. Do not use profanity.

- We do not restrict you being employed outside the company as long as those activities do not interfere with the performance of your job.

- Gambling, solicitation, or the distribution of materials is strictly prohibited during work hours. Do not post notices on the bulletin board. Should you have something of interest to share with other employees, ask your manager for approval to post.

- Do not make false, vicious, malicious statements to slander or defame any company employee, company official or owner, or government employee. Failure to observe this may result in your immediate termination.

- Misconduct off duty of such a nature as to reflect negatively on or cause embarrassment to this company may result in your immediate termination.

- Please refrain from discussing tips or money in view or hearing distance of customers and employees. There is no guarantee you will receive a gratuity.

- An employee is expected to give at least two weeks' notice before terminating employment with the company.

PERSONNEL FILES

We maintain current personnel files on all employees. It is important to keep your records up-to-date. All the information you provide us will be kept confidential. Please notify *[insert information]* about changes in your address, phone number, marital status, W-4 changes, etc.

INTERNET / E-MAIL USE

Personal use of the Internet is not allowed.

TELEPHONE USE

Personal use of the telephone is not allowed. Emergency calls to you should be limited. There is a public pay phone located *[location]*.

VACATIONS

Annual vacations are earned by length of employment and employment status and are calculated by: *[insert vacation information]*.

Vacations should be scheduled to avoid conflicts with other employees' vacations and with busy periods. The manager or supervisor must approve vacation dates at least 30 days prior to the vacation.

LEAVES OF ABSENCE

A leave of absence is an extended absence from work without loss of employment. Management must approve a leave of absence in advance. A leave of absence is without pay and subject to both state and federal law.

- **Medical Leave** — A leave of absence due to a medical condition will require a doctor's written statement indicating the medical necessity for the leave of absence as well as the estimated time needed.

- **Family Leave** — Family leave as defined by law will be granted subject to both federal and state law provisions. Qualification for this leave is at least one year of continuous service. Please submit your request in writing to your manager or supervisor. Your leave will be without pay and may be for any amount of time up to four months in length in any twenty-four (24)-month period.

Currently, companies with fewer than 50 employees are not required to offer family leave; however, you must check with the governing office or a competent attorney in this area to ensure you are in compliance

- **Maternity Leave** — *[COMPANY]* will issue a leave of absence without pay for medical complications associated with pregnancy. Maximum leave is *[length]* months. Please submit your request in writing, including your doctor's written statement.

- **Jury Duty Leave** — We encourage all employees to serve on jury panels when asked. If you are to serve on a jury, please provide written proof to your manager. You will be granted a leave of absence, without pay, to serve on the panel, as required by law.

GROUP INSURANCE

Medical Insurance: All (full-time / part-time) employees may be eligible for group medical insurance. Benefits begin on the first regular workday following a *[time]* waiting period.

The cost for medical insurance is paid as follows:

	Employee	**Dependents**
Company Pays		
Employee Pays		

The company has established this insurance benefit with you, the employee, in mind. Your contribution will be deducted from your payroll check. When you are enrolled in the group plan, you will be issued complete details about the program.

Dental Insurance: All (full-time / part-time) employees are eligible for our group dental plan. Your dental benefit plan will begin on the first regular workday following [time] waiting period.

The cost for dental insurance is paid as follows:

	Employee	Dependents
Company Pays		
Employee Pays		

WORKERS' COMPENSATION

The company pays 100 percent of this critical coverage. This insurance covers work-related injuries or illnesses. All injuries must be reported to either your supervisor or the manager as soon as they occur.

The company and its insurance carrier may not be responsible for the payment of workers' compensation benefits for an injury that arises out of an employee's voluntary participation in any off-duty recreational, social, or athletic activity that is not part of the employee's work-related duties.

SOCIAL SECURITY (FICA)

Every employee is covered under the guidelines of the social security law. These benefits are made available at your retirement and / or may provide disability or survivor's benefits. The amount deducted from your paycheck is matched by the company and deposited with the Social Security Administration for your future use under your social security number.

UNEMPLOYMENT BENEFIT INSURANCE

The company pays unemployment insurance on your behalf to both the state and federal government. These unemployment taxes are the basis of the funds that will assist you with unemployment benefits should you become eligible.

CONCLUSION

This Employee Handbook was written to inform you about our company and some of its basic policies and benefits. Policies and benefit programs described in this handbook may be changed or eliminated altogether due to a change in our business requirements or applicable legal requirements. Your management team will advise you of any changes.

Ethics Policy of Code of Conduct

Every organization should have a formal ethics policy, not only because it deters fraud, but also because it legally supports efforts to enforce ethical conduct in the workplace. Employees who have read and signed a formal ethics policy cannot claim they were unaware their conduct was unacceptable. Recommended codes of conduct for various types of organizations are commercially available, but every organization should tailor its own ethics policy to suit its business and its needs. A good ethics policy is simple and easy to understand, addresses general conduct, and offers a few examples to explain how the code might be applied. It should not contain myriad rules to cover specific situations, or vague threats such as "violators will be prosecuted to the full extent of the law." In a legal trial of a fraud perpetrator, the judge — not the company — will decide the sentence. An ethics policy or code of conduct should cover:

- **General conduct at work:** Explain that ethical and honest behavior is expected of all employees, and they are expected to act in the company's best interests.

- **Conflicts of interest:** Employees may not understand what does and does not constitute a conflict of interest, so some simple examples are appropriate.

- **Confidentiality:** Company policy on the sharing of information among employees and departments or with people outside the company.

- **Relationships with vendors and customers:** Company policy regarding doing business with a relative, friend, or personal acquaintance.

- **Gifts:** Policy regarding the types and amounts of gifts that may be accepted or given by employees during the course of doing business.

- **Entertainment:** The types of entertainment activities considered appropriate for vendors and customers and that will be accepted on expense accounts.

- **Relationships with the media:** Company policy regarding who should communicate with the media about company affairs.

- **Use of the organization's assets for personal purposes:** This section should cover personal use of the Internet while at work and use of copy machines, telephones, and company vehicles.

- **Procedure for reporting unethical behavior:** Employees should be encouraged to report any ethical violation, large or small. This section should explain how and to whom reports should be submitted, and the use of a tip hot line, if one exists.

- **Consequences of unethical behavior:** Discipline options should be clearly communicated and consistently enforced.

An ethics policy will not be effective if it is handed to each new employee and then forgotten. Review the ethics policy with employees every year, ideally as part of an antifraud education program.

Employee Fraud Prevention Checklist

Red Flags of Employee Fraud

Every day businesses lose money because an employee embezzles from the company or commits some other form of fraud, such as accepting bribes or fabricating time sheets. It is difficult to identify these individuals; only 6 percent of employees committing fraud have a previous criminal background. The following red flags are behavioral signs something may be amiss, indicating that a situation should be watched or investigated. Training managers to be aware of these red flags will make them more alert to the possibility of fraud. Remember, none of these indicators are conclusive evidence of fraud, but when combined with other factors, such as easy access to cash, accounting irregularities, loose organizational controls, a chaotic working environment, or unexplained deficits, they are signs fraud could be taking place.

____ Significant personal debt and credit problems

____ Borrowing money from coworkers

____ Creditors calling or appearing at the workplace

____ Lifestyle changes, such as the purchase of an expensive car, a new home, or a lifestyle beyond the employee's apparent means

____ Bragging about new purchases of large or expensive items

____ Carrying unusually large amounts of cash

____ Refusal to take vacation or sick leave or refusal to relinquish responsibilities when out of the office

____ Refusal to accept a promotion

____ Strong desire to retain control or unwillingness to delegate responsibilities to coworkers

____ Behavioral changes that might indicate an addiction to alcohol, drugs, or gambling, or stress over the possibility of losing the job

____ Excessive drinking, gambling, or other addictive behavior

____ Dishonesty on expense reports, or use of company property for personal benefit

____ Irritability, suspicion, or defensiveness when asked reasonable questions

____ Inability to produce documents and reports when questioned

____ Marital infidelity

____ Personal difficulties such as divorce, problems with children or parents, foreclosure, instability, or a family illness

____ Unusual relationships with coworkers, vendors, suppliers, or customers

____ Consistently comes to work unusually early or stays unusually late

____ Has authority over one or more accounting processes

____ Has unsupervised access to cash, supplies, or assets

____ Resentful attitude toward employer

___ Comes in late, leaves work early, takes excessive breaks, or falsely calls in sick

___ Physical isolation, both in the office and in personal life

___ Difficulty communicating with superiors

___ Open disregard for company policies and procedures

___ Complains about lack of authority

___ Wheeler-dealer attitude

___ Close association with other employees who have demonstrated resentful or disrespectful attitudes

___ Is under unreasonable pressure to perform from within the organization

___ Is under pressure from family or peers

___ Previous criminal record for theft or embezzlement

___ Past legal problems

___ Past employment-related problems

Conditions Under Which Fraud Occurs

Most perpetrators do not seek employment with the intent of committing fraud. When someone under the pressure of financial or personal difficulties sees an easy way out through committing fraud and finds a way to justify his or her actions, he or she begins to act dishonestly. If the opportunity did not exist, that person would not commit fraud. Just as certain red flags suggest an employee might be acting dishonestly, red flags also can point out workplace situations in which fraud could easily occur. Signs of high risk include:

___ An organization that is always operating in "crisis mode," instead of following established procedures

___ Unrealistic expectations of employees, such as unreasonably high sales targets, overly heavy workloads, or excessive production goals

___ Strained relationships between employees and their superiors

___ Lack of separation between cash-handling and accounting responsibilities

___ Too much responsibility and authority in the hands of one person

___ Poor internal controls

___ Lack of security for electronic data and computer networks

___ Employees working in isolation without supervision

___ An organizational culture that appears to overlook small lapses

Safety Policy and OSHA Compliance

It is in every business owner's interest to maintain a safe and healthy workplace. Illnesses and workplace accidents result in lost productivity and waste, low employee morale, negative media attention, costly lawsuits, and in a few instances, the closure of the business. The dangers of operating heavy machinery, climbing ladders, or working with sharp knives in a restaurant kitchen are obvious, but even an apparently safe office environment has hazards that potentially could cause serious injury.

Many small-business owners do not realize federal and state law requires them to meet certain safety standards. The Occupational Safety and Health Act, enacted by Congress in 1970, created the Occupational Safety and Health Administration (OSHA), an agency of the Department of Labor, to set and enforce workplace health and safety standards, and an independent Occupational Health and Safety Review Commission to monitor enforcement policies and review cases.

OSHA offers consultation assistance to employers who want help in establishing and maintaining a safe and healthful workplace. Largely funded by OSHA, this service is provided at no cost to the employer and is available in every state and territory. Much of the information in this section is available on the OSHA website (**www.osha.gov**).

Formulating a Safety Policy

The business owner, management, or a safety committee should formulate a written safety policy to serve as a "mission statement" in encouraging employees to work safely. OSHA offers the following suggestions for paragraphs that might be included in a safety policy:

- "The Occupational Safety and Health Act of 1970 clearly states our common goal of safe and healthful working conditions. The safety and health of our employees continues to be the first consideration in the operation of this business."

- "Safety and health in our business must be a part of every operation. Without question it is every employee's responsibility at all levels."

- "It is the intent of this company to comply with all laws. To do this we must constantly be aware of conditions in all work areas that can produce injuries. No employee is required to work at a job he or she knows is not safe or healthful. Your cooperation in detecting hazards and, in turn, controlling them is a condition of your employment. Inform your supervisor immediately of any situation beyond your ability or authority to correct."

- "The personal safety and health of each employee of this company is of primary importance. The prevention of occupationally induced injuries and illnesses is of such consequence that it will be given precedence over operating productivity whenever necessary. To the greatest degree possible, management will provide all mechanical and physical facilities required for personal safety and health in keeping with the highest standards."

- "We will maintain a safety and health program conforming to the best practices of organizations of this type. To be successful, such a program must embody the proper attitudes toward injury and illness prevention on the part of supervisors and employees. It also requires cooperation in all safety and health matters, not only between supervisor and employee, but also between each employee and his or her coworkers. Only through such a cooperative effort can a safety program in the best interest of all be established and preserved."

- "Our objective is a safety and health program that will reduce the number of injuries and illnesses to an absolute minimum, not merely in keeping with, but surpassing, the best experience of operations similar to ours. Our goal is zero accidents and injuries."

- "Our safety and health program will include:

  - Providing mechanical and physical safeguards to the maximum extent possible.

  - Conducting a program of safety and health inspections to find and eliminate unsafe working conditions or practices, to control health hazards, and to comply fully with the safety and health standards for every job.

  - Training all employees in good safety and health practices.

  - Providing necessary personal protective equipment and instructions for its use and care.

  - Developing and enforcing safety and health rules and requiring that employees cooperate with these rules as a condition of employment.

  - Investigating, promptly and thoroughly, every accident to find out what caused it and to correct the problem so that it will not happen again.

  - Setting up a system of recognition and awards for outstanding safety service or performance."

- "We recognize that the responsibilities for safety and health are shared:

  - The employer accepts the responsibility for leadership of the safety and health program, for its effectiveness and improvement, and for providing the safeguards required to ensure safe conditions.

  - Supervisors are responsible for developing the proper attitudes toward safety and health in themselves and in those they supervise and for ensuring that all operations are performed with the utmost regard for the safety and health of all personnel involved, including themselves.

  - Employees are responsible for wholehearted, genuine operation with all aspects of the safety and health program, including compliance with all rules and regulations — and for continuously practicing safety while performing their duties."

Checklist for Employers Covered by the OSH Act

Your Responsibilities as an Employer

If you are an employer covered by the OSH Act, you must provide your employees with jobs and a place of employment free from recognized hazards that are causing, or are likely to cause, death or serious physical harm. Among other actions, you must also comply with the OSHA statutory requirements, standards, and regulations that, in part, require you to do the following:

☐ Provide well-maintained tools and equipment, including appropriate personal protective equipment;

☐ Provide medical examinations;

☐ Provide training required by OSHA standards;

☐ Report to OSHA, within eight hours, accidents that result in fatalities;

☐ Report to OSHA, within eight hours, accidents that result in the hospitalization of three or more employees;

☐ Keep records of work-related accidents, injuries, illnesses, and their causes and post annual summaries for the required time. A number of specific industries in the retail, service, finance, insurance, and real estate sectors that are classified as low-hazard are exempt from most requirements of the regulation, as are small businesses with 10 or fewer employees. (See CFR 29 Part 1904.)

☐ Post prominently the OSHA poster (OSHA 3165) informing employees of their rights and responsibilities;

☐ Provide employees access to their medical and exposure records;

☐ Do not discriminate against employees who exercise their rights under the OSH Act;

☐ Post OSHA citations and abatement verification notices at or near the work site;

☐ Abate cited violations within the prescribed period; and

☐ Respond to survey requests for data from the Bureau of Labor Statistics, OSHA, or a designee of either agency.

Your Rights as an Employer

When working with OSHA, you may do the following:

☐ Request identification from OSHA compliance officers;

☐ Request an inspection warrant;

☐ Be advised by compliance officers of the reason for an inspection;

☐ Have an opening and closing conference with compliance officers;

☐ Accompany compliance officers on inspections;

☐ Request an informal conference after an inspection;

☐ File a Notice of Contest to citations, proposed penalties, or both.

CHAPTER

9

Forms and Checklists for Consultants and Independent Contractors

The checklists in Chapter 4, "Contract Basics," include a review of a service contract. This section contains sample contracts and documents used by independent contractors and their clients.

Agreements and Forms

Independent Contractor Agreement

This Agreement is entered into as of the ____ day of _____, 20____, between *[company name]* ("the Company") and *[service provider's name]* ("the Contractor").

1. **Independent Contractor.** Subject to the terms and conditions of this Agreement, the Company engages the Contractor as an independent contractor to perform the services set forth as described in this agreement, and the Contractor hereby accepts all terms.

2. **Duties, Term of Contract, and Compensation.** The Contractor's duties, term of engagement, compensation, and provisions for payment thereof have been recorded in the estimate that was previously provided to the Company by the Contractor, attached as Exhibit A. This agreement can be amended only in writing. The agreement may also be supplemented with estimates for services to be rendered by the Contractor and agreed to by the Company. All amendments and supplements will be incorporated herein as reference. All amendments and supplements are to be initialed by both parties.

3. **Expenses.** During the term of this Agreement, the Contractor shall produce a bill and the Company will reimburse Contractor for all reasonable and approved out-of-pocket expenses that are incurred in connection with the performance of the duties described herein. Expenses for the time traveling to and from Company facilities are not to be reimbursed under this agreement.

4. **Progress Reports.** The Company may request that project plans, progress reports, and / or a final report be provided by Contractor on a monthly basis. A final report will be due upon completion of the project and shall be submitted to the Company at such time. The final report shall be in such form and setting forth such information and data as is reasonably requested by the Company.

5. **Confidentiality.** The Contractor acknowledges that during the engagement he or she may have access to various trade secrets, inventions, innovations, processes, information, records, and specifications owned, used, or licensed by the Company and / or used by the Company in connection with the operation of its business including, without limitation, the Company's business and product processes, methods, customer lists, accounts, and procedures. The Contractor agrees not to disclose any of these either directly or indirectly, or use any of them in any manner, either during the term of this Agreement or at any time thereafter, except as required in the course of this engagement with the Company. All files, records, documents, blueprints, specifications, information, letters, notes, media lists, original artwork / creative, notebooks, and similar items relating to the business of the Company, whether prepared by the Contractor or otherwise coming into his or her possession, is the exclusive property of the Company. The Contractor agrees not to create any copies of the foregoing with the intent to keep them without the Company's prior written permission. Upon the expiration or termination of this Agreement, or at any time requested by the Company, the Contractor shall immediately turn over to the Company all such files, records, documents, specifications, information, and other items in his or her

possession or under his or her control. The Contractor further agrees not to disclose information about his or her retention as an independent contractor or the terms of this Agreement to any person without the prior written consent of the Company and shall at all times preserve the confidential nature of his / her relationship to the Company and of the services he provides.

6. **Conflicts of Interest; Non-hire Provision.** The Contractor represents that he or she is free to enter into this Agreement. The Contractor's signature below indicates that this engagement does not violate the terms of any agreement between the Contractor and any third party. During the entire term of this agreement, the Contractor shall devote his or her productive time, energy, and abilities to the performance of his or her duties hereunder at a level that is necessary to complete the required duties in a timely and productive manner.

7. **Right to Contractual Employment.** The Contractor is expressly free to perform services for other parties while performing services for the Company. The Contractor agrees that for a period of six months following any termination, the Contractor shall not directly or indirectly hire, solicit, or encourage leaving the Company's employment, any employee, consultant, or contractor of the Company or hiring any such employee, consultant, or contractor who has left the Company's employment or contractual engagement within one year of such employment or engagement.

8. **Right to Injunction.** The parties hereto acknowledge that the services rendered by the Contractor under this Agreement and the rights and privileges granted to the Company under the Agreement are of a special, unique, unusual, and extraordinary character that gives them a peculiar value, the loss of which cannot be reasonably or adequately compensated by damages in any action at law, and the breach by the Contractor of any of the provisions of this Agreement will cause the Company irreparable injury and damage. The Contractor expressly agrees that the Company is entitled to injunctive and other equitable relief in the event of, or to prevent, a breach of any provision of this Agreement by the Contractor. Resort to such equitable relief, however, shall not be construed to be a waiver of any other rights or remedies that the Company may have for damages or otherwise. The various rights and remedies of the Company under this Agreement or otherwise shall be construed to be cumulative, and no one of them shall be exclusive of any other or of any right or remedy allowed by law.

9. **Merger.** This Agreement shall not be terminated by the merger or consolidation of the Company into or with any other entity, nor by the merger of the Contractor with another company.

10. **Termination.** The Company may terminate this Agreement at any time by 10 working days' written notice to the Contractor. In addition, if the Contractor materially breaches provisions of this Agreement, is convicted of a crime, fails or refuses to comply with the written policies or reasonable directive of the Company, or performs acts of serious misconduct in connection with performance herein, the Company at any time may terminate the engagement of the Contractor immediately and without prior written notice to the Contractor.

11. Independent Contractor. The Contractor is not an employee, partner, or agent of the Company for any purpose. The Contractor is and will remain an independent contractor in his or her relationship to the

Company. The Company shall not be responsible for withholding taxes with respect to the Contractor's compensation hereunder. The Contractor has no claim against the Company hereunder or otherwise for vacation pay, sick leave, retirement benefits, social security, workers' compensation, health or disability benefits, unemployment insurance benefits, or employee benefits of any kind.

12. **Insurance.** The Contractor will carry liability insurance, including malpractice insurance, if warranted relative to any service that he or she performs for the Company, and will provide insurance policy information upon request.

13. **Successors and Assigns.** All of the provisions of this Agreement shall be binding upon and inure to the benefit of the parties hereto and their respective heirs, if any, successors, and assigns.

14. **Choice of Law.** The laws of the state of _____ govern the validity of this Agreement, the construction of its terms, and the interpretation of the rights and duties of the parties hereto.

15. **Arbitration.** Any controversies that arise out of the terms of this Agreement or its interpretation shall be settled in _____ (location) in accordance with the rules of the American Arbitration Association, and the judgment upon award may be entered in any court having jurisdiction thereof.

16. **Waiver.** Waiver by one party hereto of breach of any provision of this Agreement by the other shall not operate or be construed as a continuing waiver.

17. **Assignment.** The Contractor shall not assign any of his or her rights under this Agreement, or delegate the performance of any of his or her duties hereunder, without the prior written consent of the Company.

18. **Notices.** All notices, demands, or other communications required or desired to be given hereunder by any party shall be in writing and shall be validly given or made to another party if personally served, or if deposited in the United States mail, certified or registered, postage prepaid, return receipt requested. If such notice or demand is served personally, notice shall be deemed constructively made at the time of such personal service. If such notice, demand, or other communication is given by mail, such notice shall be conclusively deemed given five days after deposit thereof in the United States mail addressed to the party to whom such notice, demand, or other communication is to be given as follows:

Contractor: Name: _____

Address: _____

City/State/ZIP: _____

Company: Name: _____

Address: _____

City/State/ZIP: _____

DUTIES: The Contractor will perform the following duties:

_____

_____

TERM: Engagement of this contract shall commence upon execution of this Agreement and shall continue in full force and effect through date: _____ or earlier upon satisfactory completion of the Contractor's duties under this Agreement. The Agreement may only be extended by mutual agreement.

COMPENSATION: (choose A or B)

A. As full compensation for the services rendered pursuant to this Agreement, the Company shall pay the Contractor at the hourly rate of $_____ per hour, with total payment not to exceed $_____ without prior written approval by an authorized representative of the Company. Compensation will be payable within 30 days of receipt of Contractor's monthly invoice for services rendered, supported by reasonable documentation.

OR

B. As full compensation for the services rendered pursuant to this Agreement, the Company shall pay the Contractor the sum of $_____dollar amount, to be paid as follows:

_____

19. **Modification or Amendment.** No modification, amendment, or change of this Agreement shall be valid unless in writing and signed by both parties.

20. **Unenforceability of Provisions.** If any provision of this Agreement, or any portion thereof, is determined to be invalid and unenforceable, then the remainder of this Agreement shall nevertheless remain in full force and effect.

IN WITNESS WHEREOF, the undersigned have executed this Agreement as of the day and year first written above. The parties hereto agree that facsimile signatures shall be as effective as if originals.

Company   Contractor

By: _____   By: _____

Title or position_____   Title or position_____

Hiring Agreement for a Company

This Agreement is made on _____, 20 ____, between _____,
Company, of _____, City of _____, State of _____,
and _____, Hired Company, of _____, City of
_____, State of _____.

1. The *[type of business]*, as an independent contractor, agrees to furnish all of the labor and materials to do the following portions of the work specified in the Agreement between the Company and the Hired Company dated _____, 20 ____.

2. The Hired Company agrees that the following portions of the total work will be completed by the dates specified:

    Work:

    Dates:

3. The Hired Company agrees to perform this work in a professional manner according to standard practices in its industry. If any plans or specifications are part of this job, they are attached to and are part of this Contract.

4. The Company agrees to pay the Hired Company as full payment $ _____, for doing the work outlined above. This price will be paid on satisfactory completion of the work in the following manner and on the following dates:

    Work:

    Dates:

5. The Company and Hired Company may agree to extra services and work, but any such extras must be set out and agreed to in writing by both the Company and the Hired Company.

6. The Hired Company agrees to indemnify and hold the Contractor harmless from any claims or liability arising from the Hired Company's work under this Agreement.

7. No modification of this Agreement will be effective unless it is in writing and is signed by both parties. This Agreement binds and benefits both parties and any successors. Time is of the essence of this Agreement. This document, including any attachments, is the entire agreement between the parties. This Agreement is governed by the laws of the State of _____.

Dated: _____

_____   _____
Signature of Company   Signature of Hired Company

_____   _____
Name of Company   Name of Hired Company

(You may want a notary to sign and seal this agreement.)

Invoice for Independent Contractor

[Organization's Letterhead]

Invoice Date: _____

To: H. John Smith

    141 Allen St.

    New York, NY 10001

Invoice Number: _____   Billing Period: From_____ to _____

Subcontract Number: _____

Purchase Order Number: _____

Please check whether this is a partial or final invoice: ☐ Partial   ☐ Final

Budget Categories	Approved Budget	Current Billing Period	Cumulative to Date
Direct Costs:			
Salary and wages			
[List specific individuals]			
Fringe benefits [list fringe rate]			
Permanent equipment			
[List specific items]			
Travel			
[List specific trips & types of costs]			
Supplies, materials & other direct costs			
[List specific items or costs]			
Contractual			
[List specific contracts]			
Subtotal Direct Costs:			
Indirect / Overhead Costs (insert rate)			
Total Direct & Indirect Costs:			

TOTAL AMOUNT OF THIS INVOICE: $_____

[Insert contact information for preparer of invoice:]

Insert name of person who prepared invoice _____   Telephone: _____

Insert address _____   E-mail: _____

Networking Log

Contact / Networking	Phone Number	Address	Telephone	E-mail	Date of Contact and Follow-up

CHAPTER 10

Marketing and Public Relations

Marketing refers to the efforts made by a business to find and attract customers. A marketing strategy should be part of your initial business plan, although you may discover new strategies as your business develops. The type and scale of your marketing effort depends on the nature of your business. A local landscaper might advertise primarily by word-of-mouth, with satisfied customers referring the business to their friends. An Internet sales business would need to buy online advertising, perhaps backed up by television or radio ads. A restaurant or retail store relies on prominent signs and ads in local newspapers to attract customers' attention. Study how similar businesses market themselves — would their strategies work well for you?

Develop a comprehensive marketing plan and review it every year to see whether it is having the desired result, then add new strategies, and retire those that are too costly or do not seem to work. New methods of advertising emerge every year, and prices for some services are decreasing as new technologies become available. For each marketing strategy, develop a way to measure your customers' response. You may have been asked, "how did you hear about us?" at a retail store cash register or while making an online purchase. That business is gathering information so it can calculate its return on investment (ROI) for the advertising it has purchased.

Marketing Strategy Checklist

Your marketing strategy should include:

- ☐ Profile of the target consumer

- ☐ Competitive market analysis

- ☐ Distribution plans for your products

- ☐ Product price strategy

- ☐ Advertising budget

- ☐ Advertising and marketing strategy analysis to evaluate potential methods

- ☐ Your corporation vision and business objectives

- ☐ Brand uniqueness or image for your products

- ☐ Evaluation of your products and services

- ☐ Distinction of your company / products from competitors

Marketing Plan Worksheet

Do any governmental or legal factors affect your business?

_____

Do your prices properly cover costs?

_____

How can you compete in this market?

_____

Is your pricing in line with your image?

_____

What advantages does your product have over the competition?

_____

What are your strengths and weaknesses in comparison to competitors?

_____

What can you do better than your competitors?

_____

What features will you emphasize?

_____

What is your pricing strategy?

_____

What type of image do you want for your product?

_____

What types of promotion will you use?

    Television

_____

    Radio

_____

Direct mail

Personal contacts and networking

Newspaper

Magazines

Classifieds

Phone directories

Billboard

Internet

E-mail

Trade associations

Posters and fliers

Other

Who are your competitors?

Who are your customers going to be?

Advertising Methods Analysis Worksheet

Use this worksheet to evaluate the types of advertising media that are best for your marketing plan.

TYPE OF MEDIA	TYPE OF APPROACH TO EMPHASIZE		
	Product / Services	*Special Events / Package Deals*	*Set Yourself Apart from Competitors and Become Famous*
Local (city or regional) newspapers, magazines, or specialty publications	X		
Community newspapers	X		
Local advertiser	X	X	X
College newspaper		X	X
Business networking newsletters	X	X	
Other special-interest publications		X	
Local radio shows	X	X	X
Local television shows	X	X	X
Internet	X	X	X

Branding Worksheet

1. **Identify your personal and business values.** Begin by listing both personal and business values (honesty, quality, and so on). Then create a "value statement" for your business based on this list. Keep it short. The more condensed your value statement is, the easier it will be for you to recall. In addition, the condensed value statement may be the perfect phrase to use as an advertising tagline on your marketing materials._____

   _____

   _____

2. **Create a mission statement.** A mission statement lays out the purpose underlying your work. A good mission statement is meaningful, but still short enough to remember. _____

   _____

   _____

3. **Create a vision statement.** A good vision statement will specify how you will know when you have achieved your mission statement's goal. Setting targets for yourself and then continually striving to meet them keeps you working smarter and remaining innovative as new possibilities open up.

   _____

   _____

4. **Identify your starting point.** Where are you right now, in relation to where you want to be? Write down some of the steps you already know are necessary to make your business dreams become real.

   _____

   _____

5. **Describe your market.** Understanding whom you want to reach with branding is critical, since choices of advertising, marketing, and other types of publicity will vary depending on the target market(s) you select. _____

   _____

6. **Create a positioning statement.** Positioning is your attempt to control the image of the business your customer will see. What is the impression you hope to make in the mind of your ideal customer? Will you aim to be the lowest-cost provider in your community? The top-quality provider? The friendliest, most reliable provider?_____

   _____

   _____

Press Release Worksheet

Use press releases to announce any type of news and get attention for your business. Issue a press release when you open your doors for business, when you introduce a new product or service, or when you sponsor a special community activity. The format for a press release is fairly simple:

1. First, give the main facts of the event: date, time, place, kind of event, food, and cost (if any).

    _____

    _____

    _____

2. Then, go into detail about the activities at the event. Describe what will take place when. This section should excite the reader's interest in attending your event. Consider what makes this event different from other similar events in your community. _____

    _____

    _____

    _____

3. If the event is for a charity or other cause, emphasize the cause and where the proceeds will go.

    _____

    _____

    _____

4. If the event is to promote your business, provide details on your company — when it was or will be opened, who the owners are, what kinds of services or products are provided? Include other specifics about your business, including hours and location. _____

    _____

    _____

    _____

Send the press release to all local television and radio stations with a note asking them to use it as a public service announcement. Do the same for local newspapers, including any local free newspapers. Consider sending the press release to your local Chamber of Commerce for publication in its newsletter and to other civic organizations for the same purpose.

Sample Press Release

For Immediate Release

Title: Loving Pet Care for Holiday Travelers

[City name / Release Date] — A professional dog walking and pet sitting business, *[Business Name]*, now has service to cover the *[coverage area]* just in time for the holidays. *[Owner Name]* provides expert care as a licensed pet sitting professional.

"In-home animal care is beneficial for both pets and their owners," says *[Owner Name]*. "Animals do much better in their normal, safe, and secure environment while surrounded by familiar sights, sounds, and smells. They will receive love and personal attention and are able to stick to their normal routine while eliminating the trauma of an unfamiliar environment and exposure to other animals."

[Business Name] provides a variety of services for dogs, cats, and other small animals, including private and group dog walks and doggie play groups, cat visits, in-home overnight sitting, private boarding, day care, home care, and pet taxi.

The demand for professional pet sitting and dog walking services is at an all-time high. Pet ownership is rising, pet owners are working longer hours and traveling more for business and personal reasons than ever before, and pet owners are moving away from kenneling their pets because of health concerns, making alternatives such as *[Business Name]* more attractive.

More information, a complete list of service areas, and contact information are available at *[Business Name]*'s website at *[website address]* or by calling *[phone number]*.

CONTACT:
[Business Name]
[Contact Name]
[Address]
[Phone]
[E-mail]
[Website]

Consent form for use of a testimonial

_____ *[Your Company Name]* has my permission to use my statement or testimonial, name, and credentials, or contact information on its website, in its advertising, as well as in/on _____ *[Add any additional places you may use this testimonial.]* My testimonial was provided as an honest opinion of _____ *[Company Name]*'s services / products, and I understand in writing it that I am under no obligation and am not receiving any compensation in return for my testimonial.

_____

Signature

_____

Printed Name

Conclusion

The forms and checklists in this book are samples of the documents necessary to successfully start and run your small business. Your business is unique; read over these documents carefully and customize them to suit your particular needs. Be especially careful when preparing a lease, contract, or other legal document because the words you choose might determine whether you win or lose when a dispute arises.

The companion CD-ROM contains additional legal forms and publications. Please refer to the CD-ROM if you do not find the form you need in this book. You will also find supplemental information on specific topics. The Internet is an invaluable source of information. Federal and state governments have made almost all of their documents and publications freely available on the Web, and numerous consumer advocates and professional associations offer suggestions and advice. Throughout the book, there are references to websites where you can find detailed answers to your questions. There is no reason to remain in doubt. By becoming well-informed, you can guarantee your success in your business.

CD-ROM also contains bonus forms for property managers and landlords, building contractors, project management, hospitality, nonprofit management, and marketing and public relations.

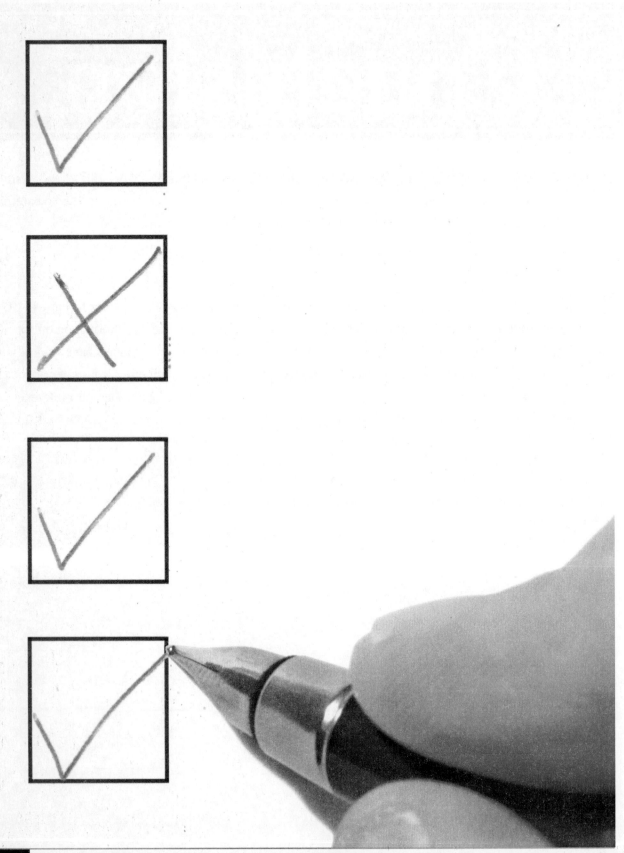

THE ENCYCLOPEDIA OF SMALL BUSINESS FORMS AND AGREEMENTS

Appendix

Directory of Contents on the Companion CD-ROM

Starting a Business

- Business Evaluation Personality Quiz
- Questions to Ask About a Franchise
- Franchisor's Disclosure Document Checklist
- Elements of a Business Plan
- Business Plan and Strategic Plan Worksheet
- Business Plan Checklist
- Sample Business Plan
- Format for Business Proposal
- Elevator Pitch
- Estimated Startup Costs Worksheet
- Startup Expenses Worksheet
- Estimated Startup Cost Shortfall
- Creating an Operating Budget Worksheet
- Budgeting Worksheet
- Startup Expenses Estimate Worksheet
- Operating Expenses Worksheet
- Sample Operating Expenses Worksheet
- Checklist for Cutting Costs
- Location Analysis
- Potential Location Checklist
- Proposed Location Rating
- Business Entity Chart
- Ownership Structure of Business Entities
- Checklist for Choosing and Registering a Business Name
- Sample Articles of Organization for an LLC
- Sample Guidelines for Articles of Incorporation
- Sample Filing for Articles of Incorporation
- Fictitious Name (DBA) Form
- Financial Statement Requirements for Business Entities
- Worksheet for a Successful Partnership
- Exit Plan Worksheet

Bonus forms for this section include:

- Furniture, Fixtures, and Equipment Estimate Worksheet

- Form W-9 — Request for Taxpayer Identification Number and Certification

Buying or Selling a Business

- Checklist for Putting Together a Search Plan
- Elements of a Selling Memorandum
- Three-Year Financial Worksheet
- Agreement for Purchase and Sale of a Business
- Checklist for New Owner of a Business

Setting Up and Running a Corporation

- Articles of Incorporation Worksheet
- Shareholder, Director, Officer, and Employee Worksheet
- Form for Corporate Minutes

Contract Basics

- Signature Box for a Sole Proprietorship Without Fictitious Name
- Signature Box for Corporation With a Fictitious Name
- Signature Box for Corporation Without a Fictitious Name
- Signature Box for General Partnership With a Fictitious Name
- Signature Box for General Partnership Without a Fictitious Name
- Signature Box for Limited Liability Company With a Fictitious Name
- Signature Box for Limited Liability Company Without a Fictitious Name
- Signature Box for Sole Proprietorship With Fictitious Name

- Checklist for Reviewing a Contract
- Checklist for Reviewing a Contract for Consulting or Services
- Checklist for Reviewing a Contract for Buying or Selling Goods
- Amendment to a Contract

Buying, Selling, and Leasing Real Estate

- Retail and Office Lease Agreement
- Commercial Lease Agreement
- Agreement to Execute Lease
- Americans with Disabilities Act — Addendum
- Agreement to Cancel Lease
- Lease Assignment
- Primary Lease Agreement
- Agreement for Sale of Commercial Real Estate
- Commercial or Industrial Property Real Estate Sale Contract
- Mortgage Form
- Balloon Mortgage Note Form
- Promissory Note A
- Buyer-Broker Agency Agreement
- Home Inspection Checklist

Bonus forms for this section include:

- Agreement to Extend Lease II
- Underlying Lease of Shopping Center
- Remodeling Agreement

Financial Reports, Accounting, and Money Management

- Questions to Ask When Researching a Bank Account

- Questions to Ask Before Setting Up Your Merchant Account
- Questions to Ask Before Seeking Outside Financing
- Personal Financial Statement
- End-of-the-Year Financial Assessment
- Balance Sheet
- Profit-Loss Statement
- Income Statement
- Sample Startup Funding Financial Statement
- Chart of Accounts
- Pricing Strategy Worksheet
- Expense Reimbursement Form
- Expense Report
- Sample Delinquent Account Notice
- Business Credit Application
- Checklist of Tax Records
- Payroll Budget Estimate
- Payroll Cost Report
- Daily Payroll Form
- Employee Turnover Rate Worksheet
- Checklist for Accounting Fraud
- Checklist for Payroll Procedures Analysis
- Checklist for Bank Reconciliation
- Checklist for Cash Receipts Analysis
- Checklist for Check Tampering
- Budget Worksheet
- Record of Personal Assets
- Personal Business Worksheet

Bonus forms for this section include:

- IRS Form 1099 MISC — Miscellaneous Income
- IRS Form 2290 — Heavy Highway Vehicle Use Tax Return
- IRS Form 4562 — Depreciation and Amortization (Including Information on Listed Property)
- IRS Form 4562 — Instructions
- IRS Form 720 — Quarterly Federal Excise Tax Return
- IRS Form 941 — Employer's Quarterly Federal Tax Return
- IRS Form1040SS — U.S. Self-Employment Tax Return
- IRS Publication 334 — Tax Guide for Small Businesses
- IRS Publication 505 — Tax Withholding and Estimated Tax
- IRS Publication 583 — Starting a Business and Keeping Records
- IRS Publication 946 — How to Depreciate Property
- IRS Schedule E — Supplemental Income and Loss
- Cash Report
- Cash Turn-in Report
- Cashier's Log
- Cashier's Report I
- Cashier's Report II
- Change Funds Report
- Checklist for Setting Up Your Bookkeeping System
- Closing Bank Account Form
- Cost of Employee Turnover
- Employer Retirement and Pension Plans
- Purchase Order
- Purchase Ledger
- Invoice
- Invoice Log
- Invoice Payment Schedule
- Credit Voucher

- Invoice II
- Real Estate Owned Worksheet

Purchasing and Inventory

- Supplier Contact Sheet
- Supplier Reference Sheet
- Vendor List
- Supplier Order Schedule
- Employee Order Request Log
- Perpetual Inventory Form
- Storeroom Requisition
- Log Checklist for Examination of Purchasing Process
- Checklist for Red Flags for Bribery in the Bidding Business Process

Human Resources

- Checklist for the Hiring Process
- Questions to Ask Before Hiring Your First Employee
- What Not to Ask Prospective Employees
- New Hire Application
- Sample Employee Hiring Letter / Agreement
- Agreement for Hiring an Independent Contractor
- General Employment Contract
- Application of Federal Law to Employers
- Direct Deposit Authorization Form
- Nondiscrimination Notice
- Checklist for Employee File
- Initial Employee Information Sheet
- Employee Contact Sheet
- Acknowledgment of Drug-Free Policy
- Technology Policy

- Confidentiality and Nondisclosure Agreement
- Checklist for Employee or Independent Contractor Determination
- Time Sheet / Time Card
- Employee Rating System
- Performance Appraisal Form
- Employee Self-evaluation Form
- Performance Evaluation Form
- Employee Satisfaction Survey
- Topics for Employee Handbook
- Sample Employee Handbook
- Ethics Policy of Code of Conduct
- Employee Fraud Prevention Checklist
- Formulating a Safety Policy
- Checklist for Employers Covered by the OSH Act

Bonus forms for this section include:

- Important Phone Numbers
- Emergency Contacts
- Authorization to Release Information
- Developing a Health and Safety Protection Plan
- Form I-9 Employment Eligibility Verification
- Internet Policy Acknowledgment Form
- Interpersonal Skills Assessment
- IRS Publication 15A — 2010 Employer's Supplemental Tax Guide
- IRS W-2 Form — Wage and Tax Statement
- IRS W-4 Form — Employee's Withholding Allowance Certificate
- IRS W-5 Form — Earned Income Credit Advance Payment Certificate
- List of OSHA Publications
- Memo I

- Memo II
- Model Safety Policy
- OSHA Handbook for Small Businesses
- OSHA Self-Inspection Checklists
- Payroll Deduction Authorization Form
- Receipt of Employee Handbook
- Recognition Preference Profile
- Résumé Sample
- Staff Calendar
- Weekly Staffing Schedule
- Where to Go for Assistance with OSHA Compliance

Independent Contractors, Freelancers, and Consultants

- Independent Contractor Agreement
- Hiring Agreement for a Company
- Invoice for Independent Contractor
- Networking Log

Bonus forms for this section include:

- To-do List
- Daily Planner
- Monthly Calendar
- Action Plan Worksheet
- Assignment of Copyright
- Client Satisfaction Survey
- Company Agreement
- Copyright Basics
- Copyright Form TX
- Meeting Agenda
- Meeting Memo for Independent Contractor
- Meeting Notification Memo
- Meeting Room Checklist

Marketing and PR

- Marketing Strategy Checklist
- Marketing Plan Worksheet
- Advertising Methods Analysis Worksheet
- Branding Worksheet
- Press Release Worksheet
- Sample Press Release

Bonus Forms

Property Managers and Landlords

- Lead Paint Poisoning Disclosure
- House Application
- Rental Application
- Residential Lease
- Roommate Agreement
- Pet Agreement
- Month-to-Month Lease Agreement
- Property Management Agreement
- Notice of Intent to Enter
- Notice of Change of Rent
- Inspection Failure Letter
- Notice of Past Due Rent
- Notice to Vacant Premises
- Payment Arrangement
- 30-Day Notice to Terminate Tenancy
- Problem Tenant Report Form

Building Contractors

- Construction Contract
- Independent Building Contractor Agreement
- Contractor and Subcontractor Agreement
- Bond of Contractor

- Bond of Subcontractor
- Pre-construction Checklist
- Contractor Invoice
- Contractor's Affidavit of Completion, Payment of Debts and Claims, and Release of Liens
- Contractor's Warranty
- Termination of Construction Contract
- Guideline for Change Orders
- Job Site Safety Checklist

Project Management

- Interview Worksheet for a Project Plan
- Phases and Processes of a Project
- Client Satisfaction Survey
- Project Plan Checklist
- Seven Super Skills for Successful Project Management

Hospitality Industry

- Restaurant Lease
- Catering Contract
- Detailed Catering Contract
- Entertainment Contract I
- Entertainment Contract II
- Restroom Checklist
- Detailed Incident Report
- Daily Incident Log
- Customer Comment Form
- Daily Sanitation Checklist
- Foodborne Illness Complaint Form
- Lost Business Report
- Employee Alcohol Policy Notification Agreement
- Service Refusal Form

- Hotel Guest Credit Application
- Hotel Registration Card
- Hotel Front Office Cash Sheet

Nonprofit Management

- Checklist for Setting Up a Not-For-Profit
- Sample Letter of Inquiry for Grant Proposal
- Sample Letter of Inquiry
- Sample Grant Proposal
- Sample Cover Letter for Grant Proposal
- Grant Proposal Review Sheet
- In-kind Donations Record and Worksheet
- Sample Individual Grant
- Volunteer Application
- Volunteer Contract
- Sample Letter for Fundraising with a Gift
- Sample Lapsed Membership Letter

Index

Code of Conduct 8, 209, 255, 282

Confidentiality Agreement 69

Consolidated Omnibus Benefits Reconciliation
Act 224

corporate minutes 6, 79, 83, 84, 280

corporation 19, 29, 49, 50, 51, 54, 57, 58, 66,
79, 80, 81, 82, 83, 86, 87, 88, 96, 110,
117, 141, 167, 270

D

diligent effort 89

E

Employee

Handbook 8, 209, 244, 245, 254, 282,
283

Polygraph Protection Act 224

Satisfaction Survey 8, 209, 241, 282

Self-Evaluation 8, 209, 239

employer identification number (EIN) 63

employment ads 210

employment contract 8, 209, 222, 282

Equal Opportunity Commission 250

Equal Pay Act 224

estate 3

estoppel 110

ethics policy 255

exit plan 6, 11, 65, 66, 279

F

Fair

Credit Reporting Act 224

Labor Standards Act 63, 224

Family Medical Leave Act 224

Federal Trade Commission 17, 31

fictitious name (DBA) 5, 11, 34, 59, 86, 87, 88,
279, 280

force majeure 92, 94

franchise 12, 15, 16, 17, 19, 20, 21, 22, 23, 31

fraud prevention 8, 209, 256, 282

G

general partnership 49, 87, 280

Genetic Information Nondiscrimination Act 224

good faith effort 31, 89

H

Hiring Agreement 8, 261, 266, 283

I

Immigration Reform and Control Act 224, 245,
250

independent contractor 92, 196, 216, 218, 219,
220, 234, 262, 263, 266

Internet-use agreement 10

R

S

U

V

W